CONTENTS

SECRET
LANGUAGE

BARRY J. BLAKE

OXFORD
UNIVERSITY PRESS

OXFORD
UNIVERSITY PRESS

Great Clarendon Street, Oxford OX2 6DP

Oxford University Press is a department of the University of Oxford.
It furthers the University's objective of excellence in research, scholarship,
and education by publishing worldwide in

Oxford New York

Auckland Cape Town Dar es Salaam Hong Kong Karachi
Kuala Lumpur Madrid Melbourne Mexico City Nairobi
New Delhi Shanghai Taipei Toronto

With offices in

Argentina Austria Brazil Chile Czech Republic France Greece
Guatemala Hungary Italy Japan Poland Portugal Singapore
South Korea Switzerland Thailand Turkey Ukraine Vietnam

Oxford is a registered trade mark of Oxford University Press
in the UK and in certain other countries

Published in the United States
by Oxford University Press Inc., New York

© Barry Blake 2010

The moral rights of the author have been asserted
Database right Oxford University Press (maker)

First published by Oxford University Press 2010
First published in paperback 2011

British Library Cataloguing in Publication Data

Data available

Library of Congress Cataloging in Publication Data
Library of Congress Control Number: 2009941610

Typeset by SPI Publisher Services, Pondicherry, India
Printed in Great Britain
on acid-free paper by
Clays Ltd., St Ives Plc

ISBN 978–0–19–957928–0 (hbk)
978–0–19–969162–3 (pbk)

1 3 5 7 9 10 8 6 4 2

ILLUSTRATIONS

ACKNOWLEDGEMENTS

I would like to thank the following for helping me write this book by supplying references, examples, suggestions, and translations: Alexandra Aikhenvald, Delia Bentley, Robert Crotty, Michael Frazer, John Hajek, Andy Pawley, Randy La Polla, Jarinya Thammachoto, Erma Vassiliou, the publisher's referees, and the ever helpful John Davey.

Quotations from the Bible are from the Authorized Version unless otherwise noted.

Translations are my own unless otherwise acknowledged.

I

ON BEING MYSTERIOUS

Philosophy is a battle against the bewitchment of our intelligence by means of language.

LUDWIG WITTGENSTEIN

anguage is a means of communication, but a good deal of language use is deliberately obscure if not actually encrypted in some form of cipher or code. This book explores the reasons for obscurity and secrecy, and touches on some of the fascinating beliefs that underlie the constraints on using language freely.

We begin our exploration in Chapter 2 with word games. Nowadays anagrams, palindromes, and word squares are generally sources of entertainment, but in the past they were often ascribed serious significance as elements of sorcery. Word games sometimes feature acrostics—texts in which a sequence of initials spells out a word or phrase. The most common case is the acrostic poem, where the initial letters of the lines form a word or phrase, but there are authors who cunningly bury all sorts of secret messages in passages of prose, as the alert reader may discover in the present text. All these features of language and others are exploited in the most popular word game of all, the cryptic crossword.

In all languages some words have more than one meaning, different words sometimes sound alike, and often a phrase or sentence can be construed in more than one way. These sources of ambiguity give scope for making puns and concocting riddles. Chapter 3 reveals that while, for us, riddles may be a childish novelty, once upon a time heroes were required to solve riddles as well as performing physical feats, and prophets found it useful to phrase their predictions in the ambiguous language of riddles.

There are times when communicating in secret is crucial. In time of war, for instance, information needs to be passed secretly between governments and military authorities. Acrostics can serve an important purpose in relation to secrecy, as we see in Chapter 4. We also consider how letters can be shuffled or replaced by other letters to form a cipher and how words can be replaced by other words in a code.

The ciphers and codes used by governments and the military are recognized as such, but some scholars claim there are anagrams, ciphers, and acrostics hidden in the Bible. They also perceive a hidden significance in the numerical properties of biblical diction. In a number of ancient languages, including Hebrew, the letters of the alphabet served as numbers, just as our Roman numerals do (CLIX can be 159 or a brand name for dry biscuits or crackers). This means one can add up the numerical values of the letters in words, which in turn creates scope for comparing totals and finding significance in the fact that certain words produce the same total.

The Bible is an example of literature dealing with belief in the supernatural—a belief which links mainstream religion with what is classified as superstition.[1] All societies believe in the supernatural, although of course not all individuals do. Large-scale societies include sceptics, agnostics, and atheists, and nowhere is this truer than in present-day western society. But we are exceptional. We may become the norm in the future, but we are anomalous by comparison with the small-scale societies that existed in the past. Scepticism is a product of civilization, which encourages recognition of more than one system of belief. Long-term observation and experiment take some of the mystery out of awe-inspiring events such as volcanic eruptions, earthquakes, tidal waves, and eclipses of the sun and moon—occurrences which past societies often attributed to supernatural powers. Belief in the supernatural accounts for some of the strongest constraints on straightforward communication, and chapters 6 and 7 are largely concerned with this. In many cultures certain words and phrases cannot be used for fear of offending a god or spirit and inviting retribution, while conversely some words and phrases are thought to have the power to enlist supernatural intervention in the physical world. Knowledge of these efficacious words and phrases—or magic words—is often restricted to initiates. Although few people in contemporary western society believe in magic, the notion of the magic word plays an important part in our culture. The spell word *abracadabra* is well known, as is the charm phrase *Open sesame*, which reflects the

---

[1] The Christians' miracle is the pagans' magic. Even within Christendom we find orthodox Christians describing as magic what heretics claimed as miracles, while Lollards and later Reformers referred to some traditional Catholic practices as magical (Kieckhefer 1994: 815).

Arabian strand in our literary heritage. Popular literature, particularly works aimed at the young, are full of magic and magic words. Think of *The Chronicles of Narnia*, *The Lord of the Rings*, and more recently the Harry Potter novels, where the magic words are mostly modelled on Latin. They include *incendio* (produces fire), *serpentortia* (conjures up a serpent), and *silencio* (silences someone).

In many cultures certain texts are considered sacred and are believed to contain records of divine revelation. The best-known examples are the Bible and the Qur'an, but there are numerous others, including some that are orally transmitted from generation to generation. Sacred texts have often been invested with the power of healing—and by this I mean not just their contents but the physical texts themselves. We read of cases where, in the hope of effecting a cure, the Bible has been placed against stricken parts of a patient's body, or where verses from the Bible have been given to a patient to eat. More often such verses have been worn in amulets or charms to avert misfortune.[2] In the early centuries of

---

[2] There is another term that vies with *amulet*, namely *talisman*. I will treat *amulet* and *talisman* as synonymous. Some writers distinguish them, but different writers use different criteria. Some take a talisman to be an amulet that attracts good fortune as opposed to warding off bad fortune, some take a talisman to contain text, while others consider a talisman to contain astrological images such as the signs of the zodiac or images of planets, and others again take a talisman to be an amulet that is used for a specific task such as guarding buried treasure (Budge 1978: 13–14; Skemer 2006: 6–9). The term *charm* overlaps with *amulet* and *talisman*. Originally it referred to an incantation, then it covered a text used in an amulet, and finally it came to denote the amulet itself, as in the modern charm bracelet.

Christianity the Bible was also thought to be a source of divination and prophecy and a guide to appropriate courses of action: devotees had only to open the Bible at random and take heed of the first verse that came to eye. St Augustine attributes his conversion to committed Christianity to this simple method.

People who work together, live in the same area, or congregate through common interests are likely to develop distinctive forms of language that are a barrier to communication with the wider language community. This differentiation is dealt with in Chapter 8. Sometimes it arises from the specialized terminology or jargon of an occupation or leisure pursuit, but often it comes from a conscious desire for demarcation from the larger community. Language is an important marker of identity and people often foster a distinctive vocabulary, particularly of a colloquial variety. Among criminals and others who tend to attract the attention of the authorities, an elaborate argot often develops, a mixture of slang and jargon. Such in-group languages serve both to bond their users and to create codes which are opaque to the authorities. They employ two means of disguise. One is a type of code in which mainstream words are replaced with substitutes: *stir* for 'jail' and *screw* for 'jailer', in two well-known examples. The other is closer to cipher, for instance, back slang, where words are pronounced backwards (so that *fish* comes out as *shif*), or Pig Latin, where initial consonants become the initial of a final syllable with the rhyme *-ay* so that 'Pig Latin', for instance, becomes *Igpay Atinlay*.

Obscurities of various kinds are common in everyday life. Many people go out of their way to be ironical or playfully abusive. Some interlard their speech with double meanings or use expressions such as, 'Were you born in a barn?' rather than 'Would you mind shutting the door after you'. Others favour euphemisms. These deviations from straight talking are covered in Chapter 9.

When people play overt language games such as cryptic crosswords and riddles the fact that there is a hidden meaning is quite clear. Often the teasing is covert, however, as when people insert passages from a previous text into their speech or writing, or choose an allusive name. Such allusions are the subject of Chapter 10. A good example of a literary allusion is the novel *White Mischief* by James Fox, better known from the 1987 film. It presents a scathing portrait of decadence among the British elite in Kenya during World War II. The title plays on *Black Mischief*, a comic novel by Evelyn Waugh published in 1932, which tends to see black Africans as a source of humour in a way that would be considered politically incorrect or somewhat racist nowadays. If one accepts this interpretation of *Black Mischief*, it gives an edge to the view of the British elite presented in *White Mischief*.

Allusions are also cleverly embedded within some fictional names. Have you ever wondered why the computer controlling the space mission in *2001: A Space Odyssey* is called HAL? Why do you think the bad guy in *The Da Vinci Code* is called Sir Leigh Teabing? These names are not arbitrary. They are enciphered allusions. Read on and all will be revealed.

2

FROM ANAGRAMS TO CRYPTIC CROSSWORDS

He who asks a question is a fool for five minutes; he who does not ask a question remains a fool forever.

CHINESE PROVERB

This chapter deals with the written form of language. It may come as a surprise to some people that writing is a comparatively recent invention. Humans have been speaking for well over a hundred thousand years, probably some hundreds of thousands of years. They have also been using hand signs, and it may be that signing predates speech. Writing was invented in Mesopotamia and Egypt far more recently, in the fourth millennium BC. It is thought that most writing systems can be traced back to these beginnings in the Near East, but writing was also developed independently somewhat later in China and Central America.[1]

---

[1] For a brief illustrated account see Blake 2008, ch. 10.

Not all humans have access to writing. Even today the vast majority of the world's languages are not written, though this is obscured by the fact that national languages such as Chinese, English, Hindi-Urdu, and Russian are written.[2] Writing is derivative, a way of representing speech, yet many people treat it as the primary form of language. There is also a lot that is arbitrary about writing. For instance, English is written in the Roman alphabet, but in theory it could be written in the Greek or Cyrillic alphabet. Spelling is also arbitrary. Words like *music* and *logic* were once spelt *musick* and *logick*, and words like *honour* and *labour* have the alternative spellings *honor* and *labor*.

Although writing is essentially a means of representing speech in permanent form and although the means of representation is arbitrary, people in literate societies become fascinated by the written symbols, whether these represent individual phonemes as in Europe, syllables as in Japanese and Korean, or words as in Chinese. People notice that there can be systematic relationships between the written form of two or more different words and between parts of different words. One such relationship is the **anagram**, where the letters of one word can be rearranged to form one or more other words. The words *prose*, *ropes*, *pores*, and *poser* are anagrams of one another.[3] Another relationship that holds for some words is that they are spelt the same way backwards as

[2] Hindi-Urdu is essentially one language. It is called Hindi in India and written in Devanagari script, and it is called Urdu in Pakistan and written in a form of Persian (ultimately Arabic) script.

[3] Some anagrams can be found in speech as in *lifer* and *filer*, where the anagrammatic relationship is simple, but in written language it is possible using pen and paper to find more complicated anagrammatic relationships.

forwards. These are **palindromes** and examples include words such as *level, madam, minim,* and *tenet*. Note that the palindromic relationship does not hold for the spoken form since there is an unstressed vowel in the second syllable, though spoken palindromes are possible, especially in monosyllabic words such as *tat, tit,* and *tot*. In some cases spelling a word backwards produces a different word; for instance, *star* spelt backwards yields *rats*. Such pairs are sometimes referred to as **mirror words** or **semordnilaps**, a term which is itself formed by reversing the word *palindromes*.

Parts of words in a phrase, sentence, or text can spell out a word or phrase. The most common example is the **acrostic** poem, where initial letters of lines spell out a name.

Written words can be arranged in patterns such as squares and the incorporation of anagrams, palindromes, mirror words, and acrostics into such **word squares** has been popular for centuries.

Today picking out word patterns is considered a form of light entertainment. There is a game called *Anagrams*, for instance, in which players have to compose anagrams using lettered tiles like those in *Scrabble*. Anagrams and palindromes are to be found mostly in cryptic crosswords, but it is interesting to note that palindromes and other forms of word play have been a regular feature of curses and charms for centuries, and in the past people have often seen hidden meanings in the formal properties of written words.

Anagrams

As mentioned above, an anagram is a word made up of the letters of another word, so that *reside* is an anagram of *desire* and vice versa. Other groups of words sharing an anagrammatic relation-ship are *Alice/Celia, amend/named, artisan/tsarina, conical/laconic, prenatal/paternal/parental, rescued/reduces,* and *listen/silent/tinsel.* There can be an anagrammatic relationship between a word and a phrase, as with *ovation/too vain* and *hitherto/other hit*; or between phrases, as with *same old story,* which yields phrases such as *delays motors* and *dreamy stools.* Anagrams are not all that difficult to find, at least in English, and nowadays anagram-producing computer programs are freely available on the Web. Although the availability of such programs threatens to take some of the fun out of finding anagrams, there is still satisfaction to be had in finding an anagram that is related in meaning to the original word or phrase. When the US government repealed the eighteenth amendment and allowed its citizens to buy alcohol again, Wyndham Lewis wrote *Tons 'o drink, even ale, for all,* an anagram of the name of the then president, Franklin Delano Roosevelt (Bergerson 1973: vii). The word *astronomers* anagrams to *moon starers* and the name of the former Conservative British prime minister Margaret Thatcher produces *Meg, the arch tartar* and an ironic *that great charmer.*

The Greek poet Lycophron of Chalcis is often credited with being the inventor of the anagram, but it is likely that anagrams were in use long before Lycophron since fairly obvious examples are found in Greek, such as χόλος (cholos) 'choler' and ὄχλος (ochlos) 'mob' (as in *ochlocracy* 'mob rule'). Anagrams were popu-lar in Ancient Greek culture and Lycophron, who lived during the reign of Ptolemy Philadelphus (285–247 BC), included an anagram of the king's name in his poem *Cassandra*: ΠΤΟΛΕΜΑΙΟΣ 'Ptolemaios' became ΑΠΟ ΜΕΛΙΤΟΣ (apo melitos) 'made of honey'. There is at least one example of something akin to an anagram that purports to predate Lycophron. It involves a simple word break, but it is an illustration of how seriously patterns of letters could be taken. When Alexander the Great was besieging Tyre, he dreamt of a satyr. One of his advisers interpreted this as a good omen because *satyros* (*Σατυρος*) could be broken up into *Sa Tyros* (*Σα Τύρος*) 'Tyre is yours', a prophecy that was fulfilled (Plutarch, *Alexander* XXIV: 8–9).

In the classical world anagrams of names were considered significant, a belief that continued into the Middle Ages. Some people believed that a person's character or fate could be discovered by anagramming the letters of his or her name, and that a curse could be lifted by rearranging the letters of the afflicted person's name (Augarde 1984: 71).

It has been common in Europe for centuries for authors to incorporate anagrams of their names into poems, and it was popular to form anagrams from biblical texts. The first example below is much quoted. It is from the Latin version of the Bible (the Vulgate). It is a good anagram in that its sense fits in with the sense of the original, but remember that with a large number of letters there are many possibilities and in the late seventeenth and early eighteenth centuries numerous anagrams with meanings related to the original were made from this verse (Sarton 1936).

> Ave Maria, gratia plena, Dominus tecum.　(Luke 1:28)
> Hail Mary, full of grace, the Lord is with thee.
>
> Virgo serena, pia, munda et immaculata.
> Virgin serene, holy, pure and immaculate.

The following is another much-quoted example. The anagram forms a possible reply to the question posed by Pontius Pilate.

Quid est veritas?   (John 18:38)
What is truth?

Est vir qui adest.
It is the man standing before you.

Scientists sometimes hid information in anagrams. In the thirteenth century Roger Bacon found it prudent to identify one of the ingredients of gunpowder in anagram form. In the seventeenth century scientists often protected their discoveries by recording them in anagrams. For instance, Galileo wrote to Kepler HAEC IMMATURA A ME IAM FRUSTRA LEGUNTUR O.Y., which means, 'These immature things are now read by me in vain'. It is an anagram of *Cynthiae figuras aemulatur mater amorum* 'The mother of loves emulates the phases of Cynthia', where the mother of loves is Venus and Cynthia is the moon. Galileo's anagram isn't a very good one since it doesn't make full sense and there are two left-over letters, but he could have unscrambled it if anyone else had claimed to have discovered the phases of Venus before his findings had been published.[4]

---

[4] Ferdinand de Saussure (1857–1913) is famous as one of the founders of structural linguistics on the basis of the posthumously published *Cours de linguistique générale*. From other unpublished notes it appears that he spent a lot of time investigating whether the names of gods and heroes in ancient poetry, songs, and prophecies were reflected in other words of the surrounding text. For instance, Saussure suggests that some of the syllables of *Aphrodite* are picked up in the following lines of the *Aeneid* (1: 403–4) where Aphrodite reveals herself to her son, Aeneas:

Ambrosiaeque comae DIvinum vertice ODorem
Spiravere; pedes vestis defluxIT ad imos

'And [her] ambrosial tresses breathed heavenly perfume from
the top

[of her head]; her clothing flowed down to the bottom of her feet'

Anagrams were sometimes formed on the names of prominent persons. The Protestant theologian we know as Calvin has the name CALVINVS in Latin, which was anagrammed to ALCVINVS. (In Latin v had the value of [u] or [w] (later [v]).) Voltaire was born François Arouet. It is thought that *Voltaire* is an anagram of *Arouet L(e) J(eune)* 'Arouet the Younger'. The letters 'u' and 'v' were once interchangeable, and also the letters 'i' and 'j'. The practice of forming anagrams from people's names was so popular at one time in France that Louis XIII appointed Thomas Billon as court anagrammist.

Today anagrams are very common in pop music circles. The French singer and songwriter *Pascal Obispo*'s name is an anagram of *Pablo Picasso*. The English rock band *Sad Café* released an album called *Façades* (1979), and American singer and songwriter Mike (*Michael*) *Doughty* released an album called *Haughty Melodic* (2005).

Anagrams are used in popular fiction from time to time. In Dan Brown's best-selling novel *The Da Vinci Code* (2003, film version 2006), the lines *O, draconian devil* and *Oh, lame saint* written in blood on the body of the murdered curator of the Louvre are anagrams of *Leonardo da Vinci* and *The Mona Lisa* respectively. The central ideas of *The Da Vinci Code* can be found in an earlier book, *The Holy Blood and The Holy Grail* by Michael Baigent, Richard Leigh, and Henry Lincoln (1982). One of the characters in

The syllables that are thought to reflect syllables of *Aphrodite* are picked out in capitals. The procedure is so open-ended as to be vacuous, but Saussure's work has attracted a lot of attention and is often discussed under the label 'anagram', as in Samuel Kinser's 1979 paper 'Saussure's Anagrams: Ideological Work', from which the above example is taken.

The Da Vinci Code is Sir Leigh Teabing, whose name echoes those of two of the earlier authors (the surname being an anagram of Baigent).

Palindromes

A **palindrome** (Greek *palin-dromos* 'back running') is a word, phrase, or any other sequence of symbols that reads the same in either direction. The earliest examples are from a Greek poet of the third century BC, Sotades, whose name is perpetuated in the alternative label for palindromes, namely 'sotadics'. Words like *eke, eve, deed, level, madam, peep, reviver, rotor, racecar, rotator, tenet,* and *tot* are palindromes, as are the names *Anna* and *Glenelg* (Scottish and Australian place name) and the name of the pop group *ABBA*, who had a palindromic hit entitled *SOS*. *Malay-alam*, the name of a Dravidian language spoken in southern India (Kerala state), is also a palindrome.[5] Palindromes are not universal and their frequency depends on the word shapes that are possible in a language. In most Australian languages, for instance, all words begin with a consonant and end in a vowel, so there are no palindromes. However, these languages were spoken and signed, but not written, and an interest in palin-dromes seems to be confined to cultures with written forms of language. Japanese is written with Chinese characters and syllabic signs (which are ultimately derived from Chinese characters). When words are written in syllables, it is relatively

[5] There are about a score of languages with short palindromic names including Atta, Ewe, Idi, Obo, and Ulu.

easy to find palindromes, e.g. *shinbunshi* 'newsprint' does not read as a palindrome in Roman orthography, but the syllables *shi-n-bu-n-shi* form a palindrome.

A phrase or a sentence can be a palindrome, as in the much-quoted examples *Able was I ere I saw Elba* and *Madam, I'm Adam*, and the more natural *Was it a car or a cat I saw?* If we take whole words rather than individual letters to be the relevant units, then a sentence such as *Fall leaves after leaves fall* is a palindrome.

Some Christian churches, both Byzantine and western, contain fonts for holy water, particularly baptismal fonts, bearing the following Greek inscription:

NIΨONANOMHMATAMHMONANOΨIN

which breaks up into:

NIΨON ANOMHMATA MH MONAN OΨIN
Nipson anomemata   me   monan   opsin.

This means 'Wash the sins not only the face' and is a palindrome in Greek. In the transliteration from the Greek alphabet it is not quite a palindrome, but note that *ps* (*Ψ*) is one letter in Greek. The only other unfamiliar letter in the inscription is *H*, which looks like a capital 'h', but is *eta* or 'long e'.

A Latin example of a palindrome is *sum summus mus* 'I am the mightiest mouse', where *sum* is 'I am', *summus* 'highest, greatest', and *mus* 'mouse'. Composing palindromes, mainly in Latin, was popular in the late sixteenth and early seventeenth centuries. Augarde (1984: 98) quotes examples such as the lawyer's motto *Si nummi, immunis*, literally, 'If money, immune', i.e. 'If you pay, you will be free from prosecution', and the motto of a woman banished from the court of Queen Elizabeth for alleged impropriety: *Ablata at alba* 'Banished but blameless'.

For the most part finding palindromic words or composing palindromic phrases and sentences is a form of light entertainment. Some devotees display great ingenuity in finding long palindromes covering more than one sentence. In the past, however, palindromes have figured in the language of magic, and many have taken reversibility to be significant (Stewart 1979: 70). In the world of Ancient Greece and Rome it was common to try and bring misfortune to one's enemies by inscribing curses on lead tablets (see also Chapter 6). These contain lots of mysterious words and phrases, mostly gibberish as far as the users were concerned, but likely to be garbled words from Hebrew and possibly other languages such as Egyptian. Some of these *voces mysticae* or *voces magicae* ('mystic words' or 'magic words') are palindromes. As Ogden (1999: 49) writes:

> One sort of *vox magica* well suited to the curse tablets was the palindrome: such words remained magically proof against the retrograde writing common on curse tablets. They appear in various lengths, but they are often very long indeed, and are the favourite bases for the formation of isosceles triangles, since they retain their symmetry and palindromic nature at each stage of reduction.

One palindromic *vox magica* in use among the Gnostics of the third and fourth centuries AD was the Greek palindrome *ΑΒΛΑΝΑΘΑΝΑΛΒΑ* (in Roman alphabet ABLANATHANALBA with Θ transliterated by the digraph TH). This was popular in amulets. It may be from Hebrew *ab lanath* 'Thou art our father', but this is not certain (Budge 1978: 207). The example in Figure 1

```
IAE OBAPHRENEMOUNOTHILARIKRIPHIAEUEAIPHIRKIRALITHONUOMENERPHABOEAI
 AE OBAPHRENEMOUNOTHILARIKRIPHIAEUEAIPHIRKIRALITHONUOMENERPHABOEA
  E OBAPHRENEMOUNOTHILARIKRIPHIAEUEAIPHIRKIRALITHONUOMENERPHABOE
    OBAPHRENEMOUNOTHILARIKRIPHIAEUEAIPHIRKIRALITHONUOMENERPHABO
     BAPHRENEMOUNOTHILARIKRPIHIAEUEAIPHIRKIRALITHONUOMENERPHAB
      APHRENEMOUNOTHILARIKRIPHIAEUEAIPHIRKIRALITHONUOMENERPHA
       PHRENEMOUNOTHILARIKRIPHIAEUEAIPHIRKIRALITHONUOMENERPH
        RENEMOUNOTHILARIKRIPHIAEUEAIPHIRKIRALITHONUOMENER
         ENEMOUNOTHILARIKRIPHIAEUEAIPHIRKIRALITHONUOMENE
          NEMOUNOTHILARIKRIPHIAEUEAIPHIRKIRALITHONUOMEN
           EMOUNOTHILARIKRIPHIAEUEAIPHIRKIRALITHONUOME
            MOUNOTHILARIKRIPHIAEUEAIPHIRKIRALITHONUOM
             OUNOTHILARIKRIPHIAEUEAIPHIRKIRALITHONUO
              UNOTHILARIKRIPHIAEUEAIPHIRKIRALITHONU
               NOTHILARIKRIPHIAEUEAIPHIRKIRALITHON
                OTHILARIKRIPHIAEUEAIPHIRKIRALITHO
                 THILARIKRIPHIAEUEAIPHIRKIRALITH
                   ILARIKRIPHIAEUEAIPHIRKIRALI
                    LARIKRIPHIAEUEAIPHIRKIRAL
                     ARIKRIPHIAEUEAIPHIRKIRA
                       IKRIPHIAEUEAIPHIRKI
                        KRIPHIAEUEAIPHIRK
                          IPHIAEUEAIPHI
                           PHIAEUEAIPH
                             AEUEA
                              EUE
                               U
```

1. Shrinking word.

is one of the long ones that Ogden alludes to, which was used as the basis of an isosceles triangle or shrinking word. It is written out and then repeated below with the edge letters missing. These repetitions and reductions of the edges continue until only the middle letter is left. In the Roman alphabet version given here $\varLambda$ is transliterated L, Θ is transliterated with the digraph TH, and Φ with the digraph PH (Gager 1992: 95).[6]

As Gager notes, a palindrome produces the same word when reversed, so if you discovered that someone had cursed you with a palindrome, you could not simply counter the curse by reversing it.

The notion of the palindrome, especially palindromic poetry, has become popular in eastern Europe over the last few decades, and an iconic relationship between reversibility of form and reversibility of meaning has been explored (Greber n.d.). Palindromic poems consist of palindromic lines, but the term 'palindromic poetry' is also applied to poems in which the whole poem is one long palindrome (first word equals the last, second word equals the second last, etc). The thirteenth-century poet Baudin de Condé wrote poems of this type.[7] The term is also applied to poems where the sequence of lines is palindromic (first line equals last line, second line equals second last line, etc.).

Semordnilaps

Closely related to the palindrome is a word that yields another word when spelt backwards. Examples include *paws/swap*, *star/rats*, *diaper/repaid, reward/drawer*, and *tiler/relit*. The term given to such 'mirror words' is **semordnilap**—that is, *palindromes* in reverse. Word-play enthusiasts can have a lot of fun with semordnilaps. A word in one language may produce a word in another when

[6] The palindrome is Greek-looking, but identifying words is problematic. One can perhaps see *phrēnē* 'mind', *mouno* 'vulva', *thilari* 'nipple' (cf. *thēlē*), *kriphia* 'hidden', and *litho-* 'stone'.

[7] For examples see Augarde 1984: 104.

reversed—as in the case of the name of the forty-fourth American president, *Obama*, which yields the Latin *amabo* 'I will love' when reversed. In another variation, the phrase *stressed desserts* is a palindrome consisting of a semordnilap pair.

Although for most people these pairs of mirror words are just a minor linguistic novelty, there are people who see significance in the fact that *dog* is the reverse of *God*, which is strange when you consider the fact that this relationship holds only for English and only in the modern spelling. If we go back to the Middle Ages we find that while *God* was spelt *God*, *dog* was spelt *dogge* (earlier Old English *docga*). In seventeenth-century witch trials the claim was often made that the devil appeared in the form of a dog, a belief that seems to have been prompted by a chance linguistic relationship.

Acronyms and Acrostics

Words and phrases can be formed from the initial letters of a phrase or longer text. In such cases we refer to the new word as an **acronym**. A well-known example is *scuba*, which is derived from 'self-contained underwater breathing apparatus'. In the Middle Ages the acronym *agla* was popular as a magic word. It is an acronym for the Hebrew *Atah gibor leolam adonai* 'Thou, O Lord, are mighty forever'. Alternatively it is interpreted as *Atah gabor leolah, adonai* 'Thou art powerful and eternal, Lord'.

Similar to the acronym is a word, phrase, or longer text that can be read from the initials of words in a larger text. This is called an **acrostic**. The term is derived from Greek *akros* 'pointed, at the tip' (as with *acro-nym*) and *stichos* 'a line or verse'. An acrostic is usually a short verse composition in which the initial letters of lines or stanzas form a word or phrase. Here is a short example from Ben Jonson (1572–1637), in which the initial letters of the lines spell *wolf*.

To Doctor Empiric

When men a dangerous disease did 'scape,
Of old, they gave a cock to Aesculape.
Let me give two, that doubly am got free
From my disease's danger, and from thee.

Acrostics were popular in Akkadian and other Mesopotamian cultures, and among the Greeks and Romans. The prophecies of the Erythraean Sibyl were issued on leaves, so arranged that the initial letters made up a word or phrase. This is not entirely unexpected given that those involved in the occult seemed regularly to favour various word patterns. In the *City of God* (18:23) Augustine recalls being shown a Greek verse purportedly from the Erythraean Sibyl, in which the initials form an acrostic spelling out 'Ιησους Χριστος Θεου Υίος Σωτηρ' (Iesus CHristos THeou Uios Sōter) 'Jesus Christ, son of God, saviour'. It is scarcely credible that this verse actually came from the Erythraean Sibyl: it is much more likely to derive from an imitator. But the example is remarkable in that the initials of these words spell 'ΙΧΘΥΣ' (ICHTHUS) 'fish', so we have an acrostic within an acrostic. Augustine sees 'fish' as standing for *Christ* since, as he writes, Christ lived in the abyss of mortality like a fish in the depths of the ocean. He does not mention that the fish was a commonly used symbol among the Christians of the Roman empire.

Here is a Latin acrostic from the classical period. It is interesting in that it employs the first consonant and vowel of the proper names in the first two lines to make up *pedicare* 'to bugger'. It is number *lxvii* in a collection known as *Priapea* dedicated to Priapus, a God charged with guarding and increasing the fertility of livestock and gardens. The poem is of a type displayed in gardens. It is to be read as if spoken by Priapus and it is a threat directed against any would-be thief who should enter the garden.

Penelopes primam Didonis prima sequatur
    et primam Cadmi syllaba prima Remi,
quodque fit ex illis, mihi tu deprensus in horto,
    fur, dabis: hac poena culpa luenda tua est.

The initial syllable of Dido follows the initial syllable of Penelope,
    and the initial syllable of Remus follows the initial syllable of Cadmus,
And that's what will happen to you caught in the garden.
    That, thief, will be the penalty you'll have to pay me.

Acrostics remained popular among leading literary figures throughout Europe in the Middle Ages and Renaissance. In 1599 John Davies (1569–1626) wrote *Hymnes to Astraea* containing twenty-six poems that all contained the acrostic *Elisabeth Regina*, and in 1637 Mary Fage published *Fames Roule*, which contained over four hundred acrostic poems in honour of leading figures of the day. Each poem was headed by an anagram of the subject's name. The following example is quoted in Stevenson and Davidson (2001: 262–3). It is addressed to Carolus Stuart, i.e., Charles the First, represented as SOL, the sun, and Maria Henrietta, the queen consort, represented by Vesta, the Roman goddess of the hearth.[8]

[8] As noted earlier in the text letter *v* does double duty as [u] and [v], hence V in CAROLVS and STVARTE.

> to their most excellent majesty of
> Great Brittaines Monarchy
> CAROLUS-MARIA-STUARTE
> anagramma
> AU! VESTA, TRAC SOL, MARRY

> Cheerly firme Vesta, clad in verdant Green,
> Au! is an emblem of our glorious queen;
> Rendring a stable, fast, well knotted heart,
> On our great SOL plac't, thence not to depart:
> Likely a higher Goddesse cannot be,
> Vesta like, ruling in her chastity,
> Shining in virtues gracious increase.

> Much glory hath this Vesta, but no peace
> Au! doth to her true soul remain,
> Returning till she doth her SOL retain;
> In whom she doth delight, whom in her pace
> Admiring she doth follow in true trace.

> So Vesta traceth SOL, and did not tarry
> Til their united graces they did marry,
> Vertues conjoined thus, SOL in his heat,
> And Vesta in her chast, and plenteous great
> Rare right increase, doth truly multiply,
> Thrusting so forth a great posterity,
> Ever to last unto eternity.

Since the seventeenth century, in Britain at least, acrostics have ceased to interest serious poets, and they have come to be regarded as a marginal curiosity which is popular only among those who like word games.

Not all acrostics are to be found in verse. They also occur in prose. In *Hypnerotomachia Polyphili* (*Polyphilo's Strife of Love in a Dream*), a famous example of early printing (1499), the decorated letters at the heads of the chapters spell out POLIAM FRATER

FRANCISCUS COLUMNA PERAMAVIT 'Brother Francesco Colonna loves Polia'. The work is written in Italian, but the acrostic is in Latin.

The hidden word in an acrostic can be made harder to find by putting the letters in any fixed position other than the beginning of each line. An acrostic in which the last letters of each line make up a word is called a **telestich**. If the first and last letters of lines form words, then we have a double acrostic. There are also triple acrostics with a name running down the middle of the lines as well as at the ends. Varying the position of the relevant letters within the lines produces even more difficult acrostics. For example, the letters could appear in the first position of the first line, the second position of the second line, the third position of the third line, and so on. In fact, Edgar Alan Poe worked the name *Frances Sargent Osgood* into a poem using this method.[9] It is easy to imagine a more subtle pattern known only to the sender and intended recipient. The typical acrostic is a literary device rather

---

[9] The most extreme form of acrostic is the *carmen figuratum* in which a hidden text forms a figure or pattern within a text. The term *carmen figuratum* also applies to a text, usually a poem, where the words are laid out to form a pattern. In the Greek Anthology there are six poems with the line length varied so that they form a pattern representing the subject of the poem (e.g., wings), and a number of the curse tablets from the Roman empire contain words and letters arranged in shapes. In the Middle Ages poems were sometimes written in the form of a cross. More recent examples of this kind of poem can be found in the work of the nineteenth-century Uruguayan poet Francisco Acuña de Figueroa, and in Guillaume Apollinaire's *Calligrammes: Poems of Peace and War* (1918). John Cage moves the lines of some of his poems to the left or right in order to produce an acrostic running down the centre of the page. Such verse is sometimes referred to as visual poetry or concrete poetry.

than an attempt at serious deception, but cases where the pattern is complicated fall under the heading of steganography, which is discussed in Chapter 4.

Some Jewish and Christian scholars claimed to have found words, phrases, and sentences by examining the sequence of initial letters in the Bible. They took these acrostics to have been hidden there deliberately rather than to be the result of chance. Examples are given in Chapter 5.

There are literary works known as *abecedarians* in which the sequence of first letters spells out the alphabet. Acrostics of this type appear in the Hebrew Bible in the Lamentations of Jeremiah and some of the Psalms. In Psalm 119, for instance, the first eight verses all begin with aleph, the second eight with beth, the third eight with gimel, and so on through the alphabet.[10]

> The label 'acrostic' is also used for a type of crossword where you fill in the answers not in a sequence across or down, but in a number of designated positions scattered over the matrix. When the puzzle is completed, words can be read either horizontally or vertically. In the following example the first clue is *fancy* and the answer is *whim*, so you fill in *w* in the cell numbered 27, *h* in the cell numbered 30, *i* in the 32 cell, and *m* in the 17 cell. The second clue is *chase* and the answer is *hunt*, so you put *h* in the 22 cell, *u* in the 38 cell, *n* in the 33 cell, and *t* in the 26 cell. I will leave the rest for readers to complete. You should employ two methods. First, try to find the answers to the clues, and second, look at the emerging

[10] Richard Coate has pointed out to me that Jim Cladpole translated all the abecedarian psalms into the Sussex dialect, preserving the acrostic system. The manuscript dates to 1938 and it is published as *De A.B.C. Psalms put into de Sussex dialect and in due A.B.C. feshion* by Jim Cladpole, edited by Richard Coate (Brighton: Younsmere Press, 1992).

text and try to estimate which letters are likely in various unfilled positions. Your guesses can be filled in in the numbered spaces opposite each clue. Some will help choosing the right answer for the clues. You should finish up with a text that reads horizontally from left to right.

1	2	3	4		5	6	7		8		9	10	11	12
13	14		15	16	17	18		19	20	21		22	23	24
	25	26		27	28	29	30		31	32	33	34	35	36
37	38	39	40											

2. Acrostic crossword.

fancy:	$\overline{27}$ $\overline{30}$ $\overline{32}$ $\overline{17}$	aromatic plant:	$\overline{24}$ $\overline{10}$ $\overline{13}$ $\overline{15}$
chase:	$\overline{22}$ $\overline{38}$ $\overline{33}$ $\overline{26}$	side:	$\overline{34}$ $\overline{21}$ $\overline{6}$ $\overline{31}$
strike:	$\overline{5}$ $\overline{25}$ $\overline{12}$	girl's name:	$\overline{9}$ $\overline{23}$ $\overline{3}$ $\overline{16}$
wash:	$\overline{18}$ $\overline{2}$ $\overline{29}$ $\overline{20}$ $\overline{14}$	club:	$\overline{1}$ $\overline{8}$ $\overline{39}$ $\overline{40}$
neat:	$\overline{11}$ $\overline{28}$ $\overline{7}$ $\overline{4}$	donkey:	$\overline{37}$ $\overline{19}$ $\overline{36}$

Word Squares

A popular form of word play over the centuries has been forming **word squares**, often referred to as **magic squares**, though that term usually refers to a square containing numerals arranged so that the sum of all columns and rows is the same. The word square can be filled in in any systematic way. In Figure 3 a simple example is

S	T	A	R
T	A	M	E
A	M	E	N
R	E	N	T

3. Word square.

shown where the words *star*, *tame*, *amen*, and *rent* can be read vertically as well as horizontally.

One kind of word square found in curse tablets from the Greek and Roman worlds was a square (*plinthion*) formed by as many repetitions of a word as there were letters, with each repetition being offset from the previous one by one position. The square in Figure 4 is from a curse addressed to the spirit EULAMŌ seeking his aid in ruining the performance of rival athletes (Gager 1992: 60).

The notion of a systematically filled-in rectangle must have been credited with some secret power, for word squares were used in amulets as well as in curses. The square shown in Figure 5 is from a medieval amulet. It features one of the Hebrew names of God, namely *Elohim* (אלהים), which can be read by

E	U	L	A	M	Ō
U	L	A	M	Ō	E
L	A	M	Ō	E	U
A	M	Ō	E	U	L
M	Ō	E	U	L	A
Ō	E	U	L	A	M

4. Eulamō square.

5. Elohîm square.

ל = l, ה = h, י = î, מ = m. For practical purposes א is a silent consonant supporting the vowel [e], which is not shown. The vowel [o] is not shown either. The Hebrew consonantal alphabet is shown in Figure 23.

ם	י	ה	י	ם
י	ה	ל	ה	י
ה	ל	א	ל	ה
י	ה	ל	ה	י
ם	י	ה	י	ם

starting in the middle with א (aleph) and proceeding to any corner by any series of horizontal or vertical steps (Budge 1978: 234).

Squares made up of the consonants of Yahweh, namely יהוה YHWH, the most sacred name of God, were also used.[11] Heinrich Cornelius Agrippa von Nettesheim (1486–1535) in his *De Occulta Philosophia Libri Tres* (*Three Books on Occult Philosphy*) describes a medal with יהוה written in the form of a square and surrounded by a wish. According to Agrippa, for the medal to be effective in protecting the wearer it had to be made of pure gold or virgin parchment. The ink had to be made from the smoke of a consecrated candle or incense mixed with holy water by an artist purified from sin (Shumaker 1972: 149).

One square that has figured prominently over the centuries in discussions of word patterns is the **sator square** and it brings together the palindrome, the acrostic, and the anagram. It is illustrated in Figure 6. The words are Latin and they form a palindrome: SATOR AREPO TENET OPERA ROTAS. When aligned in a square, they form a multiple acrostic so that words can be read vertically as well as horizontally. Starting in the top left-hand

[11] Note that Hebrew is read from right to left and in biblical Hebrew the vowels were not represented. Some further details are given in Chapter 5.

S	A	T	O	R
A	R	E	P	O
T	E	N	E	T
O	P	E	R	A
R	O	T	A	S

6. Sator square.

square one can read down the first column (the initials), then the second column, then the third, and so on. Moreover, all of this can be done by starting in the bottom right-hand corner and reading right to left or up each column in turn. The word *arepo*, an anagram of *opera*, is otherwise unknown and is usually taken to be a proper name, perhaps one that was made up to complete the square. The translation would be 'The sower, Arepo, holds the wheels with difficulty', taking *opera* to be the ablative of *opera* 'pains, effort, exertion, labour'.

The oldest known example of a sator square is one excavated from the ruins of Herculaneum, which, along with Pompeii, was destroyed by an eruption of Vesuvius in 79 AD. Other examples have been found from various parts of Europe including Scandinavia and Britain dating from the late Middle Ages and Renaissance. There are sator squares in the Runic alphabet and in the Hebrew alphabet. It would appear to be just an ingenious novelty, but it has been treated as having supernatural powers and has been used, mainly as a text in an amulet, to ward off or heal the bite of a rabid dog or snake, and to cure fever or toothache. Among the Pennsylvania Dutch it was used to ward off cattle disease. Some grimoires (handbooks of magic) recommend writing the words of the square in blood and immersing them in holy water for use in amulets. Along with various Christian prayers, the sator square was also placed on the abdomen of a woman about to give birth (McBryde 1907).

The square has been the subject of scores of learned papers, mostly involving attempts to interpret it as a Christian message. For example, it has been noted that there is an anagrammatic relation with the Latin words *pater noster* 'our father' and the letters *a* and *o*, which are equated with the Greek alpha and omega as in 'I am Alpha and Omega...' (Rev.1:11). In order to get the anagram to work you need to take *paternoster* and the letters *a* and *o* twice, but use *n* only once. This can be achieved by writing the words in the form of a cross with *n* doing double duty at the intersection of the vertical and horizontal lines. This arrangement is shown in Figure 7.

The sator square is certainly ingenious in the way it combines the palindrome, the acrostic, and the anagram, though the use of the apparently arbitrary name *Arepo* could be considered cheating. Whether it was originally concocted with a serious purpose is debatable. Certainly palindromes were popular in curses, perhaps, as mentioned above, because they could not be reversed, but this square came to be used as a charm rather than a curse. There is no evidence that it has a Christian origin—in fact the early date of the oldest example virtually precludes that possibility—but attempts to interpret it as Christian have been persistent. C.W. Ceram, writer of popular books on archaeology, suggests reading the text boustrophedon (i.e. left to right and right to left) and repeating *tenet*. This yields *Sator opera tenet* and *Tenet opera sator*. Word order is not critical in Latin and both sentences mean literally 'The sower holds works', which Ceram takes to refer to God. His

7. Paternoster cross.

suggestion echoes those of numerous others who have interpreted the square as having Christian significance.

The sator square remains popular in occult literature. In chapter 97 of Umberto Eco's *Foucault's Pendulum* a character appears under the name *Sator Arepo* and is asked if he knows the final answer behind the 'Sublime Anagram'. In chapter 113 an initiand to a secret society is questioned *Quid facit Sator Arepo*? 'What does Sator Arepo do?'

Lipograms and Univocalics

Sometimes authors set out to compose texts where there are constraints on which letters can be used. One such variety is the **lipogram**, a text in which certain letters have been deliberately avoided (Greek *lipagrammatos* 'missing letter'). The earliest known lipograms were written by a Greek lyric poet of the sixth century

BC, Lasus, who wrote several poems omitting sigma. Other examples exist in Greek and Roman literature as well as in modern European languages and Persian. It is easy enough to compose a text that omits low-frequency letters such as *q*, *x*, and *z*, but much more difficult to compose a text of any length omitting a high-frequency letter, in particular a vowel. In English letter *e* presents the ultimate challenge. It has the highest frequency of any letter and is not only used on its own to represent a vowel, but also as a silent letter in combination with other vowel letters in words such as *mate*, *mete*, *mite*, *mote*, and *mute*.

Astonishing as it may seem, whole novels have been written without using *e*. There is Ernest Vincent Wright's 50,000-word *Gadsby* (1939) and the French novel *La Disparition* 'The Disappearance' (1969) by Georges Perec (1936–1982). An English translation of this work by Gilbert Adair is entitled *A Void*. While Perec had to avoid the masculine form of the definite article in French (*le*) and the plural (*les*), he could at least use the feminine (*la*), but Adair could not use *the*.

Perec was a member of OuLiPo (*Ouvroir de Littérature Potentielle*, or 'Workshop of Potential Literature'), a Paris-based group of writers founded in 1960 by Raymond Queneau and François LeLionnais. Other well-known members were the Italian writer Italo Calvino and the American Harry Matthews. OuLiPo tries to expand literature by borrowing formal patterns from such other domains as mathematics, logic, or chess. Perec's own books range from novels to collections of crossword puzzles, from essays to parodies, from poetry to word games.

Mark Dunn's *Ella Minnow Pea* is a story about a fictional island nation off the southern Atlantic coast of the USA where there is a monument to Nevin Nallop, the inventor of the pangram *The quick brown fox jumps over the lazy dog*. This sentence was used by the communications company Western Union for testing its equipment because it contains all the letters of the alphabet. In Dunn's story the pangram appears on the base of the monument, but with age letters progressively fall off, and as each one falls off the government bans its use. *Ella Minnow Pea* originally bore the subtitle 'a progressively lipogrammatic novel', reflecting the fact that as the government bans the use of more and more letters, the letters are omitted from Dunn's text.

James Thurber (1894–1961) wrote a novella for children (and adults), *The Wonderful O*, about another island nation, Ooroo, where pirates take over and ban the letter *o*. The island is renamed *R*, *coats* become *cats* and *poets pets*. While Thurber's text is not lipogrammatic, the citizens of Ooroo (or R) are forced into lipogrammaticy.

Some writers have attempted to compose prose or verse texts using just one particular vowel. Such writings are called **univocalics**. Perec followed his lipogrammatic novel with a short univocalic work, *Les Revenentes* 'The ghosts', in which *e* was the only vowel used. (The normal spelling of *revenent* is *revenant*.) Here is an example from an English work in which *e* is the vowel.

> Men were never perfect, yet the three brethren Veres were ever esteemed, respected, revered, even when the rest, whether the select few, whether the mere herd, were left neglected.[12]

[12] From *Eve's Legend* by Lord Holland (1824), featured in W.T. Dobson, *Poetical Ingenuities* (1882), quoted in Augarde 1984: 112.

Cryptic Crosswords

Anagrams, palindromes, acrostics, and riddles all come together in the cryptic crossword. Practically every newspaper in western countries carries at least one crossword puzzle. The first crossword was made up by a journalist, Arthur Wynne, and it appeared in a Sunday paper called the *New York World* on 21 December 1913. A decade later crosswords became a real craze, first in the USA and then in Britain. The early crosswords were of the simpler type where the clues are synonymous words or phrases. By the mid-twenties the cryptic type began to appear, in which the clues are deliberately obscure and ambiguous, often with the least likely reading being the correct one. Some of the early cryptic-crossword compilers in Britain took their pseudonyms from some of the infamous Grand Inquisitors of the Spanish Inquisition, *Torquemada*, the first, *Deza*, the second (written backwards as *Azed*), and *Ximenes*, the fourth.

Perhaps the most general principle used in cryptic crosswords is that clues tend to refer to the sequence of letters that make up a word rather than to the meaning. For instance, the clue might be 'Stop a left in headgear'. To get the answer, *halt*, you need to put 'l' for 'left' inside 'hat', rather than looking for a word that means to block a left (punch) with a hat or a cap.

Like the jokesmith, the crossword maker often employs puns and other humorous devices. For instance, the clue for *stalemate* might be 'Perhaps partner of long standing'. In the eighteenth century Dr Johnson was critical of an impoverished university for being too lavish in distributing degrees, claiming that it was hoping to become rich by degrees. This is retold as a joke, but this same pun can be found in cryptic crossword clues. One example I came across was 'drink gets to dances by degrees', and the answer was *rumbas*, i.e., rum (drink) plus BA degrees.

Sequences of letters are also broken up into meaningful sequences irrespective of whether this division is etymologically justified. A word like 'tablecloth' obviously consists of *table* and *cloth*, but the crossword compilers will break 'penchant' into *pen-chant* and 'tarpaulin' into *tar-paul-in* if it suits them. The clue for *penchant* might be 'Inclination to write song', and the clue for *tarpaulin* might be 'Pitch man in for cover'. Crossword makers are also likely to ignore word boundaries if it suits them. The sequence of letters in the word *therapist* can be broken into *the rapist*. The clue might be 'psychologist who harms women'.

The crossword, whether cryptic or simple, employs at least one point of linguistic knowledge, namely letter frequency. A cunning crossword compiler manages to put the less common letters such as *k*, *q*, and *x* between black squares rather than at word intersections, since knowing the position of one of these letters is a big help to the solver.

Here are a few more tricks of the trade:

- Finding 'words' within words. *Leastwise* looks as if it means 'very foolish', so the clue might be 'Very silly, however'. *Laterally* looks like 'late rally'. The clue could be 'Delayed court exchange on the sides'. *Restrain* could be broken into *rest* and *rain*, so the clue might be 'Hold back the remainder before the shower'. Sometimes just part of a word might be identified as a word; for instance, the first three letters of *catalogue* could be identified with 'cat'. A Melbourne hardware chain does this in its advertising. It includes a dog in its commercials and refers to its *dogalogue* rather than catalogue.

• Puns are common. A clue might be 'Short period of enchantment' and the answer would be *spell*. The answers are often phrases. The clue might be 'Free and naked' and the answer would be *Have nothing on*.

• Anagrams are very popular in cryptic crosswords. The presence of an anagram is usually signalled by words such as *muddled*, *confused*, *scrambled*, or simply *out* or *off*. The answer to the clue 'Is the map-room's shape changing?' is *metamorphosis*, which is an anagram of 'Is the map-room's'. The word *changing* does double duty since it indicates the presence of an anagram and supplies the meaning.

• Palindromes crop up too. A clue such as 'raise in either direction (3,2)' would yield *put up*.

• Semordnilaps also feature. A clue such as 'rodents return to light up the sky (4)' would yield *star* (from *rats*).

• Acrostics are also used. A clue such as 'The artist starting the entertainment began with discernment' (5) yields *taste*. The terms 'odds' and 'evens' often refer to the sequence of odd numbered or even numbered letters in neighbouring words. The clue 'odd spouse in trouble' would give *SOS*, i.e. the first, third, and fifth letters of *spouse*.

• Words such as 'leader' and 'head' often refer to an initial, so 'ringleader' might refer to 'r', the initial of 'ring', and 'airhead' is to be interpreted as 'a', the head of 'air'. The clue 'airhead in bright chopper' might thus yield the answer *cleaver*. 'Bright' is *clever*, and if you put *a* in it you can get *cleaver*, which is a chopper. Note that *in* refers to the sequence of letters. Of course you can't take this for granted. The clue could also refer to something being in a chopper, with *chopper* referring to a helicopter.

• The expression 'nothing' can refer to the letter *o*. The clue 'muddled bassets get nothing for deadly dust' is to be interpreted as an anagram of *bassets* plus an *o*, to yield *asbestos*. Other ways of referring to letter *o* are 'love' (zero in tennis), 'duck' (zero in cricket), 'round', or 'circle'.

• Words such as 'clipping' or 'beheading' can refer to the removal of letters to produce another word. For instance, the clue 'a creature beheaded and still healthy' produces the answer *hale*. You have to come up with *whale* as the creature and then behead the word.

• Words such as 'edges', 'limits', and 'extremes' often refer to the first and last letters of a word. 'Extremes of bamboo smell' could be a clue for *BO* (body odour). The answer to the clue 'Traveller ends first inspection through petty details' is to be built up by taking *tr* (the letters at the ends of *traveller*), *i* (the 'first' letter in *inspection*), plus *via* 'through' to yield *trivia* 'petty details'. Words like 'front' and 'end' refer to the first and last letters of a word respectively. Thus 'Popular Front' might refer to *p*, and 'end of world' might refer to *d*.

• Words like 'middle' and 'central' often refer to letters in the middle of a word. 'The middle of the month in the wager is crooked' could be a clue for *bent* (*n*, the middle letter of *month*, in *bet*, a synonym for 'wager').

• Where a sequence of letters is indicated by the clue, these letters might not occur together. For instance, in the clue 'Very quietly edge in and deck out' for *primp*, one has to put *rim* (edge) inside *pp* (pianissimo, see below).

• Words such as 'returning' or 'going back' usually refer to taking a sequence of letters and reversing them. The clue 'a star eager to get back' yields *diva*. You have to think of the word *avid* and then reverse it.

• Words like 'in' often refer to the answer being contained within a word or phrase. For instance, 'South American race found in castle' might be a clue for *Inca* (in-ca(stle)).

• Where the answer is a homophone, the clue will often include words like 'sounds like'. For instance, 'Queen's rule sounds as if it might break drought' would give *rain* (sounds like *reign*).

• Letters are often designated by roman numerals: IV (4), V (5), VI (6), IX (9), X (10), XI (11), L (50), C (100), D (500), and M (1000).

• The crossword compiler needs ways of referring to particular letters and common sequences of letters. Here are some conventional

methods. In the case of the first entry (and other similar ones) the
sequence 'a French' will normally be part of the wording of the clue.
For instance, the clue might be 'a French frock to take off' and the
answer *undress* (un-dress).

a French	un(e)
a German	ein(e)
artist	ra (Royal Academician)
circle	o
company	co
debts	ious (I-owe-you-s)
direction	n, s, e, w (points of the compass)
doctor	dr, mo (medical officer), md, mb
duck	o (zero in cricket)
Edward	ed, ted
gold	au (Latin: *aurum*), or (French *or*)
iron	fe (Latin *ferrum*)
learner	l
left	l, port(side)
loud	f (*forte*)
love	o (zero in tennis)
measure	em, en (printer's measures)
model	t (Model T Ford)
of French	de
one	a, i
point	n, s, e, w (points of the compass)
princess	di (Princess Diana)
right	r, star(board)
road	rd

round	o
queen	er (Elizabeth Regina)
quiet	sh(ush), p (Italian: *piano*)
sailor	tar, ab (able-bodied seaman)
silver	ag (Latin: *argentum*)
soft	sh(ush), p (Italian: *piano*)
street	st
the French	le, la
the German	der, die, das
the Italian	il, la
the Spanish	el, la
very loud	ff (Italian: *fortissimo*)
very soft	pp (Italian: *pianissimo*)
way	st (street), rd (road), via

And now for an example for readers to solve. The solution is in the appendix at the back of the book.

8. Cryptic crossword.

Across

1. British Rail on company horse (6)

4. A wager on the crags for those who help (8)

9. Give cheek to tart for mouth (6)

10. Mob rushes off with headless venerable scholar after postage (8)

12. Where bet was laid in intervarsity boat race (2,6)

13. Post office in Northern Territory in charge of Black Sea (6)

15. Light rain you could barbecue on (4)

16. Every monopoly sounds like a hotel for cars (4,6)

19. Commercial goals let you in (10)

20. Silver artist in India (4)

23. Wear the French around your loins (6)

25. Nonsense to applaud pitfall (8)

27. '. . . for himself' but hopefully includes women (5,3)

28. Saint tears to pieces (6)

29. He leaves to try a hill (8)

30. Wild flower used to catch birds (6)

Down

1. Feel nauseous after receiving short invoice and debts (7)

2. Love soft for one in bottom brings censure (9)

3. 151 very loud point makes steep rock faces (6)

5. Wager one bet but comes second (4)

6. See 22 down (8)

7. It's open above model (5)

8. Silent century confused but can apply design (7)

11. Interruption construed as unlawful entry (5,2)

14. Perfumes from TV stations without direction (7)

17. Fatal result of beastly encounter (5,4)

18. One stupid degree (1,5,2)

19. Gold FBI model will increase (7)

21. A soft sitter is one who places side by side (7)

22. and 6 dn. Four dimensional? (6,8)

24. Shortens sail to avoid rocks (5)

26. Roman orator made feline duck (4)

3

TALKING IN RIDDLES

For words, like Nature, half reveal
And half conceal the soul within.

TENNYSON, *IN MEMORIAM* V

Riddles

The Nature of the Riddle

In present times we tend to treat riddles as a form of light
amusement to be found in Christmas crackers or in books of
jokes aimed at children. However, in the traditional literatures of
Europe and most of Asia solving riddles was one of the heroic
challenges, along with feats of physical strength. This tradition is
carried on in some modern fiction. In Dan Brown's popular novel
The Da Vinci Code the hero is presented with a riddle that asks him
to find 'the orb on the tomb of a knight the pope interred'. The
pope is Alexander Pope, who wrote a eulogy for the knight,

Sir Isaac Newton, and the orb is the apple, which Newton is supposed to have used in the experiments which led to his theory of gravity. The hero realizes the answer to the riddle is APPLE. This supplies the combination to the alphabetical lock on a cryptex, a cylinder containing a message.

In many societies riddling is a form of verbal art practised by adults, often in community riddling sessions, and riddles are frequently serious rather than comic. They figure among the traditional store of wisdom and have a function analogous to proverbs such as *An apple a day keeps the doctor away*, *A stitch in time saves nine*, or *Waste not, want not*. Riddles are reported from all parts of the world, though examples from Australia are scanty. In some societies riddles are put to inductees in initiation rites; in others riddles are exchanged at wakes (Burns 1976: 143). Prophets often speak in riddles or use vague or equivocal language, which makes it easier for them to claim to have been misinterpreted if their predictions go unfulfilled.

The oldest examples of riddles we know of are Sumerian and date back to the third millennium BC, but given that children begin to play with language as soon as they have mastered it, I would suggest that humans probably did the same once they had acquired language, and that riddles have a long ancestry which predates written records.

The following example is a prototypical riddle in our culture:

> What has eyes, but cannot see?
> A potato.

A typical riddle contains at its heart an unspecified subject or topic about which information is supplied in an obscure, often metaphorical form. Here the metaphor lies in the use of *eyes*, whose primary reference is organs of sight, for the shoots on the surface of a potato, an example of polysemy. In this riddle, as in many, there is an apparent contradiction, because we naturally take *eyes* in its primary sense. The contradiction is resolved by the answer, which allows us to see that *eyes* has been used in its extended sense (Georges and Dundes 1963: 112; Taylor 1943: 130).

The next riddle also appears to contain contradictions. It is spoken by a watch, and the contradictions arise from the alternation between *go* and *stop* used in their primary sense and with reference to a watch operating or not operating.

> I went to Turkey, and I stopped there, and I never went there,
>   and I came back again.

This example also illustrates two common features of riddles not found in what for us is the prototypical riddle. First, it is in statement form. A question may be added (*What am I?*) or just left implicit in the context. Secondly, the subject is personified and speaks in the first person.

Sometimes a riddle will be introduced by a conventional formula. In English the line *Riddle me, riddle me, ree* is often used to introduce a riddle in rhyme. The following riddle refers to some kind of berry.

> Riddle me, riddle me ree,
> A little man in a tree;
> A stick in his hand,
> A stone in his throat,
> If you read me this riddle
> I'll give you a groat.

Such formulas are found in African cultures. Among the Lamba, for instance, the riddler invites someone to try and answer a riddle by saying *Tyo*, which means 'Guess the riddle'. Acceptance of the game is expressed in the phrase *Ka kesa* 'Let it come' or *Ka mu leta* 'Bring it' (Harries 1971: 381). Among the Mbeere of Kenya the riddler asks *Gwata ndaĩ* 'Catch this riddle' and one accepts the challenge by replying *Nagwata* 'I catch' (Glazier and Glazier 1976: 192). In Vietnamese the optional formula to introduce a riddle is *Đố X* 'I challenge you, X' and the optional question that follows is *Là cái gì?* 'What is it?' (Nha Trang Pensinger 2001).

Although a typical riddle involves metaphor, it is possible to have a riddle that is literal, and which relies on the fact that particular properties can be common to a number of referents. The lines of the following riddle (which refers to a blackberry or bramble) can be taken literally, but there is a partial change of subject after line one. The white flowers are the subject of line one, whereas in the other three lines subject is the fruit: successively green, red, and black.

> First I am as white as snow,
> Then as green as grass I grow,
> Next I am as red as blood,
> Lastly I'm as black as mud.

One of the oldest recorded riddles is found in the Bible (Judges 14:14). After killing a young lion with his bare hands, Samson saw that bees had swarmed and built a hive in the carcass, so he proposed the following riddle to the Philistines:

> Out of the eater came something to eat;
> out of the strong came something sweet.

Like the blackberry riddle, this riddle does not depend on metaphor, but on vagueness. 'The eater' could be any creature that eats; 'something to eat' could be anything edible, and so on. There is really no way anyone who had not seen the honey in the lion could have solved the riddle, but the Philistines obtained the answer from Samson's wife, Delilah.

The blackberry example and the translation of Samson's riddle also illustrate another feature of riddles, namely that they often have formal properties such as metre and rhyme. The most common type of verse found in Vietnamese riddles has a line of six monosyllables followed by a line of eight monosyllables with a rhyme between the last syllable of the first line and the sixth one of the second line. In Vietnamese almost all words are monosyllabic or consist of combinations of monosyllables. The answer to the following example is a coconut (Nha Trang Pensinger 2001):

> *Sông không đến, bến không vào*
> *Lơ lửng giữa trời làm sao có nước?*
> It neither goes to a river nor comes to shore,
> It is suspended in air, but somehow has water in it.

In the Efik language of Nigeria and Cameroon there are proverb-like riddles (see example on p. 59) in which the answer normally echoes the tonal pattern of the question (Simmons 1958) and in the older Germanic languages riddles were in alliterative verse (illustrated on p. 53). Some riddles have a pattern of parallel statements rather than metre or rhyme, as in the following riddle describing a coffin (Taylor 1943: 133):

> The man that make it, he don't use it.
> The man that buy it, he don't use it.
> The man that use it, he don't know it.

There are two types of riddle found in Europe that are not common elsewhere. One is a riddle that depends on a pun or word play in the answer rather than a metaphor in the question. This type is sometimes called a conundrum.

> Why did the ram go straight ahead?
> Because he didn't see the ewe turn.
>
> What did Mrs Cook say when Captain Cook died?
> That's the way the cookie crumbles.
>
> Why did the fly fly?
> Because the spider spied 'er.
>
> Why do ducks go under water ?
> For divers reasons.

The other type simply demands clear thinking.

> A man looks at a portrait and says the following:
>   Brothers and sisters have I none,
>   But that man's father is my father's son.
> Whose portrait is he looking at?

Indian riddles frequently incorporate word play, perhaps not surprisingly given that traditional Indian literature is full of puns and so forth. In the collection of Amir Khusro (1253–1325), for instance, we find examples like the following one where the answer, namely *na:khu:n* 'finger- and toe-nails', appears within the riddle itself as the sequence *na:khu:n* (Vatuk 1969: 145).

> bi:sõ   ka: sir   ka:ṭ diya:
> twenty of head   cut off
> na: ma:ra: na: khu:n kiya:
> not killed nor blood made.

The heads of twenty were cut off,
There was no killing or bloodshed.

In another type two languages are used, Persian in the first line and Hindi in the second. The answer is *sada:*, which can be interpreted as *sada:* 'voice' in Persian and *sada:* 'always' in Hindi (Vatuk 1969: 148).

Quvat-e ru:h   ci:st
strength of.soul what.is

Pya:ri   ko kab   dekhiye
beloved to when should.see

What is the strength of the soul?   *sada:* the voice
When should one see one's beloved?   *sada:* always

Most riddles are part of oral culture, but in a literate society it is possible for riddles to depend on the written form. In English, for instance, there are riddles such as, 'What does it take to turn a lad into a lady?' The answer is 'y' (Green and Pepicello 1980: 26).[1]

Riddles for Heroes

The ancient literature of Europe and Asia is full of stories where heroes are asked to solve riddles or compete in solving riddles. It is not certain that riddles were ever posed to heroes in real life, but Maranda (1976: 127), quoting Ganander in *Aenigmata Fennica*, mentions that in the past in Finland suitors were required to answer three riddles to prove themselves worthy of winning the

---

[1] For more complete discussion about defining and classifying riddles, see, for instance, Burns 1976; Georges and Dundes 1963; Green and Pepicello 1984; Hamnett 1967; Maranda 1976; and Taylor 1943.

maiden of their choice. In chapter 6 of *The Banquet of the Seven Sages* Plutarch mentions a story about the king of Ethiopia challenging the king of Egypt to solve a riddle in a contest for territory that lay between the two kingdoms, and the Byzantine scholar Maximus Planudes (1260–1330) relates a duel of riddles in his *Life of Aesop* between Lycerus, king of Babylon, and Nectanebo, king of Egypt. There is also a story that the oracle at Thebes posed the following riddle to anyone arriving in the city:

> What animal is it that in the morning goes on four feet, at noon on two, and in the evening upon three?

As the story goes, the riddle remained unsolved for years and all who attempted to solve it and failed were devoured by the Sphinx. When Oedipus arrived, he solved the riddle, pointing out that it referred to a human, who crawls on four limbs as a baby, walks on two legs as an older child and adult, and uses a walking stick in old age.

In the folklore of Europe and Asia maidens are often protected by riddles. There is an example in Puccini's opera *Turandot*, the libretto of which comes from a Persian collection of stories, *The Thousand and One Days*, via an adaption by Schiller. The story also exemplifies the power of a name, which is further illustrated in Chapter 7.

> A prince of Tartary falls in love with an icy-hearted Chinese princess, Turandot (originally *Turan-dokht* 'daughter of Turan' with *dokht* being cognate with English *daughter*), but to be successful a suitor must answer three riddles. Suitors who fail are beheaded. Undaunted the prince accepts the challenge. To the first of Turandot's riddles, 'What is born each night and dies at dawn?', the prince answers, 'Hope'. To the second riddle, 'What flickers red and warm like a flame, but is not fire?', the

prince answers, 'Blood'. The third riddle is 'What is like ice, but burns like fire?' The prince answers, 'Turandot'. All three answers are correct. Turandot, who has made up the three supposedly unanswerable riddles to protect herself from men, is horrified and begs to be let off, and the prince offers her a way out. If she can find out his name by sunrise, he will forfeit his life. Morning comes and Turandot has not found out the prince's name. She must marry him. But when the prince kisses her, she begins to feel stirrings of love. The prince reveals that his name is Calaf, son of Timur, thus placing his life in Turandot's hands and relying on her new-found feelings of love to save him. Fortunately his gamble pays off.[2]

A heroine protected by riddles can be found in the Latin novella *The History of Apollonius, Prince of Tyre*, though the young woman in this instance is not a maiden. The story was popular in the Middle Ages and was incorporated into several works, including Gower's *Confessio Amantis*. In the story King Antiochus carries on an incestuous relationship with his daughter and keeps suitors at bay by proposing a riddle that they must solve if they wish to marry her. If they fail, they are beheaded. The riddle is

> Scelere vehor, maternam carnem vescor.
> I am carried away by crime. I feed on maternal flesh.[3]

Apollonius solves the riddle. He says to the king, 'When you say, "I am carried away by crime", look to yourself, and when you say,

---

[2] In the original story a servant tricks Calaf into revealing his name.

[3] There is in fact a further line to the riddle, which is obscure, namely, *Quaero patrem meum, meae matris virum, uxoris meae filiam: non invenio* 'I look for my father, the husband of my mother, the daughter of my wife and I find not'. Note also that *vescor* would have taken an ablative complement not an accusative one in classical Latin.

"I feed on maternal flesh", look to your daughter'. Antiochus does not play fair. He tells Apollonius that he is wrong and sends someone to kill him.

In the Norse sagas characters are often faced not only with physical trials but also with riddles. In *Hervarar Saga ok Heiðreks* King Heithrek swears that if an accused man can ask a riddle he cannot answer, the man will go free. One such accused is Gestumblindi, who makes a sacrifice to Odin (Óðinn) seeking his help. Odin appears to him in the guise of Gestumblindi and the two change clothes. Odin presents himself before the king as Gestumblindi and proceeds to ask the king a number of riddles. Two of these are given below. The subject of the first is a spider and of the second a die or dice. The letters þ (thorn) and ð (eth) are both to be read as *th* in this and in subsequent examples from Old Norse and Old English.

Hvat er þat undra,	What is the wonder
er ek úti sá	Outside I saw
fyr Dellings durum;	Before the Doors of Day
fætr hefir átta,	Feet it has eight
en fjögur augu	And eyes four
ok berr ofar	And it carries its knees
kné en kvið?	Higher than its stomach?
Heiðrekr konungr,	King Heidrik,
hyggðu at gátu.	Guess the riddle.
Hvat er þat dýra,	What is the beast
er drepr fé manna	That slays men's wealth
ok er járni kringt utan;	And encased in iron
horn hefir átta,	Eight corners it has
en höfuð ekki,	But no head
ok fylgja því margir mjök?	And much depends on it?
Heiðrekr konungr,	King Heidrik,
hyggðu at gátu.	Guess the riddle.

The king answers all the riddles put to him, and in the end Odin, in frustration, asks a question to which only he can know the answer, namely, 'What did Odin whisper in Balder's ear before Balder was placed on his funeral pyre?' At this the king realizes the riddler must be Odin himself, so he draws his sword and attempts to kill him. Odin escapes by turning himself into a falcon, though the king manages to hack off his tail feathers.

European Riddles

Riddles in verse were popular with the Greeks and later with the Romans. Cleobulina of Rhodes (also known as Eumetis), who lived in the sixth century BC, was famous for her riddles or enigmas (αἴνιγματα) in hexameter verse. In chapter 6 of Plutarch's *Banquet of the Seven Sages*, she responds to Aesop's question about what people would think if pipe-makers used asses' bones in place of bones of fawns with a riddle about the unlikelihood of the bones of an ass, a gross animal, being suitable for harmony.

Some classical riddles incorporate other forms of word play. The following is a palindrome.

In girum imus nocte et consumimur igni.

It means 'Into the circle we go by night and are consumed by the fire'. There is no metaphor, just a lack of explicit subject. The answer has not been recorded but is probably *moths*.

In the following example the subject is a palindrome, namely *āra* 'altar'. Note that this palindrome would not hold for classical spoken Latin since the first vowel is long and the second short. It works in later Latin, where the length distinction had been lost, and it works in the spelling since vowel length was not represented.

Si me retro legis, dicam tibi semper id ipsum.
Una mihi facies ante retroque manet.

If you read me backwards, I say ever the same.
I present one face forwards and backwards.

In the following example the subject is the proper name *Eva*, which can be reversed to yield the imperative verb form *ave* 'hail'.

Si me retro legis, faciam de nomine verbum.
Femina cum fuerim, imperativus ero.

If you read me backwards, I shall make a verb from a noun.
Feminine I was, imperative I shall be.[4]

There is a collection of a hundred Latin riddles or *Aenigmata* by an otherwise unknown author, Caelius Firmianus Symphonius, probably of the fourth or fifth century, perhaps earlier. These consist of three lines of Latin hexameters, with elegant and clever phrasing (Ohl 1928). The subject of each is given, so they do not seem like riddles.

XVI. Tinea

Littera me pavit, nec quid sit littera novi;
in libris vixi, nec sum studiosior inde;
exedi Musas, nec adhuc tamen ipsa profeci.

16. Bookworm

Letters fed me, but I did not know what a letter was.
I lived in books, but I am no wiser for it.
I consumed the Muses, but nevertheless I have not yet progressed.

[4] These examples are taken from the introduction by Elizabeth Peck (née Hickman DuBois) to her edition of *The Hundred Riddles of Symphosius* posted on the web under *Lacus Curtius. Symphosius. Aenigmata. Elizabeth Peck's Introduction*. The riddles were found in Leyden by Lucian Müller in a manuscript of Ausonius, a fourth-century Latin poet.

These were popular in the late Roman empire and the Middle Ages and some of them were incorporated in the *History of Apollonius of Tyre* mentioned above.

Riddles remained a major form of entertainment in the Middle Ages. In England, Bede (673–735) composed riddles, as did his contemporaries Boniface, Hwætberht, and Tatwine (or St Tatwin). There is also a collection of riddles by Aldhelm (640–709), abbott of Malmesbury and later bishop of Sherborne, a collection that owes a great deal to Symphonius. All these writers wrote in Latin. Our knowledge of riddles in Old English comes from a collection of ninety-odd riddles in a manuscript known as *The Exeter Book*, written around the end of the tenth century (Williamson 1977). They range in length from one line to over a hundred. They are all in the common verse mode of the time, namely alliterative verse with two stresses to the half-line and at least one alliteration between the half-lines. Here is a short riddle on the same subject as the one from Symphonius quoted above. The title is not stated, but with *moððe* 'moth' in line one and *wyrm* 'worm' in line three, there is little left for the reader to work out.

> Moððe word fræt.   Me þæt þuhte
> wrætlicu wyrd,   þa ic þæt wundor gefrægn,
> þæt se wyrm forswealg   wera gied sumes,
> þeof in þystro,   þrymfæstne cwide
> ond þæs strangan staþol.   Stælgiest ne wæs
> wihte þy gleawra,   þe he þam wordum swealg.

Words the moth ate,   and it seemed to me
A curious deed,   when that wonder I heard,
That the worm swallowed up   the words of a man

Thief in the night,   his glorious speech
And its strong support.   The thieving stranger
Was no whit the wiser   for the words he swallowed.

Such obscurity as there is derives from ambiguity in *words*. The
bookworm eats the physical words, the parchment and ink, but we
normally understand words as meaningful elements drawn from
the mental lexicon. As we saw in the previous chapter, this kind of
ambiguity is also the stock in trade of the composer of cryptic
crosswords.

Most of the riddles in *The Exeter Book* are serious. One of them
poses a question at length, which is along the lines, 'What is that
wonder that wanders through the world, bringing weeping, something no creature çan escape?' The answer is, in summary, 'Age is
on earth altogether mighty, destroying everything, biting iron with
rust and doing the same to us'. Another in the first person
describes the life of a piece of animal skin that becomes a page of
the Bible. It is soaked, deprived of its hair, covered in the tracks of
a bird's pride (a quill pen), and bound. In its final state it offers
wisdom and virtue.

Some of the riddles in *The Exeter Book* have two interpretations,
one respectable and the other bawdy. Riddle XXV can be taken to
refer to an onion, but there is an X-rated alternative.

Ic eom wunderlicu wiht,   wifum on hyhte,
neahbuendum nyt;   nængum sceþþe
burgsittendra,   nymþe bonan anum.
Staþol min is steapheah,   stonde ic on bedde,
neoþan ruh nathwær.   Neþeð hwilum
ful cyrtenu   ceorles dohtor,
modwlonc meowle,   þæt heo on mec gripeð,

ræseð mec on reodne,   reafað min heafod,
fegeð mec on fæsten.   Feleþ sona
mines gemotes,   seo þe mec nearwað,
wif wundenlocc.   Wæt bið þæt eage.

A wonder am I   to women a joy,
To neighbours a need.   To none
Bearing ill   save one who'd kill.
In the bed I stand   tall and straight,
But rough below.   Sometimes dares
A wilful woman   grab me she will,
Raze me red,   ravage my head,
Clench me close.   She'll suffer soon
From meeting with me   and beating me,
*Wounden-locked woman   will get a wet eye.

*wound as in wound up, i.e. plaited or braided

Vulgar ambiguity like this is common in riddles. In this case the respectable answer may came to mind first, but in many cases the vulgar interpretation is the first to suggest itself. The innocent answer may then be given in an attempt to embarrass the person to whom the riddle has been posed. For instance, a common contemporary riddle asks *What is it a man can do standing, a woman sitting down, and a dog on three legs?* The obvious response is 'urinate', but the answer is 'shake hands'.

Educational texts in the Middle Ages were often in the form of a dialogue between teacher and student, and riddles appear in some of these dialogues. One such text is from the English scholar Alcuin (Ealhwine c.735–804), who was invited to the court of Charlemagne and among other duties acted as mentor to Charlemagne's second son, Pepin (Pippinus). It is a dialogue between Alcuin and Pepin in most of which Alcuin answers questions with kennings. Kennings are compounds such as *whale-road* for 'sea' or phrases describing an object, a creature, or some phenomenon. These kennings are not always transparent and they often have a riddle-like quality. Here they are given as answers to questions. In other words these pairs of question and answer are like riddles in reverse with the obscurity in the answer.

P. Quid est aer?	A. Custodia vitae.
What is breath?	The guard of life.
P. Quid est vita?	A. Beatorum laetitia, miserorum moestitia, exspectatio mortis.
What is life?	The joy of the blessed, the grief of the unhappy, a waiting for death.
P. Quid est mors?	A. Inevitabilis eventus, incerta peregrinatio, lacrimae viventium testamenti firmamentum, latro hominis.
What is death?	An inevitable outcome, an uncertain journey, the tears of the living, the fulfilling of the will, the thief of Man.
P. Quid est luna?	A. Oculus noctis, roris larga, praesaga tempestatum.
What is the moon?	The eye of night, the giver of dew, the prophet of the weather.

In the following example, however, Alcuin presents Pepin with a riddle, and Pepin answers with a kenning. The referent is an arrow. The word *feminam* 'female' refers to the feminine gender of the Latin *sagitta*.

A. Vidi feminam volantem, rostrum habentem ferreum, et corpus
   ligneum et caudam pennatam, mortem portantem.
   I saw a something female flying with an iron beak, a wooden
   body, and a feathered tail carrying death.

P. Socia militum.
   A soldier's ally.

Riddles became popular in France and England in the seventeenth century. They were usually in verse and the emphasis was on elegance of expression. Here is an example from Jonathan Swift (1667–1745). The subject is obviously the moon. Note in passing that in Swift's time *quarter* could still rhyme with *Tartar*, the first vowel not having acquired rounding from the preceding [w].

> I with borrowed silver shine,
> What you see is none of mine.
> First I show you but a quarter,
> Like the bow that guards the Tartar;
> Then the half, and then the whole,
> Ever dancing round the pole;
> And true it is, I chiefly owe
> My beauty to the shades below.

Non-European Riddles

As noted at the beginning of the chapter, riddles are found in numerous cultures around the world. Outside Europe most riddles are instructive rather than amusing. They are often proverb-like, and like proverbs they belong to a familiar repertoire and commonly play a prominent part in community gatherings. One person might pose the question and the audience give the answer, though the terms 'question' and 'answer' are not always appropriate, as can be seen from the examples below.

In sub-Saharan Africa riddles are an important cultural form. Most riddles are from a traditional repertoire so the addressee is not set the task of trying to decode the riddle. Even where a new riddle is invented, the solution is offered (Messenger 1960: 226). In one type found among the Nyanga of the Congo, a proverbial-style utterance is followed by an explanation in fixed form (Harries 1971: 389).[5]

> Who desires a beauty clothes her.
> That is to say, however plain she may be, they will desire the
>   woman you clothe.

I take the 'explanation' to mean that a plain woman can be made desirable by appropriate clothing and accessories.

Among the Anang of southeastern Nigeria there are similar riddles. The example below begins with an apparent reference to a pepper tree, but the reference is metaphorical (Messenger 1960: 230).

> The pepper tree growing next to the well does not bear ripe fruit.
> Women from Obonukwa do not marry because they have 'strong
>   head'.

People passing to and from a well will pluck the peppers from any tree growing near the well and eat them, not allowing them to mature into desirable spicy fruit. The village of Obonukwa lies on the border of Ibo territory and the Anang believe the women have picked up bad

---

[5] No introductory frame is used with these Nyanga pairs, and for that reason Harries does not consider them as riddles (Harries 1971: 388).

Ibo habits such as indulging in pre-marital sexual relations. They are plucked prematurely and do not grow into desirable fruit.

In the next example the relationship between the two parts is not apparent without extra information (Messenger 1960: 228).

> A piece of firewood burns.
> Darkness brings evil thoughts.

There is an analogy between a piece of firewood continuing to burn into the night and evil thoughts that arise when one lies down to sleep. These thoughts are attributed to evil spirits, and the proverb is a warning to be on guard against such spirits.

A similar type is found among the Efik (Simmons 1958: 130).

> Pepper burns my throat.
> The world loved me when I was a child.

An immature pepper can be chewed whole, but a ripe pepper is spicy and used only as a condiment. Children are sweet and treated well, but old people are not always treated so well.

Among the Dusun of Borneo riddles play a traditional part in educating the young, rather as proverbs do for us. The one below concerns the sacrifice for a divination ritual (Williams 1963b: 151, Riddle 58).

> Q. White is the goat and black is the pig.
> No use for one to die,
> The two virgins must die together.

> A. The pig and the goat must die together to make the ritual right.

The next one teaches about the role of the headman in settling disputes (Williams 1963b: 141, Riddle 3). The answer is phrased in general terms, but in the context of local culture it would be understood as meaning the headman.

Q. The cloth is unravelled and no one can mend it but Iangkutide, who spends a day repairing it.

A. One who settles cases at law.

The Rebus

A **rebus** is a representation using pictures or icons instead of words. The word *rebus* comes from the Latin expression *Non verbis sed rebus* 'Not by words, but by things'. The earliest systems of writing, which developed in Mesopotamia, Egypt, China, and Central America, all started with pictograms such as a drawing of a hill to represent a hill or an ideogram such as a pair of legs to represent the notion of walking or going. Obviously most words do not lend themselves to these methods of representation, so pictograms and ideograms came to be used for syllables or words that sounded the same as words that had a pictorial representation. An example in English would be to represent *lionize* by a pictogram of a lion and a pictogram of two eyes, exploiting homophony between *lion-* and *lion*, and between *-ize* and *eyes*. A representation of this type is a rebus.[6]

Since the Middle Ages the rebus has been popular in heraldry, a process known as canting. Nicholas Breakspeare (1100–1159), who became Pope Adrian IV, had a broken spear in his coat of arms. One family with the surname Bowes had bows that you tie in theirs, and another family with the same name had bows of the kind that shoot arrows. The late mother of the present queen of

[6] See ch. 10 of Blake 2008.

England was born Elizabeth Bowes-Lyon and her coat of arms contains bows (of the shooting type) and lions. The coat of arms of Princess Beatrice of York retains part of this motif with an overlay of three bees (bee-trice).

In the nineteenth and twentieth centuries rebuses were popular in books of word puzzles and the like. Over the last decade or so it has become popular to send messages by mobile phone, a context in which brevity is at a premium. Lots of abbreviations are used, as is the rebus principle in using C for 'see', U for 'you', 2 for 'to', 4 for 'for', and 8 for 'ate' or more often for the syllable -*ate* in words like *later*, so that *See you later* could be texted as CUL8R.

The Charade

A development of the elegant verse riddle was the charade, in which clues were given to the letters or syllables of a word rather than to the complete referent. Here is an interesting early example from Swift's one-time lover, Esther Vanhomrigh (*c*.1688–1723).[7] It has something of the rebus about it in that it finds homophones for the syllables of *Jonathan Swift* in the first three lines.

Cut the name of the man who his mistress denied,	
And let the first of it be only applied	Joseph → Jo
To join with the prophet who David did chide;	Nathan
Then say what a horse is that runs very fast,	Swift
And that which deserves to be first put the last;	Put the adjective last

---

[7] Swift gave Esther Vanhomrigh the name *Vanessa*, which he made up by taking the first syllables of her surname and given name and adding the feminine ending.

Spell all then, and put them together, to find
The name and the virtues of him I designed.
Like the patriarch in Egypt, he's versed in the state;
Like the prophet in Jewry, he's free with the great;
Like a racer he flies, to succour with speed,
When his friends want his aid or desert is in need.

Charades became popular in England in the late eighteenth century. Here is perhaps the most-quoted example. It is by Catherine Maria Fanshawe (1765–1834), and it refers to the letter H.

'Twas whispered in Heaven, 'twas muttered in Hell,
And echo caught faintly the sound as it fell;
On the confines of Earth, 'twas permitted to rest,
And in the depths of the ocean its presence confessed;
'Twill be found in the sphere when 'tis riven asunder,
Be seen in the lightning and heard in the thunder;
'Twas allotted to man with his earliest breath,
Attends him at birth and awaits him at death,
Presides o'er his happiness, honor and health,
Is the prop of his house and the end of his wealth.
In the heaps of the miser, 'tis hoarded with care,
But is sure to be lost on his prodigal heir;
It begins every hope, every wish it must bound;
With the husbandman toils, and with monarchs is crowned;
Without it the soldier and seaman may roam,
But woe to the wretch who expels it from home!
In the whispers of conscience its voice will be found,
Nor e'er in the whirlwind of passion be drowned;
'Twill soften the heart; but though deaf be the ear,
It will make him acutely and instantly hear.
Set in shade, let it rest like a delicate flower;
Ah! Breathe on it softly, it dies in an hour.

In chapter 9 of *Emma* Jane Austen introduces an elaborate charade that plays a part in the plot. Mr Elton is invited to submit a charade for the amusement of Emma and her protégé, Harriet. He delivers the following:

> My first displays the wealth and pomp of kings,
> Lords of the earth! their luxury and ease.
> Another view of man, my second brings,
> Behold him there, the monarch of the seas!
> But ah! united, what reverse we have!
> Man's boasted power and freedom, all are flown;
> Lord of the earth and sea, he bends a slave,
> And woman, lovely woman, reigns alone.
> Thy ready wit the word will soon supply;
> May its approval beam in that soft eye!

Emma interprets the first two lines as referring to *court*, and the next two to *ship*. These are united in the fifth line to form *courtship* and the last lines carry on the courtship, which Emma mistakenly believes to be aimed at Harriet, though in fact she herself is the object of Mr Elton's affection.

The charade with purely verbal clues lives on in collections of word games for children, but in the nineteenth century another form of charade came into vogue, probably first in France, and that is what most people today think of when *charade* is mentioned. This is a game in which someone seeks to represent a word or phrase in mime. The actor usually starts by indicating the category of phrase to be represented. She might pretend to open a book to indicate a book title, pretend to sing to indicate a song title, or wiggle the upraised index and middle fingers of each hand to represent quotation marks and thereby indicate a well-known phrase or quote.

The next step is to signal the number of words by holding up fingers and then to hold up one finger to indicate the first word to be represented, then two fingers to indicate the second word, and so on. More interestingly the miming can operate on the basis of syllables. The number of syllables is indicated by laying the appropriate number of fingers of one hand on the other arm, and the first syllable is then indicated by laying one finger on the arm, the second syllable by laying two fingers on the arm, and so on. The breaking up of a word into syllables allows the rebus principle to be employed. There is also a convention for indicating words or syllables that sound the same as the target. A hand cupped behind the ear is the conventional gesture for indicating 'Sounds like'.

There are also ways of representing the two most common forms of inflection in English. Plural is indicated by linking the little fingers, and past tense is indicated by waving your hand over your shoulder as if you are brushing away a fly. In all there are forty or so conventions for indicating characteristics of the word or phrase to be guessed.

Equivocation and Prevarication

The idea that supernatural beings can communicate with humans is widespread. Supposed communication can come through such things as viewing the flight of birds or the entrails of a slaughtered animal. In modern times there are still people who claim to be able to tell the future from the distribution of tea leaves in the bottom of a cup or the fall of dice. The thread connecting these possibilities is chance. Where an outcome is not determined, there is scope for seeing the influence of supernatural forces in the result. Dreams and drug-induced hallucinations have long been a favoured source of prophecy since they involve the brain producing a scenario without any conscious determination on the part of the dreamer or hallucinator. In the case of dreams, supernatural forces have often been perceived as being at work.

In most societies communication from the spirit world is believed to reach only a select few, variously called oracles, sooth-sayers, shamans, priests/priestesses, witches/warlocks, or witch doctors. In the Ancient Greek world there were **sibyls** who issued prophecies. The term *sibyl* was ambiguous in that it could refer to the office of sibyl, the particular person holding the office, or the succession of sibyls who held the office over the centuries. The sibyls were women who inhabited caves or shrines, and their succession may have gone back to pre-Hellenic times. The best-known sibyl was the Delphic Sibyl, who lived on the side of Mount Parnassus; other well-known sibyls included the Ery-thraean Sibyl of Ionia in the Aegean and the Cumaean Sibyl, who lived in caves near Vesuvius. They were said to have uttered their prophecies in a state of induced frenzy, making strange, inarticulate sounds, a kind of glossolalia. However, Cicero points out (*De Divitatione*, LIV) that the prophecies of the Erythraean Sibyl were written out so that the initial letters of the sections formed words, i.e. they were acrostics, which indicates artful presentation even if preceded by spontaneous enlightenment. The sibyls were also said to have written their prophecies on sheets which they placed outside their caves. This meant the prophecies could be scattered by the wind, which might have added a degree of obscurity, a desirable result from the point of view of the sibyl, who needed to be vague, since obviously an explicit prophecy runs the risk of being disproved and thereby ruining the reputation of the prophet.

A good example of the vagueness and ambiguity of typical prophecy can be found in the story of Croesus, king of Lydia, who consulted the Delphic Oracle in 550 BC about his chances of success if he attacked the Persian empire. The Delphic Oracle, like the Delphic Sibyl, lived on Mount Parnassus. Croesus was told he would destroy a great empire. He also asked whether his kingdom would be long-lasting. The Oracle replied:

> Wait till a time shall come when a mule is monarch of Media;
> Then, thou delicate Lydian, away to the pebbles of Hermus.

Croesus thought the idea of a mule (*ēmionos*) becoming king of the Medes so fantastic that the prophecy must mean his kingdom would last indefinitely. He went ahead and attacked the Persians and was defeated. He had destroyed a great empire, his own. When he remonstrated with the Oracle, he was told that he should have enquired which empire was meant, and the Oracle also said that he had misunderstood about the mule. Cyrus was a mule because his mother was a Mede and his father a Persian (Herodutus 1: 53–5, 91). A mule is a hybrid of horse and donkey, so the Oracle had used *mule* in a metaphorical sense.

A curious fact about the sibyls is that they were accepted as a genuine source of revelation by early Christians, who were otherwise intent on stamping out any traces of pagan belief. Augustine, for instance, in *The City of God* (18: 23), quotes Lactantius, who in turn quotes an unnamed sibyl as having prophesied Christ's suffering, death, and resurrection. The most famous case of a pagan prophet being accepted as a source of Christian revelation is that of Virgil's fourth eclogue, part of which reads as follows (lines 4–14):

Ultima Cumaei venit iam carminis aetas;
magnus ab integro saeclorum nascitur ordo.
iam redit et Virgo, redeunt Saturnia regna,
iam nova progenies caelo demittitur alto.
tu modo nascenti puero, quo ferrea primum
desinet ac toto surget gens aurea mundo,
casta fave Lucina; tuus iam regnat Apollo.
Teque adeo decus hoc aevi, te consule, inibit,
Pollio, et incipient magni procedere menses;
te duce, si qua manent sceleris vestigia nostri,
inrita perpetua solvent formidine terras.

Now is come the last age of the Cumaean [Sybil's] song: the
great cycle of the ages is born anew. Now returns the virgin,
returns the reign of Saturn: now from high heaven a new
generation descends. You, chaste Lucina, with the birth of this
boy, in whom the iron race now ceases, and the golden one
arises over all the world, grant your favour; Now your Apollo
reigns. And in your consulate, in yours, Pollio, shall this glory of
the age begin, and the great months begin to roll. Under your
rule any traces of our crime [will] vanish and free the world from
perpetual fear.

This was written about 40 BC, between the assassination of
Julius Caesar (44 BC) and Octavian's victory over Antony at
Actium (31 BC). It is uncertain who the Wunderkind is (the
typical problem of the vagueness of prophecy) and discussion
has raged for two thousand years. The possibility of its referring to Jesus Christ is raised regularly. It is unlikely that Virgil
would have had any knowledge of or interest in Jewish Messianic prophecy. Those who have taken the lines as referring
to Christ assume that Virgil was granted a revelation. This
explains his respected status in the Middle Ages. Virgil's
Aeneid was used for bibliomancy (see page 160), and Dante

has Virgil as his guide to Hell and Purgatory in *The Divine Comedy*.[8]

Sibyls figure in Christian art and there is a reference in the *Dies Irae*, which was part of the text of requiem masses until it was eliminated by the Second Vatican Council (1962–5).

> Dies ira, dies illa
> solvet saeclum in favilla
> teste David cum Sibylla.[9]
>
> Day of wrath is that day
> When ends the world in fire's decay
> As David and the Sibyl say.

As mentioned above, oracles and fortune tellers tend to be equivocal or vague, and with good reason, since precise predictions can easily prove wrong. Sometimes they speak in riddles and, if the few examples that have been preserved are any indication, they regularly use metaphors, as in the mule example.

---

[8] Those who take Virgil's poem to be a messianic prophecy are encouraged by parallels with Isaiah. Virgil predicts that in the Golden Age to come there will be an abundance of nature and an absence of sudden death: 'No great lions will the herds have to fear . . . the snake shall die and the deceiving poisonous plant'. Isaiah had predicted a similar abundance (7: 21–25) and a similar period when, to use Tennyson's phrase, nature would no longer 'be red in tooth and claw'. 'The wolf also shall dwell with the lamb, and the leopard shall lie down with the kid; and the calf, and the young lion and the fatling together; and a little child shall lead them' (11:6).

[9] The phrase *dies ira, dies irae* first appears in the Vulgate translation of Sophonias/Zephaniah 1: 15. It was incorporated in a number of medieval poems. The 'final version' quoted here, at least the version that was used in requiem masses, is attributed to Thomas of Celano.

There is a well-known example of equivocation in *Macbeth*. Macbeth seeks to know what the future holds for him and consults three witches, who summon up apparitions. An apparition of a bloody child gives Macbeth the following assurance (IV.1):

> Be bloody, bold and resolute; laugh to scorn
> The power of man, for none of woman born
> Shall harm Macbeth.

Then another apparition gives a further assurance:

> Macbeth shall never vanquish'd be, until
> Great Birnam Wood to high Dunsinane hill
> Shall come against him.

Macbeth takes the first prediction to mean that no man can harm him since all men are born of women, and since he knows that woods cannot walk, he takes the second prophecy to mean he can never be defeated. However, when Macduff's forces attack Macbeth they cut down branches from Birnam Wood and carry them to Dunsinane as camouflage, so in a sense Birnam Wood does come to Dunsinane. And Macduff can be regarded as not having been born of woman because he was 'from his mother's womb untimely ripp'd'—in other words, delivered by Caesarian section. Here is the exchange in which Macbeth learns how the prophecy deceived him (V.8).

> MACBETH Thou losest labour:
> As easy mayst thou the intrenchant air
> With thy keen sword impress as make me bleed:
> Let fall thy blade on vulnerable crests;
> I bear a charmed life, which must not yield,
> To one of woman born.

MACDUFF   Despair thy charm;
           And let the angel whom thou still hast served
           Tell thee, Macduff was from his mother's womb
           Untimely ripp'd.

MACBETH   Accursed be that tongue that tells me so,
           For it hath cow'd my better part of man!
           And be these juggling fiends no more believed,
           That palter with us in a double sense;
           That keep the word of promise to our ear,
           And break it to our hope. I'll not fight with thee.

In a modern rewriting of *Macbeth* by Peter Moffat in the *ShakespeaRe-Told* UK television series (2005) the witches are replaced by rubbish collectors who assure Macbeth that he is safe by telling him pigs will fly before he is defeated. This quotes the saying 'Pigs might fly' and sounds like a watertight guarantee. But when Macduff comes to confront Macbeth, a police helicopter is heard overhead. Pigs might fly indeed!

Riddles for the Reader

Here are is a variety of riddles for those readers who would like to try their hand. The answers are in the Appendix.

1. Why is a publican like a prisoner?
2. Why is the figure nine like a peacock?
3. What gets wetter the more it dries?
4. If you have me, you want to share me. If you share me, you haven't got me. What am I?
5. What can run but never walks, has a mouth but never talks, has a head but never weeps, has a bed but never sleeps?

6.   My life can be measured in hours,
              I serve by being devoured.
                   Thin, I am quick
                   Fat, I am slow
                  Wind is my foe.
                   What am I?

7. What is it the more you take away the larger it becomes?

8.   Old Mother Twitchett had but one eye,
              And a long tail which she let fly;
              And every time she went over a gap,
              She left a bit of her tail in a trap.

9. I have many feathers to help me fly. I have a body and head, but I'm not alive. It is your strength which determines how far I go. You can hold me in your hand, but I'm never thrown. What am I?

10. What always speaks the truth but doesn't say a word?

11. Why are naked people hard to see?

12. What's the greatest worldwide use of cowhide?

4

CIPHERS AND CODES

It may well be doubted whether human ingenuity can construct an enigma which human ingenuity may not by proper application resolve.

EDGAR ALLAN POE, 'THE GOLDEN BUG'

Over the centuries people have often felt the need to record information secretly. Those involved with occult lore or with science often recorded their knowledge in secret writing. Plutarch mentions that the priests of Delphi had records of old oracles preserved in secret script (*Lysander* 26: 2), and in the late Middle Ages and Renaissance it was common to encrypt critical details of new discoveries, including new recipes. People regularly find the need to communicate secretly. Governments need to be able to keep their communications secret from other governments, especially in time of war. In both war and peace commercial enterprises need to keep new inventions, new models, new marketing strategies, and the like secret from competitors, and planned cost-cutting measures secret from trade unions. Criminals and those involved in plots obviously need to be able to communicate in secret, as do clandestine lovers. In the famous Indian erotic classic, the *Kama Sutra*, which was probably put together in the second century AD, women are advised to gain a knowledge of ciphers for communicating with lovers. In the nineteenth century lovers often placed encrypted messages in the personal columns of newspapers, although these were not very secure and there was a risk of pranksters cracking the cipher and sending false replies. Young people often use codes and ciphers, partly to conceal communication from parents or teachers and partly just for fun. It is interesting to note that nowadays there are websites that allow you to encrypt and decrypt messages. For anyone interested, and not seriously worried about security, this is a boon. It saves a lot of tedious encryption and decryption letter by letter. But the same computer technology that enables people to perform low-level encryption also enables governments and commercial enterprises, both legitimate and criminal, to achieve a level of sophisticated encryption undreamt of a generation ago. Whenever we use our computer to do our banking or pay our bills, we are entrusting the security of our account to such a system.

Secret communication can be in any medium: sign, speech, or writing. Disguised speech in forms such as Pig Latin and back slang is described in Chapter 8. This chapter deals with writing, which allows much more elaborate forms of encryption than speech.[1] Modern writing includes the typewriter, the teleprinter, and more significantly the computer.

[1] The forms of disguising written language are generally very different from those found with speech. Kahn (1966: 75) mentions a form of

There are basically two ways of concealing the content of a written message. The first method is to hide one message inside another. This is known as **steganography**. The other method is to encrypt a message. This can be done either using a cipher or a code (or a mixture of the two). A **cipher** involves transposing the letters of plain text as in an anagram or replacing them by substitute letters from the same alphabet, another alphabet, or a set of non-alphabetic symbols. A **code** involves employing substitutes for words or phrases. Morse code is a misnomer since this system is in fact a form of cipher. Each letter is allotted a pattern of long and short sounds: a · —, b — · · ·, e ·, i · ·, etc.[2]

One form of secret writing is private shorthand. Systems like this have a long history; one was used by Cicero (the Roman writer, not the World War II spy!). In many forms of shorthand the distinction between cipher and code is blurred since symbols are substituted for letters, for common sequences of letters such as (in English) -*ing*, and for common words such as *the*. In the Hunan province of China women developed a secret form of writing known as *Nu-shu* 'women's writing'. It was a syllabic script using derivatives of Chinese characters and some other components such as dots and arcs. It circulated only among women and

substitution used in India that existed in spoken and written form. From the information he gives it seems it was basically a spoken form that could be written in the same way that we might write Pig Latin.

[2] A reader has pointed out that phrases or sentences such as 'It's snowing down south' to indicate that a woman's petticoat is showing are examples of code. In cases like this there is no exact non-coded expression. 'Your petticoat/slip is showing' would be the closest equivalent in this case.

9. Scytale.

was used for communication and for literature. It was not only written but also embroidered in fabric and incorporated in painted artwork. It fell into disuse after the Chinese Communist Revolution made literacy available to women.

Steganography and encryption are probably as old as writing. Plutarch records that when the Spartans wanted to recall the general, Lysander, they wrote the order on a strip of parchment and wound it around a staff. They wrote the message in lines along the length of the staff, then unwound the strip of parchment and gave it to a messenger. When Lysander received the strip, he wound it around his baton and was able to read the message. The staff used was called a **scytale**. Anyone intercepting the messenger would find a strip of parchment in which there were columns of jumbled letters (Plutarch, *Lysander* 19:4–7).[3] This was a primitive form of transposition. Figure 9 illustrates the general idea. Note that unless the text covers all the available space, the strip will contain sequences of letters (*pivo*, *llef*, etc. in Figure 9) separated by spaces, which would make it easy to align the sequences. It would help to use gibberish to fill up all the available

[3] See also Thucydides 1:131, which mentions a scytale message sent to recall the general, Pausanias, who was suspected of colluding with the Persians.

space and thus produce a continuous sequence of letters on the strip.

In the Middle Ages it was generally believed that knowledge of subjects such as astrology, alchemy, theology, and magic should be restricted. Roger Bacon suggested using enigmatic phrases, secret words and alphabets, abbreviations, and a mixture of languages. Simple ciphers were sometimes used, as in the following example, where each vowel is replaced with the following consonant (Kieckhefer 1989: 141). Note that the whole text is not enciphered, just the critical words.

> So that you may see what others cannot see, mix the bile *de cbttp mbscxlp* (= *de catto masculo* 'of a male cat') with the fat of an entirely white *gblllnf* (= *galline* 'hen') and anoint your eyes with it.

The Roman alphabet used here did not distinguish *i* and *j* or *u* and *v*, *k* was not used, and *w* did not exist, so that the next consonant after *u* was *x* and the next consonant after *i* was *l*.[4]

The use of secret alphabets or idiosyncratic symbols, which was one of Bacon's suggestions, was popular in the Middle Ages, since it was an easy option when texts were hand written. The fourteenth-century poet Chaucer enciphered a few sections of his *Treatise on the Astrolabe* with some special symbols. Around this

---

[4] A later writer who could be said to have followed Roger Bacon's advice by using secret alphabets and a mixture of languages was Samuel Pepys (1633–1703), who used both methods in his diary. He wrote in a form of shorthand devised by Thomas Shelton and he used French and Spanish vocabulary in describing his amorous adventures: *I . . . had her main, which elle did give me, . . . and did hazer whatever I voudrais avec l'*, which did plaisir me grandement ('I had her hand, which she did give me, . . . and did do whatever I wanted with it, which did pleasure me greatly').

time a strong interest in all forms of secret writing was spreading through Europe. This interest ran hand in hand with a curiosity about magic, and from time to time ciphers and codes that seemed impenetrable were held to be the work of the devil.

By the time of the Renaissance nations and city-states in Europe, including the Vatican, regularly encrypted diplomatic correspondence, and by the seventeenth century it was common for nations to have code-breaking bureaus known as black chambers. From that time the success or failure of secret communication was to play an important part in history. For example, in 1587 Mary, Queen of Scots, was executed by Queen Elizabeth I of England for treason. Mary was condemned on the basis of evidence obtained from enciphered messages circulating between her and her supporters. These ciphers were cracked by Thomas Phelippes, in the employ of Elizabeth's principal secretary, Sir Francis Walsingham.

One problem with successfully decrypting an enemy message is that if you act on the information obtained, your action is likely to indicate to the enemy that you are decrypting their messages, which will drive them to adopt a more secure system and cut off your potential source of information. A famous example of this occurred in World War I. Early in 1917 the British intercepted and decrypted a telegram from Arthur Zimmermann, the German foreign minister, to the German ambassador in Mexico. Anxious to prevent the entry of US troops into the war on the Western Front, Zimmermann suggested to the Mexican government that they attack the United States and try to regain territory lost in 1848. The British passed the contents of this telegram to the United States so as to inflame public opinion against Germany, but they had to cover the fact that they had broken a German code, so they arranged for a spy to steal a copy of the decoded message from the German embassy in Mexico.

In some instances it is necessary to ignore what has been learnt from breaking an enemy cipher or code even if it means letting people die. During World War II the British broke a new cipher used by the Germans, which revealed among other things that Germany was going to shoot down a commercial airliner flying from Lisbon to London in the belief that Winston Churchill would be on board. In fact well-known actor Leslie Howard was on the flight, along with his accountant, Alfred Chenalls, who happened to look like Churchill. The British hoped to gain a significant strategic advantage from Germany's continued use of the cipher in question, and therefore did not wish to reveal that they had broken it. As a consequence they took no steps to delay or protect the flight, instead allowing events to take their course. The plane was shot down (Wolfe 1970: 11–15).

Steganography

The practice of hiding a secret message inside another message is known as **steganography**. One way, which is of no linguistic interest, is to render the secret message invisible. Many a child has dabbled with invisible ink, often lemon juice, which can be made visible by applying heat, and anyone familiar with spy stories will know about microdots, which are photographs of documents reduced to the size of a full stop and placed in a non-secret document.

Most secret communication involves some form of encryption using either a cipher or a code, but one of the problems with this is that if you are captured with an encrypted text in your possession, you are likely to be put under duress to reveal the underlying message. But if the presence of a message is concealed, the bearer can remain free of suspicion. Herodotus relates the story of a Greek living in the Persian empire who got word of Xerxes' plans to invade Greece. To warn the Spartans he took two waxed tablets, removed the wax, wrote his message, and then covered the message with a new coating of wax. A messenger was able to take the tablets to Sparta without discovery by the guards keeping watch over the roads. According to Herodotus the Spartans did not know what to do with the tablets until Gorgo, the widow of Leonidas (the hero of Thermopylae), suggested removing the wax. One wonders why the messenger did not advise this. Perhaps he had not been told, in case he was tortured by the Persian guards (Herodotus, Book VII, chapter 239).

In Chapter 2 the acrostic was introduced as a literary device rather than a means of serious deception, but, as indicated there, an elaborate acrostic can provide some measure of secure communication. During the civil war in seventeenth-century Britain a certain royalist, Sir John Trevanion, was incarcerated in Colchester Castle. One day his gaoler handed him the following message from a friend (Smith 1955: 25–6):

> Hope, that is ye beste comfort, cannot much, I fear me, help you now. That I would saye to you, is this only: if ever I may be able to requite that I do owe you, stand not on asking me. 'Tis not much that I can do, but what I can do, bee ye verie sure I wille. I knowe that, if dethe comes, if ordinary men fear it, it frights not you, accounting it for a high honour, to have such a rewards of your loyalty. Pray yet that you may be spared this soe bitter, cup. I fear not that you will grudge any sufferings; only if

> bie submission you can turn them away, 'tis the part of a wise
> man. Tell me, an if you can, to do for you anythinge that
> you wolde have done. The general goes back on Wednesday.
> restinge your servant to command.

On the face of it it seems an innocuous message, the sort of thing a friend might write to someone in jail and in danger of execution. But if one takes the third letter after each punctuation mark, then a hidden text is revealed. These letters have been underlined and they spell out the following message:

> panel at east end of chapel slides

In 1499 Johannes Trithemius (1462–1516) compiled a work entitled *Steganographia,* which circulated in manuscript form for over a century until it was published in 1606. The reason for the delay in publication was that it was placed on the Index of Prohibited Books by the Vatican on the grounds that it was an occult work. Trithemius illustrates a simple form of steganography in which one reads every second letter of the text, ignoring the first and last words. An example is given below, from the introduction to a message.

> *pamersiel* anoyr madrisel ebrasothean abrulges itrasbiel nadres
> ormenu itules rablon *hamorphiel*

Ignoring the first word, which indicates which system is being used, and starting with the second letter of the next word, one reads *Nym die ersten Bugstaben de omni uerbo*, a mixture of German and Latin that translates into 'Take the first letter of every word' (the letters are underlined in the example above). The words in which the message is hidden are *voces mysticae*, traditional magic words, or at least they look like such (Shumaker 1982: 100). The first word, *pamersiel*, is the name of the chief spirit of the east, and still figures in occult lore today. Much of Trithemius' work is couched in the language of the occult and the passage quoted here looks like a conjuration of spirits so it is no surprise that the *Steganographia* was banned on the grounds that it dealt in communication with devils.

This system is straightforward from the decrypter's point of view, but it would take some ingenuity to compose a sensible text in which every second letter was prescribed. Trithemius also described another system in which one extracts the hidden message by taking the initial of the fourth word from the end of the text and then going backwards through the text taking the initial of every fourth word; then repeating the process starting with the third last word, then with the second last word, and finally with the last word. Again this is easy for someone to read if they have the key, but it is extraordinarily difficult to compose a reasonable text with the initials of all the words prescribed in advance (Shumaker 1982: 103–4). The method is not really practical where there are time constraints. Trithemius gives an example in Latin, a language allowing considerable freedom of word order, which makes the task somewhat easier than it would be in most languages.

Steganography occasionally turns up in crime and espionage fiction in the form of a short message inserted somewhere in a larger text. A rather general phrase such as 'in the final analysis' is used to alert the intended recipient to where the message begins. The recipient then reads the initials of the following words.

A modern form of steganography is employed in recordings. It has become common since the 1960s for words to be recorded backwards on tracks of popular songs, mostly rock. The technique is known as **backmasking**. The words, phrases, or sentences can only be heard by playing the track in reverse. Christian fundamentalists in the United States have claimed that satanic messages are being passed subliminally into the minds of listeners. It is true that some bands, possibly provoked by the Christian fundamentalists, have inserted some ungodly messages in reverse, including a reverse version of the Lord's Prayer, but there is no evidence that anyone can pick up the secret message, even subliminally, from a normal playing of the track.

Substitution Ciphers

For the purposes of keeping whole texts secret, the most widely used system is a **cipher** (also cypher), which involves replacing each letter by a different letter or symbol. In the jargon the plain text (the original) is said to be **enciphered**. The process of recovering the plain text is **decipherment**. If the cipher is secure, the message can be deciphered only by the intended recipient armed with the **key**. If it is not secure, someone who intercepts the message may be able to 'crack' or 'break' the cipher. With codes as opposed to ciphers there are analogous terms, **encode** and **decode**. The terms **encrypt** and **decrypt** are broader and apply to ciphers and codes.

One of the earliest known ciphers is the one used by Julius Caesar for confidential passages in his private letters to friends. The method was quite simple: for each letter of the plain text he substituted the letter three places on in the alphabet, so that *a* became *d*, *b* became *e*, and so on (Suetonius: *De Vita Caesarum, Divus Julius 56*). Here is the full set of substitutions. Note that there are 23 letters in the Roman alphabet, there being no *j*, *u*, or *w*. Letter *i* had the values [i] and [y] according to its position in a word, and *v* had the phonetic values [u] and [w] (later [v]). The letter *k* is included here, but it was used only in transliterating Greek words. Here and in subsequent illustrations I follow the convention of using lower case for plain text and small capitals for encrypted text.

```
a b c d e f g h i   k l   m n o p q r s t v x y z
D E F G H I K L M M O P   Q R S T V X X Z A B C
```

Here is an example from one of Caesar's letters to Cicero in which he says, 'Let this be the new way of conquering that we fortify our position by mercy and generosity'.

haec nova sit ratio vincendi vt misericordia et liberalitate nos mvniamvs.
LDHF QRZD XMX ZMQHQGM ZX PMXHVMFRVGMD HX OMEHV-DOMXDXH QRX PZQMDPZX

There are twenty-three possible Caesar ciphers using the Latin alphabet, twenty-six using our Roman alphabet. None of them is particularly secure since by trial and error an interceptor is likely to discover the principle. One might seek to scramble the cipher alphabet, but such a cipher is still vulnerable to analysis on the basis of letter frequencies. Although the Caesar cipher is the simplest and least secure of ciphers, it is still in use today in some internet forums, where only superficial security is required.

One method of producing a cipher alphabet somewhat less systematically related to the plain text alphabet is to use a code word, a practice that has been in use since the seventeenth century.

A code word or phrase, in this instance *March first*, is written below the plain text alphabet starting under *a* and omitting any repeated letters. The remaining letters are then filled in in sequence as follows:

```
a b c d e f g h i j k l m n o p q r s t u v w x y z
M A R C H F I S T B D E G J K L N O P Q U V W X Y Z
```

Of course the letters of the cipher alphabet could easily be more thoroughly scrambled, but if a number of messages need to be sent over a period of time, the cipher needs to be changed, preferably daily, and there has to be a way of informing the intended recipients what the cipher alphabet for a particular day is to be. The use of a set of code words circulated in advance is one way of doing this.

Here is a short military message enciphered with the alphabet shown above.

> send reinforcements to brigade hq asap. enemy armoured battalion reported moving south.
> PHJC OHTJFKORHGHJQP QK AOTIMCH SN MPML HJHGY MOG-KUOHC AMQQMETKJ OHLKOQHC GKVTJI PKUQS

In this example the word breaks of the plain text have been maintained, which would provide an aid to anyone trying to decrypt the message without the key. In practice messages are normally transmitted in blocks of five characters. This provides greater security, but it is also done for practical reasons. Random characters are hard to handle in blocks of more than five. One tends to lose one's place in typing long sequences. Here is the same message in five-letter blocks with a null (letter *c*) added to complete the last block.

PHJCO HTJFK ORHGH JQPQK AOTIM CHSNM PMLHJ HGYMO
GKUOH CAMQQ METKJ OHLKO QHCGK VTJIP KUQSC

All substitution ciphers that encipher each letter of the plain text
by the same cipher letter (monoalphabetic ciphers) are vulnerable
to breaking on the basis of frequency analysis. Figure 10 gives
approximate relative frequencies for the letters of English over a
variety of types of text.

In order to decipher a substitution cipher without the key one
determines the frequency of the letters in the cipher alphabet and

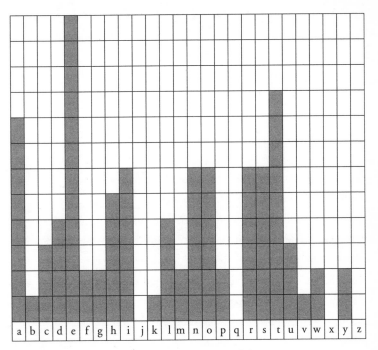

10. Approximate relative frequencies of letters in English.

seeks to match them with the plain text alphabet on the basis of frequency. For long messages in normal English, this method would produce quick results. In practice the frequencies in a particular genre may be different from those based on a large body of different types of text. For instance, military messages with frequent references to HQ would mean the low-frequency letter *q* would have a greater than normal frequency. A bigger problem is small sample size. If there are only one or two short messages, it is unlikely the frequencies in these messages will give a clear guide to the plain text. Here are the frequencies for the message given above:

a	2	h	10	o	7	v	1
b		i	2	p	4	w	
c	5	j	6	q	6	x	
d		k	7	r	1	y	1
e	1	l	2	s	2		
f	1	m	6	t	4		
g	4	n	1	u	2		

This suggests that *H* in the cipher alphabet is *e* in the plain alphabet, which happens to be correct. The letters *M, C, J, K, O,* and *Q* are likely to correspond to *t, a, i, o, n, s, r,* or *h*, but a lot of trial and error is required to determine the precise correspondences. The key reveals that the last letters of the alphabet are enciphered as themselves. These are low-frequency letters and this shows up in the frequency count.

A cryptanalyst also looks for common digraphs (*th, er, on, an*) and common trigraphs (*the, and, tha, ent, ion, tio, for, nde, has*), as well as for common words such as *and, the, of, in, to,* and *that.* It is interesting to note that *que* is the most common trigraph in Spanish and is also very common in French, while *che* is the most common trigraph in Italian. These are the equivalents of *that* in English, so their high frequency is predictable. The frequency of *que* is further increased by the fact that it is the Spanish word for *what.*

Chronogram

In a number of ancient languages including Hebrew, Greek, and Latin letters of the alphabet served as numerals. In the Middle Ages Jews took to indicating the date of death in epitaphs and the date of publication in books by choosing Hebrew phrases such that the date could be read from the initials. This practice then spread to other Europeans, who used letters for their Roman numeral value: I 'one', V 'five', X 'ten', L 'fifty', C 'hundred', D 'five hundred', and M 'thousand'. For instance, an epitaph for Queen Elizabeth I has the form *My Day Closed Is In Immortality* in which the capital letters MDCIII give the date of her death, 1603.

The Arabic scholar al-Kindi (801–873 AD) wrote on almost every field of knowledge including cryptanalysis, and he is credited with being the first to point out that transposition and substitution ciphers can be broken on the basis of frequency analysis.[5] A later Muslim scholar, al-Qalqashandi, published an encyclopaedia in the fourteenth century that included a section on cryptology.[6]

[5] Al-Kindi also introduced Indian numerals to the Muslim world, those same numerals that found their way to Christian Europe where they are known as Arabic numerals.

[6] Qalqashandi acknowledges a debt to al-Mausili. In fact the debt is to generations of Muslim scholars who developed an interest in cryptology from working on religious texts such as the Qur'an.

He included information on the frequency of letters and sequences of letters, and he pointed out that one could use multiple substitutions for high-frequency letters to defeat cryptanalysis on the basis of letter frequency.

These ideas made their way to Europe and by the beginning of the fifteenth century it was standard practice to include 'homophones' as they were called, i.e. cipher equivalents for particular plain text letters, mainly high-frequency letters. Obviously more than twenty-six letters were needed, so pairs of digits were used. Another method of frustrating frequency-based analysis was to encipher pairs or trios of letters. Again digits were used. The Argenti family, who were in charge of the Vatican ciphers in the late sixteenth and early seventeenth century, were probably the first to disguise some common sequences, for instance, by eliminating *qu*, by writing double consonants as single ones, and by other deliberate misspellings. They also used lots of nulls (dummies or fillers), which disturbed the natural distribution of letters (Kahn 1966: 113).

A more secure form of substitution cipher is a **polyalphabetic** one in which plain text letters are enciphered by more than one alphabet. Polyalphabetic ciphers came into use in Italy in the fifteenth century. A widely used polyalphabetic substitution was one devised by Johannes Trithemius in the early sixteenth century and popularized later in the century by the French diplomat Blaise de Vigenère (1523–1596). Twenty-six different alphabets were used, each one offset by one place from the preceding one so they formed a 'Vigenère square' as shown in Figure 11.

The procedure for enciphering the plain text is as follows. Find the first letter of the plain text in the leftmost column and read across the row until you find the column headed by the first letter of the key. In the example below the plain text is 'remain in position' so the first letter is *r*. The key is PINCER and the *r*-row intersects with the P-column at a cell filled by *g*, so *g* is the first letter of the cipher text. The second letter of the plain text is *e* and the second letter of the key is I; the *e*-row meets the I-column at *m*, so *m* is the second letter of the cipher text. Here is an illustration of the full encipherment. The keyword is shorter than the text, so it is repeated as many times as is necessary. An alternative would be to

A	B	C	D	E	F	G	H	I	J	K	L	M	N	O	P	Q	R	S	T	U	V	W	X	Y	Z
B	C	D	E	F	G	H	I	J	K	L	M	N	O	P	Q	R	S	T	U	V	W	X	Y	Z	A
C	D	E	F	G	H	I	J	K	L	M	N	O	P	Q	R	S	T	U	V	W	X	Y	Z	A	B
D	E	F	G	H	I	J	K	L	M	N	O	P	Q	R	S	T	U	V	W	X	Y	Z	A	B	C
E	F	G	H	I	J	K	L	M	N	O	P	Q	R	S	T	U	V	W	X	Y	Z	A	B	C	D
F	G	H	I	J	K	L	M	N	O	P	Q	R	S	T	U	V	W	X	Y	Z	A	B	C	D	E
G	H	I	J	K	L	M	N	O	P	Q	R	S	T	U	V	W	X	Y	Z	A	B	C	D	E	F
H	I	J	K	L	M	N	O	P	Q	R	S	T	U	V	W	X	Y	Z	A	B	C	D	E	F	G
I	J	K	L	M	N	O	P	Q	R	S	T	U	V	W	X	Y	Z	A	B	C	D	E	F	G	H
J	K	L	M	N	O	P	Q	R	S	T	U	V	W	X	Y	Z	A	B	C	D	E	F	G	H	I
K	L	M	N	O	P	Q	R	S	T	U	V	W	X	Y	Z	A	B	C	D	E	F	G	H	I	J
L	M	N	O	P	Q	R	S	T	U	V	W	X	Y	Z	A	B	C	D	E	F	G	H	I	J	K
M	N	O	P	Q	R	S	T	U	V	W	X	Y	Z	A	B	C	D	E	F	G	H	I	J	K	L
N	O	P	Q	R	S	T	U	V	W	X	Y	Z	A	B	C	D	E	F	G	H	I	J	K	L	M
O	P	Q	R	S	T	U	V	W	X	Y	Z	A	B	C	D	E	F	G	H	I	J	K	L	M	N
P	Q	R	S	T	U	V	W	X	Y	Z	A	B	C	D	E	F	G	H	I	J	K	L	M	N	O
Q	R	S	T	U	V	W	X	Y	Z	A	B	C	D	E	F	G	H	I	J	K	L	M	N	O	P
R	S	T	U	V	W	X	Y	Z	A	B	C	D	E	F	G	H	I	J	K	L	M	N	O	P	Q
S	T	U	V	W	X	Y	Z	A	B	C	D	E	F	G	H	I	J	K	L	M	N	O	P	Q	R
T	U	V	W	X	Y	Z	A	B	C	D	E	F	G	H	I	J	K	L	M	N	O	P	Q	R	S
U	V	W	X	Y	Z	A	B	C	D	E	F	G	H	I	J	K	L	M	N	O	P	Q	R	S	T
V	W	X	Y	Z	A	B	C	D	E	F	G	H	I	J	K	L	M	N	O	P	Q	R	S	T	U
W	X	Y	Z	A	B	C	D	E	F	G	H	I	J	K	L	M	N	O	P	Q	R	S	T	U	V
X	Y	Z	A	B	C	D	E	F	G	H	I	J	K	L	M	N	O	P	Q	R	S	T	U	V	W
Y	Z	A	B	C	D	E	F	G	H	I	J	K	L	M	N	O	P	Q	R	S	T	U	V	W	X
Z	A	B	C	D	E	F	G	H	I	J	K	L	M	N	O	P	Q	R	S	T	U	V	W	X	Y

11. Vigenère square.

use alphabetic order for the remainder of the encipherment. Trithemius' original conception simply used the alphabets in succession. There was no keyword.

plain text (left-hand column)	r e m a i n i n p o s i t i o n
key (top row)	P I N C E R P I N C E R P I N C
cipher text (cells in table)	G M Z C Q E X V C Q A Z I Q B P

Repeating the keyword is a weakness. Consider the following message, which is to be enciphered by the Vigenère square using the keyword PINCER. If a sequence of plain text occurs more than once and if the start of that sequence happens to correspond to the same letter in the keyword, there will be a repeated sequence in the cipher text. This is illustrated below, where the word *the* is to be enciphered with the keyword sequence PIN at the beginning of the text and again eighteen letters later. This happens again twenty-four letters later, where the word *they* happens to begin where the keyword begins.

```
P I N C E R P I N C E R P I N C E R P I N C E R
t h e m i n i s t E r w i l l s e e t h e a m b
a s s a d o r t o m o r r o w a n d t h e y w i
l l d i s c u s s D r a w i n g u p a n a g r e
e m e n t f o r l E n d i n g a i d t o t h e i
r n o r t h e r n N e i g h b o u r
```

Interceptors would note these intervals and also the intervals between the two-letter repeats in the cipher text resulting from *ss* and *nd* being enciphered by the same key sequence (all these are shaded). They would note that the intervals were all multiples of six; they would conclude that six different alphabets had been used, and they would make six different frequency distributions. One would be for the first letter, the seventh, the thirteenth, etc. The second would be for the second letter, the eighth, the fourteenth, etc., and so on. If there was enough material to throw up reasonable frequency distributions, then informed guesses could be made about likely plain text equivalents, and with some trial and error it is likely the plain text could be recovered.

A longer keyword gives greater security, but is still vulnerable to frequency analysis. However, the Vigenère square was used as a field cipher as late as the nineteenth century by the Confederate army in the American civil war and by other armies in other campaigns. Field ciphers need not be fully secure. They carry tactical information and need to be secure only for as long as it takes to do such things as move troops.

If a longer keyword provides greater security than a short one, the logical extension of this principle is to have a keyword that is as long as the message. One way of accomplishing this is to use another text. In Graham Greene's *Our Man in Havana* the protagonist is given a copy of *Lamb's Tales from Shakespeare*. To encrypt or decrypt a message all he needs to know is the agreed starting point for a particular day. He then proceeds to add the key text to the plain text by taking *a* to be equal to 1, *b* to 2, *c* to 3, and so on. Adding *b* (2) and *d* (4) yields *f* (6). The system is cyclic so that adding *x* (24) and *d* (4) yields *b* (2), i.e. 28 minus 26. Although this is an improvement on the method described in the previous paragraph, it is still vulnerable. Someone intercepting a message in the *Lamb's Tales* system could try subtracting common sequences of letters such as *the*, *-ing*, *-ious*, or *-ment* at various points of the message. If they were persistent enough, or better if they had a computer, they would find little bits of plain text, and they might eventually be able to piece together some or all of the plain text or the key text. The ultimate solution is a random key that is used once only. This is discussed below.[7]

Steganography can be combined with a cipher. Johannes Trithemius (1462–1516), mentioned earlier as the compiler of *Steganographia*, gives examples of a text in which one takes the initial of every second word and then applies a Caesar shift. For instance, the text *Tuis respondere litteris gauderem, ita Xhristus me gaudere faciat; transmitteremque...* ('I would be glad to reply to your letter, as Christ makes me glad, I would send...') yields **rgxgt**, but if we substitute the letters two places back in the alphabet for each of these letters respectively, we get *Peter* (Shumaker 1982: 105).

In 1508 Trithemius published a second work on cryptography called *Polygraphia*. This contained an ingenious combination of cipher and steganography. The system was imitated by Giovanni

---

[7] Vigenère also developed the notion of taking the plain text itself as the key. This is a form of **auto-key**. It usually works like this. A keyword is used to supply an offset. In the example below the keyword HEAT is aligned with the first four letters of the plain text and is followed by the plain text. The intended recipient receives the cipher OJUVHHE etc. and subtracts the keyword HEAT to recover the first four letters of the plain text (getb). These four letters are then subtracted from the next four letters of the cipher text (HHEV) to reveal the next four letters of the plain text (ackt), which are then subtracted from the next four letters of the cipher text, and so on.

```
Plain   g e t b a c k t o b a g h d a d ...
Key     H E A T G E T B A C K T O B A G ...
Cipher  o j u v h h e v p e l a w f b k ...
```

	1		2		3		4		5		6
a	Recepi	a	literam	a	honorate	a	et	a	illustrissime	a	Petre
b	Accepi	b	epistolam	b	ornate	b	ac	b	clarissime	b	Alberte
c	Habui	c	chartam	c	humane	c	atque	c	excellentissime	c	Carole
d	Vidi	d	paginam	d	sincere	d	-que	d	eruditissime	d	Francisce
e	Novi	e	paginas	e	docte	e	etiam	e	felicissime	e	Federice
f	etc.		etc.		etc.		etc.		etc.		etc.

12. Della Porta's cipher and steganography.

Baptista della Porta in *De Furtivis Literarum Notis* 'Concerning Secret Letter Signs', published in 1563, and it is from this work that the above illustration is drawn via Shumaker (1982: 110–11).[8] A large number of alphabets is provided and against each letter is a Latin word. A simplified version appears in Figure 12. Six alphabets are given and only the first five letters of each. The process of encipherment involves using the alphabets in succession. For instance, to encipher the phrase *bad ace*, one uses the first alphabet to encipher *b*, which yields *Accepi*, the second alphabet to encipher *a*, which yields *litteram*, the third alphabet to encipher *d*, which yields *sincere*, and so on, until we have *Accepi literam, sincere et excellentissime Federice* 'I have received [your] letter, sincere and most excellent Frederick'. The ingenuity lies in the fact that the words in each alphabet are mutually substitutable so that as we move across the alphabets we produce acceptable sense. All the words in column one are verbs in the first person, perfect aspect, compatible with the words in the second column, which are

[8] Della Porta had a number of suggestions for improving the security of ciphers and codes. One was the use of synonyms for common words and names and the other was varying the spelling.

variations on the theme letter/epistle. The words in columns three and five are all flattering adjectives in the vocative case linked by co-ordinating conjunctions in column four and relating to a personal name in the vocative case in column five. The numerous alphabets are all designed so that encipherment produces acceptable text and disguises the presence of a hidden message.

In Book VI of *The Advancement of Learning* Francis Bacon gives an interesting example of a combination of cipher and steganography. The cipher component consists of a binary representation of the alphabet using only the letters *a* and *b*, predating by more than three hundred years the use of binary representation in computers. Five bits are used to cater for the twenty-four letters of the Elizabethan alphabet—a practice which also predates the modern use of blocks of five in sending code or any strings of letters that do not make sense.

Bacon gives an example of the biliteral alphabet with the Latin word *Fuge!* 'Flee!'

    aabab baabb aabba aabaa

As a cipher this is a straightforward substitution, but it is hidden inside a message using two alphabets, the *a*-alphabet and the *b*-alphabet. There are slight differences in the form of the letters between the two alphabets, an extra serif here, an extra loop there. One takes a text, which will be sent openly, and in writing it one chooses letters from the *a*-alphabet or the *b*-alphabet so as to reproduce the sequence of *a*'s and *b*'s in the biliteral rendering of *fuge*. Bacon's example is *Manere te volo, donec venero* 'I want you to wait until I come'. In order to represent *aabab*, etc., one takes the *m* and *a* of *manere* from the *a*-alphabet, the *n* from the *b*-alphabet,

a	aaaaa	g	aabba	n	abbaa	t	baaba
b	aaaab	h	aabbb	o	abbab	u/v	baabb
c	aaaba	i/j	abaaa	p	abbba	w	babaa
d	aaabb	k	abaab	q	abbbb	x	babab
e	aabaa	l	ababa	r	baaaa	y	babba
f	aabab	m	ababb	s	baaab	z	babbb

13. Bacon's biliteral alphabet.

the *e* from the *a*-alphabet, and the *r* from the *b*-alphabet, and so on. This is illustrated below:

```
m a n e r e t e v o l o d o n e c v e n e r o
a   a b a b b a a b b a a b b a a a b a a
```

Anyone who intercepts the message sees *Manere te volo, donec venero*, but the intended recipient who is armed with the two slightly different alphabets goes through letter by letter writing down a sequence of *a*'s and *b*'s, and then marks off blocks of five and reads the hidden message from the key to the biliteral representation as in Figure 13.

There are mechanical aids to encipherment. Alberti, a genius of the Italian Renaissance, invented a simple device consisting of alphabets arranged around the edges of concentric discs. The plain text alphabet was on the larger outer disc, and the cipher text on the smaller disc. One could lock the position of the smaller disc relative to the larger one and encipher by reading from the outer alphabet to the inner. There were twenty-four different possible offsets and by revolving the inner disk after a specified number of letters one could produce polyalphabetic substitution. Alberti was perhaps the first to introduce polyalphabetic substitution. The outer disc also contained the digits 1, 2, 3, and 4 for sending coded numeral groups.

American president Thomas Jefferson invented a cipher device consisting of wheels mounted on an axle, with an alphabet on the

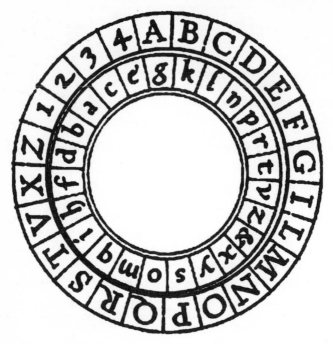

14. Alberti's cipher disk.

circumference of each wheel. It was 'reinvented' by Etienne Bazières in the late nineteenth century and became widely used. Modern versions of such a device were employed in World War II. These had twenty-five wheels each bearing a randomized alphabet, plus a blank wheel carrying a pointer. A device of this type is illustrated in Figure 15. The wheels can be assembled on the shaft in any order and this order is the key. Normally there would be a number or phrase to determine the key for a particular day. When the wheels are assembled on the shaft, they are rotated so that the first twenty letters of plain text are aligned along the guide rule. Any other row can supply the cipher text. Yes, that's right: *any other row*. The intended recipient is in possession of the key so he (or she) has the

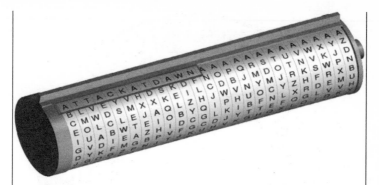

15. Jefferson-type cipher device.

wheels in the same sequence. On receiving the first twenty letters of cipher text the recipient aligns it along the guide rule and scans the other rows, one of which should contain the plain text. After the first twenty letters have been transmitted, the sender loosens the wheels and twiddles them so that the next twenty letters of plain text are aligned above the ruler.

Transposition

The other method of encipherment is to transpose the letters of the plain text. In Figure 16 the message has been written vertically in five columns from left to right. Two null letters have been added at the end to fill the matrix.

Now if the rows of this matrix are sent in five-letter blocks, the recipient or an interceptor will see the following:

mngps eihet entta tebet mtyru eotpe anhat tienn

The intended recipient will have information on how the scrambling was arranged. An interceptor will have to decide first whether

m	n	g	p	s
e	i	h	e	t
e	n	t	t	a
t	e	b	e	t
m	t	y	r	u
e	o	t	p	e
a	n	h	a	t
t	i	e	n	n

16. Transposition.

this is a transposition cipher or a substitution cipher. Since letters *e* and *t*, and to a lesser extent *a* and *n*, stand out in frequency, an interceptor will conclude that it is most likely a transposition cipher. He or she will then have to use trial and error to find the path by which the letters were scrambled. In this instance the degree of security is very low since the interceptor is likely to realize that reading the first letters of each block gives plain text, then reading the second letter of each block, and so on. Choosing any number of columns other than the five used in transmitting the message would have obscured this.

Transposition and substitution can be combined. Late in World War I the Germans used the ADFGX cipher, which combined the two principles. It involves a 5 × 5 matrix with the letters ADFGX indexing the rows and columns. The alphabet is distributed randomly over this matrix. Since there are twenty-six letters in the alphabet the Germans combined *i* and *j*, as had been done in various derivatives of Roman script. This is illustrated in Figure 17.

	A	D	F	G	X
A	f	x	g	n	o
D	p	a	q	m	z
F	w	k	b	l	c
G	v	u	d	e	y
X	r	s	t	i/j	h

17. ADFGX cipher.

Letters of plain text are enciphered using the coordinates of the matrix. Suppose we have a message 'send report asap', the first letter *s* will be enciphered as XD, the second letter *e* as GG, and so on. The result of this encipherment can be written out across a number of columns and the columns transposed according to some key. This is illustrated Figure 18, where the message has been written out across six columns.

Now if these columns are rearranged so that, for instance, columns 1 and 2 are separated, it means that the digraphs enciphering the letters of plain text are dismembered. For example, the digraph XD enciphering *s* will be split up. This was a very secure system and the Allies had limited success in breaking it.

X	D	G	G	A	G
G	F	X	A	G	G
D	A	A	X	X	A
X	F	D	D	X	D
D	D	D	A		

18. ADFGX transposition.

Codes

In 1384 Gabriele di Lavinde, who was secretary to the Avignon anti-pope Clement VII, published a book called *Liber Zifrarum* 'Book of Ciphers', in which he suggested using short groups of letters to stand for proper names of common occurrence within an enciphered message. This was probably to save time and effort, but it represents the first instance in Europe of code. As we have already seen, a code essentially operates at the word level whereas a cipher works at the level of individual letters. A mixed cipher-code of the type proposed by Lavinde is called a **nomenclator**. The box on p. 96 shows that Alberti's cipher disc included the numerals 1, 2, 3, and 4 to allow words to be encoded by a sequence of digits.

Lavinde and Alberti had in mind the use of code words within an enciphered text, but it has been common practice for centuries to insert code words in plain text. Military personnel are not allowed to reveal their whereabouts in time of war and their mail is censored. During World War II my father deposited a list of code words for likely locations in the Pacific with my mother. If he wrote that she should plant petunias in spring, this indicated he was in New Guinea. If he suggested poppies it meant he was in Borneo, and so on. This is essentially a kind of steganography. A word can stand for another word or phrase or one phrase can stand for another. For instance, I might send the sentence *I hope to get more supplies tomorrow* and the recipient might interpret this as *Enemy build up along northern coast* because he or she has been given a list of sentences and equivalents. This is a useful method for communicating with spies or resistance fighters in enemy territory. Certain phrases or sentences can be incorporated in a newspaper article, a speech, or a radio broadcast. To the uninitiated the code phrases and sentences will be taken literally, but to those who have been supplied with a list of code phrases and sentences and their equivalents, they will convey a different message.

To send a message completely in code requires equivalents for a large number of words. Since, as we have seen above, messages are normally transmitted in five-letter blocks, it is convenient to use code words of five constituents. The individual components can be letters, figures, or other symbols such as % or &, so a code word is not a word in the normal sense. A code book is like a bilingual dictionary and should consist of a list of plain text words in alphabetic order with their code equivalents and a list of code words in alphabetic order with their plain text equivalents, as illustrated in Figure 19.

The main problem with codes is the security of the code books. These are substantial and need to be distributed widely, for instance, to all the embassies of a nation or to all naval vessels in a fleet. There is always a danger that an enemy will manage to get access to one. Because of the difficulty of producing and distributing code books, a code is generally used over a long period, and a

plain → code	
army	ntlax
brigade	crpol
battalion	trips
company	xzurl
platoon	lloot

code → plain	
crpol	brigade
lloot	platoon
ntlax	army
trips	battalion
xzurl	company

19. A codebook.

large body of text encoded in the same system if intercepted by the enemy can lend itself to breaking on the basis of frequency analysis. In normal English the most common words are *a, of, to, in, it, is, be, as, to, so, the, and, for, are, but, not, you, that, with, have,* and *this,* but these frequencies may not hold for the telegraphic style often adopted in messages. Other words are likely to be frequent in certain genres, as is illustrated by the military terms in Figure 19. Providing alternatives for common words makes a code safer. Another aid to security is to scatter meaningless five-character blocks as nulls through the text.

Towards a Random Key

During the period between World War I and World War II a number of enciphering machines were developed, the best known of which is Enigma. It was patented by a German, Arthur Scherbius, in 1918 and it came into general use by the German government and armed forces in 1926. It was the size of an old desk typewriter, but it was housed in a box and was portable. The method for enciphering was to type the plain text letter by letter on a keyboard and receive in return a cipher equivalent shown by the illumination of a letter on a lampboard. The sequence of illuminated letters could be copied down and transmitted.

The heart of the machine consisted of three alphabetic wheels (upgraded to five in World War II) mounted on a shaft. When a key on the keyboard was depressed a current ran to the corresponding contact on the first wheel, then to a contact on the second wheel, then to a contact on the third wheel, and then to a contact on a reflector, which sent the current back via a different path through the wheels to the lampboard. As each letter was enciphered the first wheel moved on one place; after twenty-six letters a lug on the wheel moved the wheel to the right on one place. After this wheel had gone through a revolution, it moved the wheel to its right on one place. This provided 26 × 26 × 26 (17,576) substitutions. The three wheels could be removed from the shaft and put back in any other order, there being six possibilities (3 × 2 × 1).

In addition to this mechanism there was a plugboard on the front of the machine on which were two alphabets with a hole for each letter. (In the interest of legibility, only one is shown in the schematic diagram in Figure 20.) The operator was supplied with six short cables that could be used to connect six pairs of letters. On one day *a* in one alphabet might be linked to *x* and *c* to *s*. On another day *b* might be linked to *s* and *d* to *p*. The combination of the plugboard, the wheels, and the fact that the wheels could be mounted on the shaft in different orders meant that the machine could produce a more or less random key of enormous length.

The Enigma machine is pictured in Figure 20 along with a schematic diagram. The arrows show the passage of electric current from a key on the keyboard through the plugboard and the scramblers (the three wheels) to a reflector and back again to a lamp on the lampboard. The system is reciprocal. If typing in plain text *x* yields cipher text Y, then cipher text Y will yield plain text *x*. The same machine can be used for encryption and decryption. To communicate using Enigma the sender and receiver must have their machines set up in the same way. They must have the same settings for the plugboard, the order in which the wheels are mounted on the shaft, and the initial settings of the wheels in the scrambler.

20. An Enigma machine (schematic diagram over leaf).

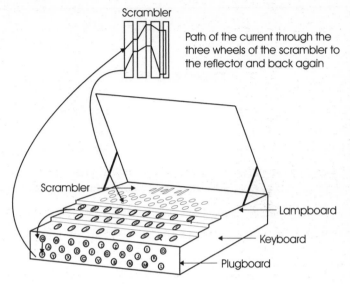

An Enigma machine with schematic view of 3-wheel scrambler.

Enigma provides a very high level of security, but not as high as the Germans believed.[9] On the eve of World War II an Enigma machine was smuggled into Britain, and the British had considerable success in reading German cipher messages by exploiting the fact that the content of messages such as weather reports is largely

[9] By 1931 the Poles were able to build a replica of an Enigma machine from documents provided by a German traitor, and from time to time they were also given the book of settings for each day. The Germans used these printed instructions to set their machines for the day, but then they sent a key for each particular message, i.e. they began by sending a three-letter sequence that was to be used for the particular message. This was an added precaution, but they sent it twice in case it became garbled in

predictable and provides a crib. This was illustrated in the film *Enigma* (2001), based on the book by Robert Harris.

One-Time Pad

Around the end of World War I somebody came up with the idea of a **one-time pad**. Machines such as Enigma aim to produce a sequence of letters that is near to random and that does not repeat. A sequence of letters that was truly random and never reused would, in theory, provide an unbreakable cipher, and this was the notion behind a one-time pad. Chunks of a sequence are distributed to users on pads of paper. If there are only two users, each of them receives a pad. A, the sender, takes a sheet from the pad and adds the sequence of letters to produce the cipher text. B, the recipient, uses his copy of the same sheet to subtract the key and obtain the plain text. The pages from the pad can be used in order or chosen according to some predetermined sequence.

transmission, so, for instance, if the message key was *gxd* they enciphered *gxdgxd* before proceeding to use this setting for the message proper. A Polish cryptographer, Marian Rejewski, was able to exploit the fact that the first and fourth letters enciphered the same plain text letter, similarly the second and fifth and the third and sixth. He noted the intervals between plain and cipher letters and using his own replica he went through every setting and noted the intervals that arose in encipher-ing the same letter twice. Over the course of a year he compiled a list of correspondences between settings and intervals, and was able to deduce the settings of the scrambler from the intervals. This enabled him to read partial messages and to deduce the substitutions made via the plugboard. For instance, if he read *kiroglam*, he might see that this is *kilogram* with *l* and *r* transposed (Singh 1999: 149–55).

Users are required to destroy the used pages immediately after encipherment and decipherment. If a page from a one-time pad is reused, a cryptanalyst who comes into possession of two or more messages enciphered with the same page has some chance of deciphering the text. We begin by assuming the plain text underlying the messages contains certain common sequences of letters such as *the*, *and*, *tha*, *ent*, *ion*, *tio*, *for*, *nde*, and *has*. Suppose we look for *the*. We assume *the* begins right at the beginning of the message, then in the second position, the third position, and so on right through the message. At each position we subtract *the* and obtain a sequence of letters that will be a part of the one-time pad at any point where *the* occurs. We then subtract each of these sequences from the second message and if that yields a likely bit of plain text, we have probably identified *the* in the first message. This is illustrated below. The first message is 'Send the supplies asap'. In attempting to break the cipher we go through the cipher text assuming *the* occurs somewhere. When we actually get to *the*, the cipher text is vxv. Subtracting *the* from the cipher text yields BPQ. When we subtract BPQ from the corresponding point in the cipher text of the second message, we obtain 'and', a likely piece of genuine plain text. If we are lucky, we will be able to find a few cases where we can identify a likely sequence in the second message and hopefully we can expand the sequences, which in turn means we will be able to work out the corresponding stretch of one-time pad and subtract this from the first message to obtain plain text. In theory we can keep expanding fragments in each message and eventually decipher both messages. In practice this would not be easy with just short messages, but in these days of computers a large number of possibilities can be tried very rapidly.

Message 1	send**t**	**he**sup	plies	asap
One-time pad	ADZYB	**PQ**LAE	MWXON	CFIJA
Cipher text	TINCV	**x**VEVU	CIGTG	DYJZ

Message 2	arm**ya**	**nd**nav	yread	ytogo
One-time pad	ADZYB	**PQ**LAE	MWXON	CFIJA
Cipher text	BVMXC	DUZBA	LOCPR	BZXQP

Although a one-time pad is theoretically unbreakable, there are two problems. One is how to generate a truly random sequence. A method used at one time by the USSR was to compose random sequences on a typewriter, but it is not hard to see that the compositor is likely to favour certain sequences of keystrokes. Some have used the lottery system in which twenty-six letters marked on chips are placed in a bowl. The bowl is shaken and a chip is drawn out blindly and recorded. It is then returned to the bowl and the process is repeated as often as needed. Nowadays random sequences are generated by computer, but true randomness is not so easy to achieve and some programs that purport to be truly random are not. The other problem is to ensure the actual pads remain secret; they are an obvious target for enemy spies. Recently the paper pad has been replaced by some form of electronic storage. A computer housed in a mobile phone can store the one-time pad and be used for encipherment and decipherment, but it is not safe from spies, and there is a problem with erasing the data.

Secret Communication in the Computer Age

Most of us make unwitting use of sophisticated ciphers, for instance when we perform banking transactions over the internet.

Computers operate in terms of binary digits (bits), and letters or numbers are represented by seven-digit binary numbers. The upper case A, for instance, is represented by 1000001 in the standard method of representation, namely the American Standard Code for Information Interchange (ASCII). Computers can carry out substitutions not only for these binary numbers, but even for the bits that compose them; moreover, they can transpose the bits in a number *and* bits in adjacent binary numbers.

Here is an example of carrying out substitution on a plain text message 'cat' with a key DOG.

1. Plain text: cat
2. Plain text in ASCII: 1000011100000110101OO
3. Key: DOG   100010010011111OOOIII
4. Cipher text: OOOO1111OOO1IIOOOOOOII
5. Key: DOG   100010010011111OOOIII
6. Plain text in ASCII: 1000011100000110001OO (same as line 2)

Adding or subtracting bits operates in the following way. If the two bits are the same, we write 0; if they are different, we write 1. In the example above the ASCII code for C is 1000011 and the ASCII code for D is 1000100. In the first position we 'add' 1 and 1 and obtain 0 as our cipher value in line 4. In the second, third, and fourth positions we add 0 and 0 and write 0 in line 4. In the fifth, sixth, and seventh positions we are adding 1 and 0, so we write 1 in each case, and so on. This might seem an odd operation that loses information, but note that performing the same operation on the cipher text (line 4) and using the same key (line 5) reveal the original plain text (line 6).

All information in a computer is represented in this way—not just letters, numerals, and other symbols but sounds and images, including moving images. At this point cryptography has little to do with language. Readers interested in following developments in cryptography in the computer age are advised to read the final chapters of books such as those by Simon Singh listed in the bibliography, and then google the technical terms for more recent information.

Voice transmission can also be encrypted. Between the world wars there were scrambling devices that separated the speech signal into five frequency bands and swapped the bands around, so that the output of the lowest frequency band, for instance, was transmitted as a higher frequency band. In another variation the speech signal was broken into short segments ands these segments were rearranged. This was analogous to a simple local transposition, rather like sending a word like *stamp* as TMASP, except that in speech the individual phonemes are not clearly separate as in writing, so a particular segment might contain part of one phoneme and part of another. Neither method was very secure and in World War II the Americans used a system called Sigsaly in which the speech signal was sampled every twenty milliseconds and its amplitude modified. Nowadays with digital representation of speech the binary numbers and the bits that compose them can be subject to transposition and substitution, as mentioned above.

Final Word

Although machines like Enigma provide a high level of security, they are too slow for use on the battlefield, where speed is the more important consideration. For this reason simple, traditional ciphers have been used in combat zones until quite recently. But there is a way of combining speed and security that does not involve any encryption and that is to use a language unknown to the enemy. The Americans used native speakers of American Indian languages to pass messages in both world wars: Choctaw speakers in World War I and over four hundred Navaho (Navajo) speakers in World War II, as well as small numbers of speakers of Choctaw, Comanche, and other languages. The speakers invented native terms for military concepts. The Comanches, for instance, called a tank a 'turtle' and a bomber a 'pregnant airplane'.[10]

The use of steganography, ciphers, and codes has largely been motivated by the practical necessity of concealing information from rivals, competitors, and enemies, but the process of devising a secure means of communication and the business of trying to break a code or cipher provides a stimulating mental challenge for the general public. Cryptographic puzzles and problems are a popular form of entertainment, and cryptology plays a part in literature. Substitution ciphers have featured in works such as Edgar Allan Poe's 'The Golden Bug', Arthur Conan Doyle's *The Adventure of the Dancing Men*, and several of Dorothy Sayers' detective novels. In the film *2001: A Space Odyssey* (1968) the

[10] Having learnt about the use of Choctaw speakers in World War I Hitler sent anthropological linguists to the USA in the 1930s to learn American languages. Knowing this, the US made little use of American languages in the European theatre of war (Wikipedia entry for *Code Talker*).

talking computer that directs the spaceship is called HAL, a name derived from *IBM* by a Caesar shift of minus one.

Ciphers to Solve

Here are two ciphers you can try to decipher for yourself (Figures 21 and 22). First make frequency counts, then compare them with the shape of the graph in Figure 10. Do the frequencies of the cipher letters match those of plain text? If so, you are faced with encipherment by transpostion: look for ways of rearranginging the text to assemble common sequences of letters and common words such as *the* and *and*. If not, you have encipherment by substitution, and you have to use a bit of trial and error in matching the high-frequency cipher letters with the high-frequency letters of English plain text, namely *e, t, a, o, i, n*.

KJNHN	QBKIK	GLOKI	SRCJA	TRCLB	NOTFL	BTUNQ	PKHNW
BTQFN	PPPYP	QNHTQ	CRTFF	YONFT	QNIQK	QBNLF	TCJQN
XQTFL	BTUNQ	CPQKS	PNTRK	INWKO	ITLOT	RQCRN	QBTQB
TPUNN	JCJSP	NPCJR	NQBNP	NVNJQ	NNJQB	RNJQS	OYUDU

21. Cipher to solve (a).

E	T	M	I	T	H	N	S	I	E
I	R	L	L	I	W	A	R	R	V
T	E	T	E	A	A	N	M	A	N
I	D	L	L	R	W	A	D	D	E
T	S	H	E	F	S	C	N	O	E
N	R	C	E	P	E	S	O	T	S
W	H	I	L	A	E	L	E	L	V
M	E	M	E	T	I	D	A	I	E
A	L	F	T	E	Y	E	H	R	R
E	P	S	E	T	R	N	A	T	I
A	O	N	D	L	N	W	L	I	N
T	O	A	K	E	T	E	U	Q	S
O	T	N	S	P	I	S	O	T	X

22. Cipher to solve (b).

5

BIBLICAL SECRETS

There shall not be found among you any one who maketh his son or his daughter to pass through the fire, or that useth divination, or an observer of times, or an enchanter, or a witch.

DEUTERONOMY 18:10

Kabbalah

Among Jewish scholars in Provence and northern Spain in the twelfth and thirteenth centuries there developed a school of mystical speculation that came to be known as the *Kabbalah* (also *Cabala, Kabalah, qabalah*). The word 'Kabbalah' means 'receiving' and it was claimed that the school was carrying on an oral tradition incorporating divine revelation to Adam and Moses. The principal notions of Kabbalah concern a model of the universe showing the relationship between God, spirits, and humans, and are not related to language, but within this philosophy there were notions about language, particularly Hebrew. These notions became influential in Christian Europe in the Renaissance and

א	ב	ג	ד	ה	ו	ז	ח	ט	י	כ
'aleph	bêth	gîmel	dāleth	hē	wāw	záyin	ḥêth	ṭêth	yôdh	kaph
'	b	g	d	h	w	z	ḥ	ṭ	y	k
1	2	3	4	5	6	7	8	9	10	20
ל	מ	נ	ס	ע	פ	צ	ק	ר	ש	ת
lāmedh	mêm	nûn	sāmekh	'ayin	pē	ṣādhê	qôph	rêš	sîn, šîn	tāw
l	m	n	s	'	p	ṣ	q	r	sh	t
30	40	50	60	70	80	90	100	200	300	400

23. The Hebrew alphabet.

Some of the letters have alternative forms that are used at the end of a word. These are used for the numbers 500 to 900 as follows: ך k 500, ם m 600, ן n 700, ף p 800, ץ ṣ 900.

still attract some interest today. Sacred texts tend to receive close scrutiny and the Hebrew Bible, particularly the first five books (Genesis, Exodus, Leviticus, Numbers, and Deuteronomy) known collectively as the Torah, were examined by Kabbalists for anagrams, ciphers, and acrostics. In Hebrew letters of the alphabet served as numerals and scholars placed values on the numerical properties of words in the Bible. These values are shown in Figure 23.

Before examples are given it should be pointed out that the Hebrew alphabet used in the Bible consists entirely of consonants. Originally no vowels were written, as we see in the earliest inscriptions, from the tenth century BC. But at some time between the tenth and sixth centuries the letter ׳ (y) came to be used for a final î and ו (w) for final û. In the period after the Babylonian exile of the sixth century the use of these letters was extended to indicate vowels within the word so that ׳ could indicate î or ê, and ו could indicate û or ô (Lambdin 1973: xxiii). Much later, around the seventh century AD, a system of 'pointing' was introduced by the Masoretes 'the bearers of tradition'. This involves subscript dots for vowels. It should also be noted that Hebrew is written right to left.

Anagrams

A linguistic feature of biblical texts that stimulated some interest was the anagram. Since biblical Hebrew was written without vowels, it is relatively easy to find anagrams. One example is between the name *Moshe* (*Moses*) and *Ha-Shem*, 'The Name'. The consonants in *Moses/Moshe* are M s[H] H (משה) and in *Ha-Shem* H s[H] M (השם). *Ha-Shem* was, and still is, one of the ways of referring to God without using the sacred name YHWH 'Yahweh' (יהוה). A notion similar to the anagram was that permutations of the letters in a word still held the essence of the word, so that all twelve cambinations of the four consonants in YHWH held the essence of the sacred name (Reuchlin 1993: 307). In Umberto Eco's novel, *Foucault's Pendulum*, one of the characters, Jacobo Belbo, has a computer program for listing all combinations of four letters which is used to identify all the permutations of YHWH (not that such a task really requires a computer). Significantly, the computer is called *Abulafia* after the thirteenth-century Kabbalist Abraham Abulafia, who placed great significance on the letters of Hebrew and the text of the Hebrew Bible.

Ciphers

Examples of cipher have been identified in the Bible, although the enciphered text consists of particular words rather than long passages. In one scheme, *Atbash*, the first letter of the alphabet is substituted for the last letter, the second for the next to last, the third for the third from last, and so forth. In Jeremiah there is a reference to a king of Sheshach in a list of kings (25:26) and there is a further reference in a prophecy about the fall of Babylon: *How is Sheshach taken!... What a horrifying sight Babylon has become!* (51:41). Sheshach has been taken to be an Atbash variant of Babel, i.e., Babylon, which the reader can check from Figure 23: *Sh* → *b*, *Sh* → *b*, and *Ch* (or *k*) → *l*. This identification of Sheshach as Babylon has been widely accepted and some translations of the Bible simply convert *Sheshach* to *Babylon*.

Other systems of encipherment identified in the Bible include *Abgad*, in which each letter in the Hebrew alphabet is replaced by the one succeeding it, so that aleph is replaced by beth, beth by gimel, and so on.[1] This system has been used in amulets. In another system, *Albam*, the first letter of the alphabet is replaced by the twelfth, the second by the thirteenth, and so on, a correspondence that can be read vertically in Figure 23. People have claimed to have found various hidden words (usually names) in the Bible using one substitution system or another. However, it seems likely that some of the 'finds' are the result of coincidence, given that in a purely consonantal system there will be many consonant sequences that correspond to more than one word or phrase, as with *Moshe* and *Ha-Shem*.

[1] The reader can see how the names Atbash, Albam, and Abgad are formed by looking at Figure 23. Aleph is to read as 'a'. Each name is based on the first two substitutions in the system. It will be seen that *Atbash* involves *t* for *a* and *sh* for *b*; *Albam* involves *l* for *a* and *m* for *b*, and *Abgad* involves *b* for *a* and *d* for *g*.

Notarikon

Followers of the Kabbalah find acrostics in the Bible, specifically in
the Torah, a practice known as **notarikon**. It involves taking
phrases or sentences from the Torah and seeing if the initials,
medials, or finals form a word or phrase. It is essentially acrostics,
but typically with acrostics the hidden names are clearly deliberate
and their distribution is systematic. For instance, in an acrostic
poem all the initials of the lines or all the initials of the stanzas will
form a word, as illustrated in Chapter 2. With notarikon, however,
the investigator searches through the text like someone trying to
break a cipher and finds that here and there a sequence of initials
or finals forms a word. From the sentence MY IOLH LNW
HS^HMIMH 'Who shall go up for us to heaven?' (Deuteronomy
30: 12) the initials form the word MILH 'circumcision' and the
final letters form YHWH 'Yahweh' (taking yôdh and waw with
their consonant value), from which it has been argued that circumcision has divine approval (Westcott 1910). The chances of an
accidental acrostic vary from language to language but are high in
biblical Hebrew and in English. The text of this book contains
hundreds of examples of three-letter and four-letter words formed
by sequences of initials, plus a few examples of longer words.

In another variation of notarikon each letter of a word is taken
to stand for another word. For instance, *mizbeaḥ* 'altar' has been
'explained' as *meḥilah zekhut berakhah ḥayyim* 'forgiveness, merit,
blessing, life' (Werbolowsky and Wigoder 1997).[2]

---

[2] The leader of the Jewish revolt against Antiochus IV Epiphanes in the
second century BC was Judah Macabee. Some believe the epithet *Macabee*

Some people claim that if one takes the line of succession from Adam to Abraham, i.e., Adam, Seth, Enosh, etc., the initial letters of the names form a sentence meaning, 'I will forgive (or "lift up") my enemies, having compassion, forgiving those made from (or "laid low in") dust a second time'. [3] Given that for the most part vowels were not written in biblical Hebrew the string of consonants derived from the initials of the names allows more than one possibility of interpretation, more so when one considers that it can be broken up into words in more than one way.

The persistence of belief in hidden acrostics in the Bible is interesting and is epitomized in a recent popular book, *The Bible Code* by Michael Drosnin (1997). Drosnin claims, 'The Bible is constructed like a giant crossword puzzle. It is encoded from beginning to end with words that connect to tell a hidden story' (1997: 25). His method of finding hidden messages is to search for words, especially proper names, phrases, and dates, by looking for sequences of letters spaced at equal intervals throughout the text. In the simplest instance one starts at the first letter of the Bible and looks for words made up of successive letters, then one looks for words made up of every second letter, every third letter, and so on. There is no limit to these intervals beyond what is determined by

---

is an acronym of *Mi kamocha ba'elim YHVH*, 'Who is like unto thee among the mighty, O Lord!' (Exodus 15:11), which was used on the standards of his army. Reuchlin (1993: 313) notes that the Gematria total for MKBY is 72, which equals the total of YHVH, but this is only true if subtotals for Y (10), YH (15), YHV (21), and YHVH (26) are added together.

[3] Information taken from the Wikipedia entry for *acrostic* where the original Hebrew is given.

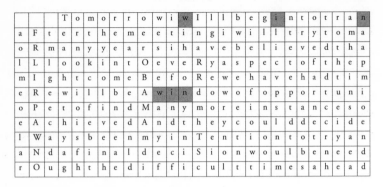

		T	o	m	o	r	r	o	w	i	w	I	l	l	b	e	g	i	n	t	o	t	r	a	n
a	F	t	e	r	t	h	e	m	e	e	t	i	n	g	i	w	i	l	l	t	r	y	t	o	m	a
o	R	m	a	n	y	y	e	a	r	s	i	h	a	v	e	b	e	l	i	e	v	e	d	t	h	a
l	L	l	o	o	k	i	n	t	O	e	v	e	R	y	a	s	p	e	c	t	o	f	t	h	e	p
m	I	g	h	t	c	o	m	e	B	e	f	o	R	e	w	e	h	a	v	e	h	a	d	t	i	m
e	R	e	w	i	l	l	b	e	A	w	i	n	d	o	w	o	f	o	p	p	o	r	t	u	n	i
o	P	e	t	o	f	i	n	d	M	a	n	y	m	o	r	e	i	n	s	t	a	n	c	e	s	o
e	A	c	h	i	e	v	e	d	A	n	d	t	h	e	y	c	o	u	l	d	d	e	c	i	d	e
l	W	a	y	s	b	e	e	n	m	y	i	n	T	e	n	t	i	o	n	t	o	t	r	y	a	n
a	N	d	a	f	i	n	a	l	d	e	c	i	S	i	o	n	w	o	u	l	b	e	n	e	e	d
r	O	u	g	h	t	h	e	d	i	f	f	i	c	u	l	t	t	i	m	e	s	a	h	e	a	d

24. A modern example of notarikon.

the length of the text. The name *Yitzhak Rabin*, that of the Israeli prime minister who was assassinated in 1995, was found with an interval of 4,772. The search can begin with the second letter of the Bible, the third, the fourth, and so on. All this means there is a good chance of finding words and phrases, and Drosnin appears to admit as much. However, he claims that when these words are found, there are often related words found nearby that constitute prophecies. Near to the name Yitzhak Rabin he finds 'assassinate' and 'Amir', the name of the assassin. The concept of 'nearness' is crucial. When a word, say a name, is found, the text is written out in lines that equal the distance between its constituent letters. In the case of *Rabin*, the lines of text will be arranged in sixty-four rows of 4,772 letters. This means that the name *Yitzhak Rabin* will appear at some point as a vertical sequence and one then surveys the area surrounding this vertical sequence.

Rather than reproduce Drosnin's Hebrew example, in Figure 24 I have shown part of an English text with *Obama* showing up as a vertical sequence. In looking at this figure one needs to think of a very large text where the letters *o-b-a-m-a* occur at intervals of, say, 1,208 and the text is written out in rows of 1,208 letters to show *o-b-a-m-a* as a vertical sequence. Note first that the sequence *win* (shaded) occurs next to the first *a* in *Obama*. Of course this contiguity exists however the text is arranged, but *win* becomes significant only when the preceding *a* is recognized as part of the sequence *Obama*. Now look at the top line of the matrix, where the word *win* can be picked out at intervals of seven. This piece of text is not near *Obama* in the original text, but comes to be near only when the text is written out with a line length matching the intervals between the letters *o-b-a-m-a*.

If a text like this had been examined in this way prior to the 2008 American presidential election, it could have been taken as a prophecy of Obama's success, even without the example of *win* that is contiguous with *Obama*. Drosnin finds a number of significant contiguities, such as the pair *Clinton* and *president*, and the four terms *Hitler*, *evil man*, *Nazi*, and *slaughter*. He describes the odds against such juxtapositions arising by chance as astronomical. My impression is that these juxtapositions are not so unlikely, particularly if we take a generous view of what is near (see the second *win* example) and allow that more than one word can be semantically appropriate to a particular name, e.g. *succeed* or *win*; *kill*, *cut down*, or *assassinate*.

Drosnin has challenged his critics to find comparable revelations in other texts, such as *Moby Dick*. One person who has taken up the challenge is Brendan McKay of the Australian National University, who demonstrates that Drosnin's method reveals a prediction of Drosnin's own assassination in Melville's novel. When Drosnin's name is written vertically using Drosnin's method, it is intersected by 'him to have been killed'.[4]

Gematria

In most ancient languages, including Akkadian, Hebrew, and Greek, the letters of the alphabet served as numerals. This meant that any sequence of letters designating a word could have a numerical interpretation, and conversely some sequences of numbers could coincide with a word. This is marginally possible with Roman numerals in English; an example given in Chapter 1 is the sequence *CLIX*, which can be 159 or a trade name for a brand of crackers. This ambivalence led to a form of numerology where the numerical properties of words, such as the sum of the numerical values of their letters, was held to be significant. Jewish scholars of the Kabbalah claimed to have found hidden meanings in the Torah by such methods.

The Greeks called the study of the numerical properties of words **isopsepha**, but it is better known as **gematria** (also gima-triyyah), a word associated with Jewish traditions but ultimately from Greek *geometria* 'geometry' (Birnbaum 1964; Werbolowsky and Wigoder 1997).[5] One of the earliest examples of gematria concerns Sargon II of Assyria. When he built Dur-Sharrukin,

[4] See various Web sites under 'Drosnin'; in particular search for 'Demise of Drosnin'.

[5] Gematria scores the occasional mention in fiction. In the 1998 film *Pi* (π) the protagonist, a mathematician who is trying to find patterns in the universe (including the stock market!), meets someone who believes in gematria and gives up his search to help his new acquaintance find patterns in the Torah.

α	β	γ	δ	ε	ς	ζ	η	θ
1	2	3	4	5	6	7	8	9
ι	κ	λ	μ	ν	ξ	ο	π	φ
10	20	30	40	50	60	70	80	90
ρ	σ ς	τ	υ	φ	χ	ψ	ω	♈
100	200	300	400	500	600	700	800	900

25. The Greek alphabet with numerical values.

present-day Khorsabad, he decreed that the length of the walls was to be 16,280 Assyrian units, a figure which equalled the numerical sum of the letters in his name. Leonides of Alexandra wrote couplets in which the numerical total of the two lines matched, or quatrains where the totals for the couplets matched (Cameron 1995: 478). Among the graffiti found in the ruins of Pompei there is one in Greek that reads 'Amerimnus thought about his lady Harmonia for good. The number of her honourable name is 45'. Another reads *Philō hēs arithmos* φμε 'I love her whose number is 545'. These numbers probably seem unromantic to us, but in a world where formal properties of words were of interest and numerology was popular, they probably had some considerable significance. The number 45 incidentally is not the value of Harmonia. As can be seen from Figure 25, the number 45 is με (*me*) in Greek and must have some reference unknown to us.

Discoveries have been made in and around Egypt of amulets containing stones engraved with the name of a spirit or god, *Abraxas* (earlier *Abrasax*). The name also appears frequently in curse tablets, often in conjunction with other names of spirits or gods. Abraxas is associated with the Basilideans, followers of Basilides, a religious teacher in early second-century Alexandria. Basilidean teaching combined ideas from a number of religious traditions including

Zoroastrianism, Judaism, and Christianity. If one adds the numerical value of the Greek letters of Abraxas or Abrasax ($A\beta\rho\alpha\xi\alpha\varsigma$ or $A\beta\rho\alpha\sigma\alpha\xi$), one obtains the total 365 (1 + 2 + 100 + 1 + 200 + 1 + 60), which corresponds to the 365 orders of spirits recognized in the Basilidean model of the universe (Budge 1978: 208). It also corresponds to the number of days in the solar year, and Abraxas was associated with the sun (Ogden 1999: 48).

Disciples of the Kabbalah developed a strong interest in the numerical properties of proper names, and they claimed that the numerical sum of the letters in words indicated hidden revelations in the text of the Bible, at least in the Torah. Interest in the numerology of the Bible and in the Kabbalah generally spread to Christian scholars of the late Middle Ages and the Renaissance.

The numerical value of a word can be obtained by adding up the value of each letter, so that יהוה YHWH has the value of 26 (y (10)+h(5)+w(6)+h(5)). As an example of seeing significance in the numerical value of a name consider the fact that in Genesis 14: 14 Abraham's servants are said to number 318 and a few verses later Eliezer is introduced as Abraham's steward (Birnbaum 1964: 123; Roth 1966). Eliezer (אליעזר) scores 318, a figure that readers can calculate for themselves from Figure 23. This does not seem to matter much, and if it is not coincidence, it may mean that the writer was indulging in some in-group communication as an exercise in ingenuity.

For a more significant example consider the interpretation given to part of Genesis 49:10:

> The sceptre shall not depart from Judah, nor a lawgiver from beneath his feet, until Shiloh shall come; and unto him shall the gathering of the people be.

The words 'Shiloh shall come' are *ShILH IBA* (with *A* for aleph) and the numerical value is 300+10+30+5 for *ShILH* and 10+2+1 for *IBA*, making a total of 358. The word *Messiah* is *MShIH* and has the same total (40+300+10+8). This leads to an interpretation that the Messiah shall come.

As mentioned above, interest in the Kabbalah was not confined to Jews, and gematria became popular among writers on magic and the occult in the late Middle Ages and the Renaissance. For instance, Heinrich Cornelius Agrippa von Nettesheim, who was mentioned in Chapter 2, claimed that the shapes, order, and numerical equivalents of the letters of the Hebrew alphabet did not arise by accident but were 'formed divinely, so that they relate to and accord with the heavenly bodies, the divine bodies, and their virtues'. Hebrew names in the Bible, including those derived from gematria, were set by God himself 'according to a number and figure which are unchangeable by reason of their eternal stability'.

A belief that there are hidden meanings in the text of the Hebrew Bible is understandable given the traditional Jewish belief that Hebrew is the original language given by God to Adam and Eve. It was believed that the language had magic properties, and that there was a connection between words of Hebrew and their referents, a connection that was lost in the arbitrary languages that sprang up after Babel (Zika 1976: 122; Shumaker 1982: 33). This idea is taken up in Chapter 6. However, it should be pointed out that the Hebrew script illustrated here came into use after the Babylonian exile (sixth century BC), superseding an earlier script. Both scripts derived from a Phoenician script, which in turn was ultimately derived from Egyptian hieroglyphs. We have already looked at innovations in the use of the letters ׳ (y) and ׳ (w) to indicate vowels. Textual diversity continued until the second century BC, around which time the numerical values of the letters were assigned (Sáenz-Badillos 1993: 76).

Whatever one may think of this type of gematria, it is strange that some people apply the practice to the Bible in translation. In English one would take the values: $a = 1$, $b = 2$, and so on down to $z = 26$. *God* would score a value of 26 (7+15+4), which might excite some devotees since this is the value of YHWH in Hebrew; but since French *dieu* would score a different value, and similarly with Italian *dio*, German *Gott*, etc., it is hard to see any rationale. A gematria enthusiast would find significance in the fact that *Jesus* and *Messiah* both score the same, namely 74, but given the number of words and phrases that can apply to Jesus, such as *Emmanuel*, *Christ*, and *Son of Man*, there is scope for coincidence. This applies more generally: there are numerous names in the Bible, quite apart from other words, and there will inevitably be instances where totals match or where one is twice another and so on.

Onomancy

Since at least classical times there has been a belief that names can be the basis of predicting someone's future. Divination using names is called **onomancy**. It overlaps with gematria in that the numerical values of letters play a part. Onomancy was widely used to predict the winner of a contest by considering the number values of the letters in the names of the contestants, the number values of the days of the week, and so on. As one commentator notes, 'The practice of onomancy was rooted in the same presuppositions noted in protective magic using magic squares and numbers, that language has a mathematical correspondence to reality' (Jolly 2002: 57).

6

WORDS OF POWER

…but speak the word only, and my servant shall be healed.

MATTHEW 8:8

The blow disappears, the word remains

YIDDISH PROVERB

Beliefs About Language

This chapter and the next are largely concerned with belief in the supernatural and belief that there is an intimate connection between the form of a word, especially a personal name, and what the word refers to. The subject of this chapter is words that are thought to have power to affect some aspect of the physical world, and in the following chapter we move on to words that are taboo.

In our society certain speech acts have power, as when a marriage celebrant says, 'I now pronounce you husband and wife' or a judge says, 'I hereby sentence you to three years' hard labour'. Society agress to confer power on formulaic utterances like these when they are used by properly authorized persons in specified circumstances. However, for most humans who have ever lived, and still for some millions living today, some words, phrases, and texts are regarded as having an inherent power to change some aspect of the environment, in particular to cure or curse, or to provide protection against unwelcome change. Some of these words and phrases have to be used in an appropriate ritual carried out by a suitable person, but the words are not considered to be arbitrary or the creations of ordinary humans like the words used by a marriage celebrant or a judge.

A moment's consideration will make it clear that there is no natural relationship between the form of a word and what it stands for. For a start there can be more than one word for the same entity. In English the words *rock* and *stone* both have much the same reference, as do *girl* and *lass* or *film* and *movie*. Moreover, there are numerous languages and most of them have their own words for any particular shared entity. What we call a *dog* in English is *chien* in French, *Hund* in German, *anjing* in Indonesian, and *inu* in Japanese. However, the belief that there is a connection between words and their referents is widespread. Even among the sophisticated Greeks the question was an open one. In Plato's dialogue, *Cratylos*, Socrates serves as arbiter in a debate in which one participant, Cratylos, argues for a natural relationship between words and meanings, while the other participant, Hermogenes, argues that the relationship is arbitrary or conventional. Anyone arguing for a natural relationship between words and referents points to onomatopoeic words, i.e., words that are imitative of a sound or the source of a sound, such as *gong*, *twang*, and *cuckoo*. There are also sets of words that exhibit sound symbolism, an apparent connection between part of a syllable and the sense. For instance, a number of words in English have the rhyme *-ump* and refer to rounded protuberances (*lump*, *rump*, *mumps*) or an impact with something rounded or heavy (*bump*, *crump, dump, thump*).

The argument fails owing to the relative scarcity of such words, but some people still believe in a natural relationship between word and referent. They will tell you *bum* is a dirty word (and children caught uttering such words have sometimes been forced to wash their mouths out with soap[1]) or that *slug* is an appropriate word for the creature it denotes because both are unpleasant (although a person who might say this probably wouldn't find any unpleasantness in words for slugs in unfamiliar languages). Some words do become contaminated by usage. *Nigger* is a good example. Originally an innocent enough word deriving from *niger*, the Latin for 'black', it has acquired unpleasant connotations by a long period of racist usage.

Most readers will be familiar with the notion of sticking pins in a voodoo doll in an attempt to harm the person the doll represents. This is part of a belief found in numerous cultures that one can affect a person or animal by means of some kind of image. Frazer (1911a: 52) calls this homeopathic or mimetic magic. A figurine may

---

[1] In the film *Georgia Rule* Grandma Georgia (Jane Fonda) puts a cake of soap in the mouth of those who blaspheme.

be made of clay, tallow, wax, wood, or dough, while an effigy can be made from reeds or grass. The link between the figurine or doll and the victim is made by taking corporeal matter or effluvia from the victim and attaching it to the image or by writing the victim's name on the image. Some form of ritual involving incantation is performed, and the image is then injured, destroyed, or placed in some inauspicious place such as a grave or a drain. An injury to part of the image, say the head, right arm, or left leg, is supposed to cause the victim pain in the corresponding part of the body.[2] If the effigy is destroyed, that is supposed to bring about the victim's death. Although such images are usually used in an attempt to harm an enemy, some have been made of a beloved and have been subjected to love charms.

An alternative to making an image is to take a body part such as hair or nail clippings, or else bodily effluvia and to subject that to some kind of ritual. This is an example of what Frazer calls contagious magic, the belief that something once in contact with or part of a creature remains part of that creature.[3]

In many cultures a name is like an effigy or a body part in that damaging the name, for instance by stabbing it or scrambling it, is

[2] Frazer distinguishes mimetic or homeopathic magic in which one produces an effect by imitating it, and contagious magic where an object has power deriving from the creature it was formerly in contact with. Both are subsumed under the widely used broader term *sympathetic magic* (1911a: 52).

[3] In Europe it was not uncommon to damage a footprint in an attempt to damage the person who made it. It was also believed that some people who were ill had had sorcery performed on their footprint and that their footprint had been taken. There were even ritual procedures for restoring the missing footprint (Clark 2002: 104–5).

thought to be capable of damaging or destroying the owner of the name. In fact the term 'owner' is not always appropriate, since in some cultures a name is not owned but is considered part of a person (examples are given in Chapter 7). Philip Peek, writing about African views of language, states, 'Deeply felt concern about names, their creation, use and avoidance, reflects this general point, in that to name something is to "know" its essence and possibly control it. Names do not simply describe; they are their referent' (Peek 1981: 27).

Many, perhaps most, cultures have myths about the origin of language. People tend to identify themselves as the original humans and take their language to be the original human language, and they often explain language diversity as the result of some later divine punishment or a natural disaster that dispersed the population. The Kaska people of western Canada, for instance, have the following story (condensed from Teit 1917: 442–3):

> Once there came a great flood, which covered the earth. The people became separated. Some were driven far away. When the flood subsided, people were now widely scattered over the world. When, in their wanderings, they met people from another place, they spoke different languages and could not understand one another. This is why there are now many different centres of population, many tribes, and many languages. Before the flood there was but one centre, for all the people lived together in one country and spoke one language.

The creation story recorded in the first chapters of Genesis has God allotting basic names for day, night, heaven, and earth, and Adam, the first human, assigning names to fauna (and presumably everything else). The language used by God, Adam, Eve, and the serpent is not specified, but is naturally taken to be Hebrew, the language of those telling the story.[4] Later, chapter eleven states that 'the whole earth was of one language, and of one speech' until God punished the people for building a tower to reach heaven (the Tower of Babel) by scattering them and 'confound[ing] their language, that they may not understand one another's speech'. This story reflects a belief that Hebrew is the original language and it gave rise to a belief in the special potency of the Hebrew language. The third-century Christian scholar Origen, for instance, believed Hebrew names had power in their original form, but lost it in transliteration or translation (Skemer 2006: 96).

This way of thinking became prominent among scholars in the Kabbalah tradition. One Hebrew text in circulation among Kabbalists was the *Sefer Yetzirah* 'Book of Creation' (also *Sepher Yetzirah*). It was attributed to Abraham, but probably dates from around the beginning of the Christian era. It contains the view that the universe was created by God through the letters of the Hebrew alphabet. One might ask who created the letters, but even setting that aside we are left with a world view that ascribes primacy to language, including the written form of language, over everything else in the universe (Winslade 2000: 84).

Kabbalah ideas about the Hebrew language became influential in Christian Europe in the Renaissance through the writings of scholars such as Giovanni Pico della Mirandola (1463–94), Johann Reuchlin (1455–1522), and Heinrich Cornelius Agrippa von Nettesheim (1486–1535). A particularly pervasive belief was that there

---

[4] Although it is a majority view that Hebrew is the language spoken by God and Adam, it is not a universal view.

was an inherent connection between Hebrew words and their referents. The following quotation from Manuel do Valle de Mouro, a sixteenth-century Portuguese theologian, captures the essence of this (Maxwell-Stuart 1999: 137).[5]

> The art of the Kabbalah is a Jewish tradition. The Jews believe that the predilections, conditions, powers and faculties of innumerable things are contained in Hebrew names in such a way that if anyone were to invoke properly the whole power of the Hebrew names, letters, accents and so forth, he could accomplish many extraordinary things. They claim that these same utterances create power over the whole universe, nature, evil spirits, angels and God himself, and that this happened because God himself or Adam, both of whom enjoyed the attributes of immortality and wisdom, gave things their substances, qualities, conditions, properties and descriptive names. Consequently, things are under the immediate control of the person who calls them by their names . . .

The view that one can exercise control via words is widespread, but this passage expresses a conviction that Hebrew embodies a unique connection between words and their referents, because Hebrew names are the real, original names.

It is easy nowadays to see this notion as misguided. Hebrew is just one of a number of Semitic languages and is not even the most conservative or nearest to Proto-Semitic, the ancestral form of Semitic. This only became clear with the development of historical linguistics in the nineteenth century, but even before that time there were those who viewed the notions stemming from the Kabbalah sceptically. A seventeenth-century Spanish writer, Francisco Torreblanca Villalpando, wrote, ' . . . for it is incredible that

[5] See also Shumaker 1972: 135, 149.

the sun, moon and other stars, the elements and things derived from them, since they lack reason, feel that divine power which lies hidden in Hebrew words, and are so affected thereby and so moved that they obey a person simply because he wills it . . . It must be said that no name, whether pronounced mentally or aloud, naturally and of themselves have such a power' (quoted in Maxwell-Stuart 1999: 138). Villalpando had his own theory about uniquely powerful language, however. He went on to contrast 'Kabbalistic words' with the words used in Christian sacraments, which he regarded as possessing a power with which they were endowed by Christ.

As we saw in Chapter 1, all societies believe in the supernatural, and all societies believe they have means of contacting the spirit world. It is common to avoid offending spirits and so avert misfortune or to seek to win their favour in obtaining cures, fertility, prosperity, and success in finding a partner. People frequently ask for help in defeating their enemies, which directly or indirectly involves the use of curses. A curse may be laid on an individual or a group of people, on animals, plants, or land. Misfortune may be invoked in the form of failed crops, famine, fire, flood, injury, or disease. In the culture of Ancient Greece and Rome it was common to inscribe curses on thin sheets of lead. These were buried near the home of a target or placed in a grave in the hope of enlisting help from the spirit of the departed. The graves of those who had suffered untimely deaths or had not been given the proper burial rites were favoured, since it was thought their spirits were likely to remain in the vicinity of the grave. These curse tablets, known as *katadesmoi* in Greek and *defixiones* in Latin, were directed at adversaries in business, the theatre, and the courts. From the second century AD onwards they were used against competitors in sport. A number of defixiones unearthed from the Roman empire are aimed at competitors in chariot races and their horses, and have been found buried near stadiums. Early curse tablets from as far back as the fourth century BC are designed to get rid of an unwanted partner or lover; from the second century AD onwards there are similar texts for acquiring a partner or lover (Ogden 1999: 4, 24). If the target is a woman, the curse may involve barrenness, miscarriage, or the birth of deformed children.

Another type of curse is one that is placed on a thief who has stolen someone's property. A number of curse tablets excavated from Bath, England, are of this type. The victim asks a deity to afflict the thief, whose identity may not be known, and to recover the stolen goods (Gager 1992: 93–4). Curses may also be directed against a potential transgressor. This is common in the Bible. The last verses of Revelation place a curse on anybody who adds to or subtracts from the foregoing text (Rev. 22:18–19):

> If any man shall add unto these things, God shall add unto him the plagues that are written in this book. And if any man shall take away from the words of the book of this prophecy, God shall take away his part out of the book of life, and out of the holy city, and from the things which were written in this book.

Methods of trying to contact or influence the spirit world have varied from culture to culture, but there are common themes. There is often a requirement that the person making contact is cleansed in some way by sexual abstinence, fasting, or, as in the case of Indian culture, long-term asceticism. A ritual often involves cleansing by fire, smoke, or water, and where sacrificial victims are used, they have to be virgin or unblemished. Timing is often significant and account is taken of such phenomena as the phases of the moon or the conjunction of the planets and fixed constellations. Where a potion is produced to cure or induce harm, it may involve using substances ranging from herbs to the body parts and effluvia of humans and animals.

A number of grimoires or handbooks of magic are extant from the Middle Ages and Renaissance, including the *Liber Iuratus* or *Sworn Book of Honorius* (thirteenth century), the *Munich Handbook* (fifteenth century), *Libri Tres de Occulta Philosophia* by Heinrich Cornelius Agrippa (1531), the *Greater Key of Solomon* (sixteenth century), and the *Lesser Key of Solomon* (seventeenth century). These combine ancient pagan procedures for magic with Judaeo-Christian beliefs and texts. Shakespeare captures the essence of this type of magic in *Macbeth* (IV. 1), when the witches recite a long and imaginative recipe for a 'hell-broth' to enlist the aid of evil spirits. Note the use of body parts of creatures that pose a threat to humans, a body part from a victim of infanticide by a prostitute (*drab*), and the addition of poison (*hemlock*). The hemlock root has been obtained at night and the gall of goat and slips of yew have been gathered during an eclipse of the moon, a most unpropitious time. The Christian element lies in the inclusion of body parts of various non-Christian peoples, who are considered evil.

> Scale of dragon, tooth of wolf,
> Witches' mummy, maw and gulf
> Of the ravin'd salt-sea shark,
> Root of hemlock digg'd i' the dark,
> Liver of blaspheming Jew,
> Gall of goat, and slips of yew[6]
> Silver'd in the moon's eclipse,

[6] On the prominence of yew in magic see Elliott 1957.

> Nose of Turk and Tartar's lips,
> Finger of birth-strangled babe
> Ditch-deliver'd by a drab,
> Make the gruel thick and slab:
> Add thereto a tiger's chaudron,
> For the ingredients of our cauldron.[7]

In the ancient Near East some illnesses were interpreted as the result of possession by an evil spirit, and exorcism sometimes involved the use of an animal or an effigy of the victim as a substitute host for the illness. The ritual was intended to transfer the evil spirit from the victim to the animal or effigy. In the New Testament there is a story of Christ casting out evil spirits from humans and transferring the spirits to a new host, namely pigs (Matthew 8:28–33). In Mesopotamia human substitutes were sometimes used for kings thought to be in danger because of an ill omen such as a lunar eclipse. The king would be dethroned and a substitute put in his place. The substitute king would be killed to fulfil the assumed prophecy and then the real king would be restored. On one occasion the real king died anyway and the substitute, who had been a gardener, retained the throne (Thomsen 2001: 71–6). There is something quaint about the notion of deceiving the spirit world by using a substitute, but stories of dealings with the supernatural are full of literal interpretations. A similar principle applies to traditional taboos. A person who breaks a taboo is usually treated as guilty even if the transgression is accidental or made in ignorance. Laws must be obeyed to the letter.

Almost all procedures for communicating with the supernatural use language, and it is this component that interests us here. It may

---

[7] In the older pronunciation of *cauldron* the 'l' was not pronounced and this word would have rhymed with *chaudron*.

be a matter of letters or characters, of words, formulas, or other short passages, or even whole works. Sacred words may have a status similar to that of sacred objects, but with more versatility. Verbal cures might be spoken in a patient's ear, or, if written, might be placed in contact with a patient's body or inscribed on food and eaten.

Letters and Symbols

To those unfamiliar with the medium writing can seem mysterious and possessed of magical powers. In literate societies not everyone can read, and this was particularly true in the past. Over the last two millennia those involved in magic have exploited the mystique writing holds, particularly for the illiterate, by using alphabets such as the Hebrew one or devising new alphabets. This was especially common during the Renaissance, when a number of derivatives of the Hebrew alphabet were introduced, such as the Malachim alphabet and the Celestial or Angelic alphabet. The latter was so called because the shapes of the letters were discerned in the pattern of constellations, on the same principle as the signs of the Zodiac (Agrippa 1992, Book III: 30).[8] More recently J.R.R. Tolkien devised an alphabet called Tengwar, which he used in *The Hobbit* and *Lord of the Rings*. He also used Germanic runes, an alphabet which is often associated with magic (see below).

When writing is introduced into a culture, one of its first uses is to record secret and sacred words. According to Ostler (2007: 44–5),

---

[8] Other alphabets to be found in Agrippa are the Theban and the Transitus Fluvii 'Passing the River', as it is normally translated. There is also the Alphabet of the Magi devised by Paracelsus and the Enochian

'As in many cases of early literacy, the offer of writing to the Romans was not taken up as a chance to begin literature; for them, as for their Etruscan tutors, the first writing seems to have been a means of making spells or formulas effective by setting them down on a permanent medium'. Writing not only allows for a permanent record of a text that is meant to be recited, it also provides the possibility of a text that operates in written form, as with the words in an amulet or charm.

Writing developed from pictograms and ideograms, and the use of logographic symbols has continued in parallel with writing proper. Commonplace examples include the international symbols for male and female toilets and the more localized symbols used by itinerants to indicate to fellow travellers the reception they can expect in given premises. These may be iconic, for example a loaf of bread to indicate the likelihood of food, or apparently arbitrary as with a dot inside a circle ⊙ to indicate the possibility of the police being called (Ward 1957: 138). At a more elevated level are the auspicious symbols in several Indian religions, particularly Buddhism. They include the endless knot, the parasol, the lotus flower, the swastika, and the dharma wheel.

In the Roman empire and in Europe over the last two millennia texts with a supernatural orientation have often been accompanied by non-linguistic symbols, many of which have no identifiable origin or meaning. Some of the better-known ones are illustrated in the box below. To these we could add the cross in various forms, which for Christians has long been a symbol of great power. This is epitomized

devised by John Dee (the court astrologer to Elizabeth I and James I) and his assistant, Edward Kelley. Further information and illustration of all the alphabets mentioned is available on the Web.

in Bram Stoker's *Dracula*, where Count Dracula shrinks from the sight of the cross and is rendered powerless, but the cross also figures prominently in Christian legend. One such story concerns Constantine, the first Roman emperor to grant official recognition to Christianity. According to Eusebius Constantine saw a vision of the cross with the words *En toutō nika* (*Εν Τουτω Νικα*) 'In this [sign] conquer' before the battle of Milvian Bridge (312 AD). Constantine's army adopted the sign and conquered the rival army of Maxentius, thereby winning the imperial crown (*Life of Constantine* 28). Constantine is also reported to have used another Christian symbol, the *chi-rho*, which consisted of the first two letters of Christ's name in Greek superimposed on one another (see box).

The ancient Egyptian ANKH symbolized reproduction and life. It has come into widespread use in popular culture since the 1960s, possibly helped by the 1954 film *The Egyptian*.

The pentagram dates back to Sumeria in the fourth millennium BC. It has been in use as an amulet throughout the Near East and in Europe ever since. In the Middle Ages and Renaissance it was popular among those practising the 'black arts' and an inverted pentagram came to symbolize the devil.

The earliest examples of the hexagram date back to around 800–600 BC. It is sometimes known as the Shield or Star of David and has long been a symbol used to designate Jews. It was commonly used as an amulet, often inscribed with sacred names. It was adopted by the Zionist movement and appears on the flag of Israel.

This symbol is the Chi-Rho and consists of a capital Greek X and a capital Greek P superimposed on one another, these being the first two letters of *ΧΡΙΣΤΟΣ* 'Christ'.

Letters seem to have a fascination quite apart from their practical use in notating words. The curse tablets of the Greek and Roman worlds contain partial alphabets, words written out in patterns, and the use of letter-like characters (Ogden 1999: 8, 48–9). In one form of palmistry described by Bartolomeo della Rocca (1467–1504) letter shapes were picked out in the lines of the palm and each letter was taken to be a predictor of character and fortune.[9]

Letters and other symbols can be combined. In some medieval charms words were written in the form of a cross. For instance, a twelfth-century English charm for nose-bleeding reads, 'For blood running from the nose, write on their forehead in the form of a cross *stomen calcos, stomen metaroru*'. This is a distorted form of the Greek *stōmen kalōs, stōmen meta thobou (theou)* 'Let us stay good, let us stay in fear (of God)'. The first phrase is written vertically and the second written horizontally, intersecting it (Barb 1948: 39).

The Germanic people acquired a form of alphabet around the second century AD (Figure 26). Its exact origin is disputed; it shows resemblances to the Roman alphabet and other Italic alphabets as well as the Greek alphabet. The letters were known as runes and the alphabet is often referred to as the runic alphabet. It is also known as the *futhark* (Scandinavian version) or *futhork* (Anglo-Saxon version), this name deriving from the first six letters of the alphabet, the digraph *th* representing a single letter *þ* (thorn). The runes were used mostly for inscriptions carved on leather or bone to record ownership or on stone to record the memory of the dead. Various forms of

[9] Quoted in Maxwell-Stuart (ed.) 1999: 28.

the runic alphabet continued to be used for inscriptions even after the Germanic people were introduced to the Roman alphabet. In Germanic countries runes remain in use for ornamental purposes and as signature-like markers in the present day, and there has been a revival of interest among New Agers with an interest in the occult because runic writing is believed to be connected with magic. The name *rune* (*rūn* in Old English) means 'secret' or 'mystery' and the runic alphabet is strongly associated with magic in the Norse sagas. When one considers that runes were the first form of writing to be introduced to the Germanic people it is not surprising that they were attributed magic properties.

It seems that individual runes were considered to possess magic properties. A possible early reference can be found in Tacitus, writing in the first century AD. He notes that the Germans practised the following custom (*Germania* 10):

> Virgam frugiferae arbori decisam in surculos amputant eosque notis quibusdam discretos super candidam vestem temere ac fortuito spargunt. Mox, si publice consultetur, sacerdos civitatis, sin privatim, ipse pater familiae, precatus deos caelumque suspiciens ter singulos tollit, sublatos secundum impressam ante notam interpretatur.

> They cut off the branch of a fruit-tree and separate the twigs, mark them with distinct characters and sprinkle them at random on a white garment. Then, the priest, if it is a public consultation, or the *paterfamilias*, if it is a private one, praying to the gods and looking up to the sky takes three, one at a time, and interprets them on the basis of the characters that were inscribed on them.

Tossing twigs in the air and choosing three at random gives the spirits scope to indicate whether or not a venture is likely to

26. The Runic alphabet.

succeed. If the characters were alphabetic they were probably runes, but they may have been non-language symbols.

In *Egil's Saga*, set in the eleventh century, when Egil Skalla-grimsson is handed a poisoned brew he stabs his hand, cuts runes on the drinking horn, and rubs his blood into the grooves. The horn splits, the poisoned brew is spilt, and Egil is thus saved (chapter 44). The saga does not record the particular runes used, but it distinctly states that Egil carved 'runes' rather than 'words'. In the Old Norse poem *Skírnismál* there is a clearer reference to the use of specific runes having power. Skirnir is sent to woo Gerthr on behalf of his master, the god Freyr. It is a wooing consisting mostly of threats and verse 37 is as follows,

Þurs ríst ek þér	Thurs I carve
ok þría stafi,	and three other runes,
ergi ok æði ok óþola;	Lust, frenzy, and frustration.
svá ek þat af ríst,	As I carve on,
sem ek þat á reist,	so I carve off
ef gerask þarfar þess.	If need be.

Here Skirnir tells Gerthr that he has carved *thurs* (a rune) and three other runes, each of which relates to a mental state. If she does not accept Freyr's offer, she will be cursed with a combination of lust and lack of satisfaction, but Skirnir points out that he can destroy the carving and thereby abort the curse.[10]

One curious practice in the Middle Ages and later was to inscribe letters, whether runic or roman, on dice and then use the dice to stamp cakes given to rabid dogs in an attempt to cure them (cf. Elliott 1957: 259).

A different combination of letters and dice featured in a form of divination practised in the Roman Empire and later in Europe. Letters were inscribed on small tiles and the tiles were selected in turn by the fall of dice, so that the resulting words were produced by chance. A variant of this system involved selection of tiles by domestic fowl or pre-literate children (Flint 1991: 218).

Magic Words and Formulas

In western culture we tend not to take the idea of magic words and formulas seriously. Secret magic formulas are none the less a recurring motif of folk tales. In Lithuania and Latvia there are stories of a maiden taken away by a snake to the bottom of a lake to marry a man who is both snake and prince. After bearing him three children she is given permission to visit her family, and the prince

---

[10] There was one 'secret' connected with runes and that was the practice of sometimes indicating them by their place in the alphabet. For instance, the twenty-four-character version of the runic alphabet was arranged in three rows of eight, as in Figure 26, and a letter could be designated by its row number and position number. These numbers could be indicated by offshoots on either side of a stem or by fins on either side of a fish (Lowe 2006: 688).

gives her and the children a magic formula which will enable them to return. Not wanting her to go back to the lake, her family get the children to reveal the formula, which they then use to summon the prince from the depths and kill him (Bradūnas 1975).

Open sesame! is familiar as the magic formula that opens the cave filled with treasure in *Ali Baba and the Forty Thieves*, and *abracadabra* is the stock example of a magic word, popular with professional magicians. *Abracadabra* appears in *De medicina praecepta* by Quintus Serenus Sammonicus, a learned writer of the late second century AD, but it is not Latin and its origin is unclear. It may have a Semitic origin, perhaps in the Aramaic phrase *avra kehdabra* 'I will create as I speak'.[11] *Abracadabra* is typical of the language of magic, first, because it is meaningless and second, because it features internal repetition, namely of the segment *abra*. Full and partial reduplication are common in magic language, as are rhythm, rhyme, alliteration, assonance, and swapping of sounds as in spoonerisms (Keane 1997: 53; Roper 2003a: 9).[12] These qualities are illustrated among the variants of a medieval formula to be used against the bite of a mad dog. These include *Pax Max D Inax* and *Pax, Max, Y, Vy, Vax*. *Pax* is 'peace' in Latin and *max* is presumably an abbreviation of *maxima* 'greatest'. The rest seems to be gibberish, but note the jingly rhyme (Elliott 1957: 260).

An early example of gibberish and word play can be found in the *De Agricultura* (160) of Cato the Elder (second century BC), where

[11] In the Harry Potter books of J.K. Rowling the killing curse, *avada kedavra*, is a variation of *avra kehdabra*.

[12] In the passage from Macbeth quoted earlier in this chapter Shakespeare uses formal features commonly found in English charms such as alliteration, rhyme, and four-beat lines (Roper 2003b: 56).

he gives instructions on how to bind a fractured limb. He stipulates that the formula *moetas vaeta daries dadaries astataries dissunapiter* must be recited during the binding process and the formula *huat huat huat ista sistas sistar dannabou dannaustra* must be recited every day until the fracture mends.

As we saw on page 16, in Ancient Greece and Rome it became increasingly common as time went on to use magic words (*voces magicae*) or words of mystery (*voces mysteriae*), as they were known (Gager 1992: 6). These include the so-called Ephesian letters, *askion*, *kataskion*, *lix*, *tetrax*, *damnameneus*, and *aision* (Ogden 1999: 47). They are words that do not make sense in Greek or Latin and they may well stem from an older language such as Egyptian or Akkadian. If so, they had probably become garbled and assimilated to yield plausible Greek forms. Some magic words appear to be made up from Greek roots, for instance *hippochthon* from *hippos* 'horse' and *chthon* 'earth'.[13]

The practice of using *voces magicae* continued in Europe throughout the Middle Ages and Renaissance. A fifteenth-century manuscript from Wolsthurn Castle in the Tyrol gives a number of recipes, procedures, and texts for cures. To exorcize a demon a priest should recite the following mixture of Latin, Greek, and meaningless gibberish into the ear of the possessed (Kieckhefer 1989: 4):

> Amara Tonta Tyra post hos firabis ficaliri Elypolis starras poly polyque lique linarras buccabor uel barton v el Titram celi massis Metumbor o priczoni Jordan Ciriacus Valentinus.

With the spread of Christianity in Europe pagan charms were replaced by Christian prayers, although the distinction is not

---

[13] More examples of magic words can be found in Luck 1985: 94–5.

always clear. Consider the following fourteenth-century text to be recited over a patient suffering toothache (Jolly 2002: 41). Prayers continued a practice common in charms, namely that of listing, but whereas pagan charms often listed a number of gods or spirits, Christian prayers often list Hebrew, Greek, and Latin epithets applying to Christ. These are often garbled, as in this example, indicating that users did not understand them completely.

> *Messias, Sother, Emanuel, Sabaoth, Adonay, Panton, Craton, Permocraten, Iskiros, agios, ymas, eleyson, Otheos, Athanatos, Alpha et Omega, leo, vermis, vitulus, agnus, homo, aries, usion, serpens, prius et novissimus, finis, Pater et Filius et Spiritus Sanctus, amen*

The 'translation' is as follows: *Messias* 'Messiah'; *Sother* = *Soter* 'saviour'; *Emanuel* (Hebrew *Im-manu-'el*) 'with-us-God' used of Christ identified with Emanuel/Immanuel, the Messiah prophesied in Isaiah 7:14; *Saba'oth* '[God of] hosts'; *Adonay* 'my Lord'; *Panton* + *Craton* = *Pantokratōr* 'Almighty'; *Permocraten* = ?; *Iskiros* = *Iskyros* 'strong' or 'violent'; *agios* 'holy'; *ymas* looks like *hymas* 'you', but should probably be taken to be *hēmas* 'us' and construed with the following word, *eleyson* 'have mercy', to yield 'Have mercy on us'; *Otheos* is *ho Theos* 'the God' written as one word; *athanatos* 'immortal'; *Alpha et Omega* first and last letters of the Greek alphabet referring to Christ as in Revelations 1:18, etc.; *leo* 'lion'; *vermis* 'worm'; *vitulus* 'calf'; *agnus* 'lamb'; *homo* 'man'; *aries* 'ram'; *usion* possibly containing the root *sios* 'holy' or *Siōn* 'Sion'; *serpens* 'serpent'; *prius et novissimus* = *primus et novissimus* 'the first and the last' (Rev. 1:17); *finis* 'end'. The final phrase, *Pater et Filius et Spiritus Sanctus, amen* 'Father, Son, and Holy Ghost, Amen', is a standard formulaic ending for a prayer. Some of these epithets seem natural enough, but others such as *leo*, *vermis*, *vitulus*, *aries*, and *serpens*, which appear odd to us, 'reflect a learned tradition of types that is especially developed in twelfth-century sermons and mystical thought' (Olsan 1992: 129).[14]

This example provides a good illustration of the distortion that occurs when words are passed down through generations who are unfamiliar with the languages involved, a distortion that can also be observed in the transmission of rhymes and lyrics. But however garbled they might be, unfamiliar words doubtless had a certain value by the very fact that they were mysterious and seemed to have an exotic heritage. In some instances the distortion may have been deliberate. To quote Aristotle, 'Discourse must be made to sound exotic, for men are admirers of what is distant' (*Rhetoric* 1404b). Many of the recorded magic texts were written by professional workers of magic (Greek *magoi*, Latin *magi*) and these magicians doubtless found it useful to impress their clients with some kind of mysterious mumbo jumbo.[15]

Pagan and Christian elements continued to be mixed long after Christianity became dominant in Europe. In the Anglo-Saxon *Nine Herbs Charm* from the tenth or eleventh century a reference to a myth in which Woden kills a snake occurs alongside a reference to Christ having formed two herbs, chervil and fennel, when he was on the cross (*Lacnunga* LXXIX–LXXXII in

[14] A number of prayers similar to the one quoted here consist of a string of Greek and Latin words that can apply to Christ. These include *gloria* 'glory', *panis* 'bread', *pastor* 'shepherd', *propheta* 'prophet', *via* 'way', and *vita* 'life'. See, for instance, Hymn 71 in Hewett (ed.) 1861: 54.

[15] See, for instance, Endicott 1991: 126 writing about Malay spells.

Pettit ed. 2001; Weston 1995: 279). A similar confusion of pagan and Christian lore characterizes an Old English text setting down the ritual for restoring land that has been bewitched. It involves taking samples of soil and produce and having Christian prayers said over them, partly in Old English and partly in Latin, but some of the instructions are clearly pre-Christian. The samples have to be taken before dawn (*on niht aer hyt dagige*) and one must recite prayers facing east and then turning in the direction of the sun (*sunganges*). In northern Europe actions carried out in the direction of the sun were supposed to produce a favourable result, while those carried out in the opposite direction (*wythersŷnes* 'widdershins') were thought to produce the opposite result. The church adopted numerous pagan practices designed to invoke supernatural protection of crops and livestock or to guarantee fertility. Samples of produce such as milk and honey were taken to mass and blessed with appropriate Bible passages such as 'Be fruitful and multiply' (Genesis 1:22).[16]

The Christian prayer quoted above lists epithets that apply to Christ in the fashion of a litany. The words are deemed appropriate but are presumably not thought to possess any intrinsic power. However, Renaissance scholars who embraced the Kabbalah believed in the power of Hebrew names, above all YHWH, the sacred name of God. Johann Reuchlin (1455–1522) in his *De Verbo Mirifico* (*On the Wonder-Working Word*, 1494) developed the fanciful notion that the name of Jesus was even more powerful. He wrote

[16] Pagan practices survived alongside Christian ones. The church never managed to eradicate 'magic'. Flint (1991: 394ff.) argues that the church deliberately tolerated some traditional practices so as not to alienate people.

YHWH as IHUH (taking the vocalic values of the semi-vowels) and Jesus as IHSUH and noted that IHUH contained no true consonants since God was spirit, but IHSUH contained a true consonant because Jesus was God made flesh (Zika 1976: 132; Kieckhefer 1989: 149).[17] Agrippa von Nettesheim (1486–1535) took up this view and suggested that *Jesus*, the most efficacious of all names, could be used in amulets (Shumaker 1972: 135, 149–50). The four-letter Hebrew name of God was known as the *Tetragrammaton* and the word *Tetragrammaton* was sometimes inserted in late medieval and Renaissance prayers as a kind of Christian equivalent of a magic word. During the course of the first millennium the three magi who figure in Matthew's account of Christ's nativity acquired names: Caspar, Melchior, and Balthasar. Eventually these names came to be inserted in prayers, as if their very inclusion increased the efficacy of the prayer.[18]

Some of the tendencies noted above, namely the use of mysterious words, often garbled, and the mixing of the pre-Christian and Christian, survived until fairly recently and may persist today. In nineteenth-century Yorkshire a charm against witches included pentagrams, the words *Alga* [*Agla*], *El*, *Naglah*, *Adonai*, and *Sadai*, and the phrases *Hoc in vince* 'In this [sign] conquer' and *Jesu Christi Rex Judaeorum* 'Jesus Christ, King of the Jews' (Rushton 1980: 117). After the Reformation Latin was largely confined to the Roman church, at least in religious contexts, and became a language of *voces mysticae*, a wholly mysterious language. In the eyes

[17] In *The Art of the Kabbalah* Reuchlin wrote, 'The tetragrammaton is sufficient in itself to perform miracles and prodigies ... a name through which a man can effect miracles, by accounting as a fellow-worker and as a delegate from God' (1993: 308–9).

[18] For instance, on the Coventry Ring in the British Museum.

of some Protestants it was often associated with superstition even when used in church ritual, but as can be seen from the charm just quoted it was also used outside the church context.

Texts of Power

Literate cultures generally contain large sacred texts such as the Egyptian Book of the Dead, the Vedas, the Bible, and the Qur'an, or texts venerated for their wisdom, such as *The Analects of Confucius*, or as a source of divination, such as the ancient Chinese *I Ching* (*Yì Jīng* in Pinyin) or 'Book of Changes'. With the passage of time the language in which these works are written falls out of general use. The Hebrew of the Torah was not the spoken language of the Jews after the Babylonian captivity of the sixth century BC. By this time they were speaking Aramaic, the lingua franca of the area, but they retained Hebrew as a written language and continued to use it in ritual, as they still do.

Where a religion that begins among the speakers of one language is taken up by speakers of another language, the language of the texts will naturally be unfamiliar. In the Roman empire Greek came to be the language used in various religions, including Zoroastrianism, which originated in Persia, and the worship of Isis and Osiris from Egypt. Greek was also the medium for Christianity for several centuries, and although it was widely spoken in the eastern parts of the empire, Latin was the vernacular of the west. From the second century Christian texts began to be translated into Latin and by the fourth century Latin was the language of the church. A few centuries later vernacular Latin had split and developed into what were to become the Romance languages, and church Latin became incomprehensible. Where Christianity spread to areas such as Ireland, where Latin had never been spoken, or countries where it had ceased to be spoken, such as England in the fifth century, Latin was of course a foreign language. The Qur'an and other sacred writings of Islam are in the Arabic of the seventh century, which has come to be called Classical Arabic in distinction from the modern varieties. The Qur'an is held to be the word of God transmitted by the Archangel Gabriel to Muhammad. There is a reluctance to translate it and Muslims are expected to learn Classical Arabic. Even where sacred texts are translated, discrepancies between the translation and the vernacular can arise with language change. The Authorized Version of the English Bible is in sixteenth-century English and remained in use until the twentieth century despite becoming badly out of kilter with even the written form of the language. The short sentence *hallowed be thy name* contains an archaic subjunctive construction with *be*, the obsolete *thy*, and *hallowed*, which is of marginal currency in contemporary English.

Religious works contain rules of conduct (*Thou shalt not kill*) and exhortations to virtue (*Love thy neighbour*) of which the faithful need to be reminded. In Deuteronomy God commands the Jews as follows:

> Therefore shall ye lay up these my words in your heart and in your soul, and bind them for a sign upon your hand, and they may be as frontlets between your eyes.
> And thou shalt write them on the door posts of thine house, and upon thy gates. (Deuteronomy 11:18, 20; see also 6:8, 9, Exodus 13:9 and 13:16, and Proverbs 7:3)

This led to the Jewish practice of wearing black leather boxes, těfillīn or phylacteries, containing biblical texts on the head and left arm when praying.[19] In Jewish, Christian, and Islamic cultures it is common for short passages from the sacred texts to be displayed on public buildings or in the home. Sometimes they are used as headings for or as frames around correspondence or other written work.

Given that they are considered to be divinely inspired, texts such as the Bible and the Qur'an have often been credited with power, even miraculous power. This can be a matter of using the physical text as a means of healing, for instance, placing a Bible in contact with sick or injured persons or giving them a short text to eat. More often it is a matter of employing passages of such texts in the abstract sense in prayers, blessings, consecrations, and the like.

Among the Jews the Torah-scroll was sometimes brought in to a woman in labour or laid against a sick baby, but such practices were not confined to Jews. A fifteenth-century manuscript from Wolsthurn Castle in the Tyrol gives a number of recipes, procedures, and texts for cures. For menstrual problems a piece of parchment was to be inscribed with a short text from the mass, *per ipsum et cum ipso et in ipso* 'through Him and with Him and in Him', and placed on the woman's forehead (Kieckhefer 1989: 4). Pedro Manuel, archbishop of Leon 1523–34, condemning diviners who 'have access to secrets which it is for God alone to know, and enter a circle wherein they invoke evil spirits', mentions that they wrote 'forbidden' words on lumps and swellings in the belief that

---

[19] These texts used were all ones dealing with the prescription, namely Exodus 13:1–10, 13:11–16, Deuteronomy 6:4–9, 13–21.

these would relieve the problem.[20] Toothache charms and prayers like the one illustrated in the previous section were often tied to the patient's head (Olsan 1992: 120). These are examples of what Frazer might have called contagious magic, magic by contact (Frazer 1911a: 174–219), although they differ from sorcery involving corporeal matter, bodily effluvia, or footprints. With religious texts what is important is the supposed divine origin of the words. Their power to heal can be directed to a target by contact.

Over the whole period of written records from Ancient Mesopotamia down there are references to evil being spread by contact with dirty water or herbs or by the ingestion of poisoned food or water, most of which presumably have a rational explanation. Less rational is touching someone with a severed male organ from a bird or animal noted for its reproductive capacity in an attempt to increase potency or fertility. Touching with sacred texts can be seen as an analogous practice.

In literate cultures it has been common to place short texts in amulets or talismans.[21] Amulets are found in most, if not all, cultures (Budge 1978: 1). An amulet is meant to provide protection from some misfortune such as sickness, disease, or death. Some amulets are for special purposes such as protecting a pregnant woman from miscarriage or guarding against a difficult birth or defective offspring, some are to guard against wild animals or bites from snakes, scorpions, or spiders, and some are to provide protection from the elements or ensure fertility of crops or animals. Others again are used to provide protection for those on a journey or

[20] Quoted in Maxwell-Stuart 1999: 64.
[21] On the terms *amulet*, *talisman*, and *charm* see note 2 to Chapter 1.

anyone in a boat. An amulet is usually worn hung around the neck or attached to clothing, but some amulets are placed in dwellings or in vehicles (like a St Christopher medal). An amulet may simply contain herbs or stones thought to have magic properties, but many contained writing on papyrus, parchment, or paper, or inscribed on metal or gemstones. The writing could be a symbol such as a triangle or a pentagram, a name, or a short text. Among the Jews appropriate biblical texts were used, such as 'I will put none of these diseases upon thee, which I have brought upon the Egyptians, for I am the Lord that healeth thee' (Exodus 15:26) or 'Thou shalt not be afraid for the terror by night; nor for the arrow that flieth by day; nor for the pestilence that walketh in darkness, nor for the destruction that walketh at noonday' (Psalm 91:5–6). In recent times modern technology has been employed to make miniature versions of books of the Bible and the Qur'an small enough to be worn in pendants, although this is not a solely recent innovation. A very small version of John's gospel dating to the fifth or sixth century has been preserved. It measures approximately two by three inches and was presumably used as an amulet (Skemer 2006: 87).

The use of pagan amulets was condemned by the church (Flint 1991: 244), and even the use of biblical texts as a cure or prophylactic did not always enjoy the approval of the church. Augustine condemned the practice of placing the gospel of John on people suffering from headaches, fever, and other afflictions. The first fourteen verses of John's gospel formed a favourite text in amulets. Aquinas believed that physical texts could be used as a mnemonic, but were not sufficient in themselves. One needed to have the words in one's heart and soul, as prescribed in Deuteronomy 11:18 (see above). With any religious text or *objet* there is always the danger that it will be treated as a fetish. Not surprisingly, Luther condemned the use of biblical texts in amulets (Skemer 2006: 63–5, 67, 87).

In addition to placing physical texts in contiguity with ill or injured persons, it was also common to recite charms or prayers into the ears or mouth of a patient. The aim was to achieve penetration of the words into the patient's body, so a natural extension of the practice was to make Christian texts in edible form and administer them to patients (Clark 2002: 100). The *pax max* texts used against the bite of a mad dog (see p. 146) were inscribed on apples or bread and given to the dogs to eat (Elliott 1957: 260). A twelfth-century manuscript from Germany recommends writing prayers on wafers and eating them barefoot, an interesting blend of the Christian and pagan (Kieckhefer 1989: 70). In the Anglo-Saxon *Leechbook* (lxii) a prescription for overcoming fever involves writing the opening words of the Vulgate version of John's gospel (*In principio erat verbum* 'In the beginning was the Word') on a paten and washing them into a drink. In a later manuscript they are to be written on parchment and scraped into a bowl and administered to a person thought to be possessed by a demon (Kieckhefer 1989: 74). The choice of words in this case is motivated by the part-for-whole principle, the first words of a text bringing to mind a larger text. The power of words can also be seen in a practice reported of Swedish peasants, who would tear a page from the psalter, bake it in dough, and feed it to cattle believed to be the victims of witchcraft (Ullmann 1957: 43).[22]

---

[22] In China it has been the custom to ingest written words by writing them on rice paper and eating the paper or by burning the paper and putting the ashes in food.

In traditional Christian belief and still in the teaching of the Catholic and Orthodox churches a priest can turn bread and wine into the body and blood of Christ by using the words 'This is my body' and 'This is my blood'.[23] The consecrated bread or host became a valued source of power, and hosts were sometimes stolen and given to humans and livestock to cure a complaint or ward off disease. The value of the host could be enhanced by writing biblical texts on it (Kieckhefer 1989: 79). Consecrated hosts were also stolen for blasphemous purposes including black masses. The doctrine of transubstantiation has points in common with instances of supernatural metamorphosis in pagan and traditional mythology.

One form of charm refers to an event in which some heroic figure overcame an enemy or a malevolent force. With the spread of Christianity this genre took its heroes from the Bible or the lives of saints. In some cases a short narrative was included in the charm, and such charms are referred to as 'narrative charms', but in other cases a mere reference to a story was considered sufficient, since the story would have been well known to the patient or any other audience. A curious fact about Christian narrative charms is their propensity to use apocryphal accretions to Bible stories or entirely apocryphal stories.[24] For instance, there are numerous versions of a charm against toothache, which relates an apocryphal

[23] In Latin the words of consecration of the bread are *Hoc est enim corpus meum* 'For this is my body' (lit. this is for body mine). It has been suggested that this lies behind the mock Latin phrase *hocus pocus* used by conjurors. Some people are sceptical about this etymology, but it has some plausibility, particularly as it converts the near rhyme in *hoc est* and *corpus* to a true rhyme.

[24] A popular amuletic text in the Middle Ages was the apocryphal *Heavenly Letter* supposedly written by Christ to King Agbar of Edessa (Urfa) (Skemer 2006: 96).

story of Christ curing St Peter's toothache. The following example is from nineteenth-century Lancashire. It is a written charm meant to be worn under the clothing (Roper 2003a: 23). The Latin *fiat* means 'May it be' and the cross symbols are an indication that the sign of the cross is to be made at the points where it occurs.

> Ass Saint Peter sat at the geats of Jerusalem, our Blessed Lord and Saviour Jesus Christ pased by and sead: What eleth thee, he said Lord my Teeth ecketh. Hee sead arise and folow me and thy Teeth shall never Eake Eney moor. Fiat ✠ Fiat ✠ Fiat.

St Apollonia was also invoked in cures for toothache because she had been tortured by having her teeth ripped out. The use of these texts was often accompanied by the sprinkling of holy water on the patient, and, as with the charms and prayers against toothache mentioned earlier, the text was placed in contact with the afflicted area of the body.

Another common charm was the Veronica charm, which was used to staunch bleeding ranging from a nose bleed to excessive menstrual bleeding. Here is an example (Barb 1948: 43):

> In the name of Christ write on the forehead with the [patient's] own blood the name of Veronica. The same it is who said: If I touch the fringe of the garment of my Lord I shall be healed.

The reference is to the haemorrhaging woman who was cured by touching the hem of Christ's garment (Matthew 9:20, Mark 5:25, and Luke 8:44). In later tradition she was given the name Veronica and identified with the apocryphal woman who placed a cloth on the face of Christ as he carried his cross to Calvary, and who received a miraculous imprint of Christ's face on her cloth. These narrative charms, as they are called, all employ some kind of analogy or precedent. They often include phrases such as 'just as you cured so-and-so, please cure . . . '.

Supernatural powers have often been consulted about the future and when sacred texts are used as a source of such divination the practice is known as **bibliomancy**. This is quite different from referring to a work such as *I Ching*, which is explicitly concerned with divination. In its most primitive form bibliomancy involves standing a book on its spine, letting it fall open, and then picking a passage with one's eyes closed. The passage in question is then taken to be prophetic. The procedure is hardly random, since books tend to open wherever they have most frequently been opened in the past, so some people have suggested using dice or some other chance mechanism to determine the page. The books that have been used for this purpose have been the epics of Homer, the Old Testament among Jews, the Old Testament and New Testament among Christians, and the Qur'an in Islam. Somewhat surprisingly Virgil's *Aeneid* was also used in the late Roman empire and in the Middle Ages. This may have been partly due to the fact that it was a prestigious verse epic in Latin paralleling the *Iliad* and the *Odyssey* in Greek, but more likely because Virgil was considered to have predicted the birth of Jesus Christ in his fourth eclogue (see page 67).

St Augustine (354–430) in his *Confessions* (8.12.29) recounts having heard a voice telling him to 'pick up and read' (*tolle, lege*). He picked up the Bible, which he had been reading, and it fell open at Romans 13:13–14:

> So was I speaking and weeping in the most bitter contrition of my heart, when, lo! I heard from a neighbouring house a voice, as of boy or girl, I know not, chanting, and oft repeating, 'Take up and read; Take up and read.' Instantly, my countenance altered, I

> began to think most intently whether children were wont in any
> kind of play to sing such words: nor could I remember ever to
> have heard the like. So checking the torrent of my tears, I arose;
> interpreting it to be no other than a command from God to open
> the book, and read the first chapter I should find. . . . I seized,
> opened, and in silence read that section on which my eyes first fell:
> Not in rioting and drunkenness, not in chambering and wanton-
> ness, not in strife and envying; but put ye on the Lord Jesus
> Christ, and make not provision for the flesh, in concupiscence.[25]

He took the choice to have been divinely inspired and showed it to
his friend Alypius and his mother Monica, who had spent years
urging him to become a practising Christian. From that moment
he and Alypius became committed Christians, Augustine eventually becoming the bishop of Hippo, Alypius becoming the bishop
of Tagaste, and both of them plus Monica acquiring sainthood. It
is interesting to note that bibliomancy was later condemned, even
by Augustine himself, who presumably did not consider this
example to be in the same class as deliberately seeking guidance
by opening a book at random or as determined by the fall of dice
(Flint 1991: 223; Peters 2002: 196).

Iconicity

A sense of analogy runs through human cultures. It can be seen in
the use of voodoo-type images and in charms and prayers that use
the 'just as . . . so also' formula. Gager (1992: 26) quotes a Hittite
counter-spell that reads, 'Just as I have burned these threads and

---

[25] Pusey translation available online from Christian Classics, Ethereal
Library.

they will not come back, even so let also these words of the sorcerer be burned up'. This sense of parallelism also shows up as an iconic relation between the performance of a text or ritual procedure and the intended effect. At a simple level a charm or prayer is thought to have more chance of success the more it is repeated, hence thrice-repeated prayers, novenas, decades of the rosary, and litanies. Among Tibetan Buddhists a prayer wheel is used to multiply prayers. The traditional Tibetan prayer wheel is a small cylinder mounted on a central shaft and bearing a prayer or mantra on its surface. Each revolution of the prayer wheel provides a repetition of the prayer. Besides the hand-held prayer wheel there are prayer wheels that are turned by wind, flowing water, or the warm air rising from a candle. Nowadays there are even prayer wheels operated by electric motors or simulated by computers.

As we saw earlier, the word *abracadabra* appears in the writing of Quintus Serenus Sammonicus. He wrote that to recover from a tertian fever a sick person should wear an amulet around the neck containing a piece of parchment inscribed with a triangular formula derived from this word, which acts like a funnel to drive the sickness out of the body (Figure 27). There is meant to be an analogy between the shrinking of the word and the reduction of the fever.

This use of shrinking words was common in Hellenistic times and continued in the Roman empire and later in Europe. One shrinking word used in amulets was the Hebrew word *shebrîrî*, which was thought to cure diseases of the eye (Figure 28). Remember that Hebrew is written from right to left and originally vowels were not written (so there was no symbol for *e*), but some letters could represent long vowels, such as ׳, which represents î. The word *shebrîrî* appeared in full on the first line (ש = sh, ב = b, ר = r, and ׳ = î), then *brîrî*, *rîrî*,

```
ABRACADABRA
ABRACADABR
ABRACADAB
ABRACADA
ABRACAD
ABRACA
ABRAC
ABRA
ABR
AB
A
```

27. The abracadabra triangle.

îrî, *rî*, and finally *î*. These were recited and as the words got shorter the disease was supposed to diminish (Budge 1978: 220)

Analogous to the shrinking word is the use of a formula containing a number, usually nine. This formula is repeated with the number being reduced by one with each repetition. Like the shrinking word, this was an example of sympathetic magic. The disease or swelling was supposed to reduce as the series of numbers in the formula decreased, though it is not clear from the records what interval was allowed to elapse between repetitions (Jolly 2002: 39). Here is an example aimed at curing a skin disease (tetter) (Roper 2003a: 20).[26]

[26] The number *nine* is common in the magic of the ancient Near East and later in Europe. Budge (1978: 435) suggests that its significance derives from the fact that it is three times three. This raises the question of why *three* was significant. 'Three times' appears regularly in magic formulas, perhaps simply because it is a satisfactory number, neither too small nor

י		ר		י		ר		ב		ש
	י		ר		י		ר		ב	
		י		ר		י		ר		
			י		ר		י			
				י		ר				
					י					

28. Shebrîrî triangle.

Tetter, tetter; thou hast nine brothers,
God bless the flesh and preserve the bone,
Perish thou tetter, and be thou gone,
In the name of the father, Son and Holy Ghost.

Tetter, tetter; thou hast eight brothers, etc.

Tetter, tetter; thou hast seven brothers, etc.

If a culture includes means of invoking supernatural assistance with curses, cures, or divination, it follows that it will provide ways of countering a curse (and possibly a cure) or averting a prophesied disaster. Counter-charms and rituals intended to reverse spells sometimes entail destroying the image of a sorcerer—giving him a piece of his own medicine, so to speak.[27] A written curse can be destroyed and replaced, as is illustrated in *Egil's Saga*. Egil Skalla-grimsson visits a farmer whose daughter has been ill for some time.

too large. This may be the same reason why narrative jokes tend to have a tripartite structure with the punchline in the third episode. The fact that three is a small odd number may be significant in contexts where symmetry is not required. An example of the use of multiples of three in the context of prayer can be seen in the Catholic nine-day prayer, the *novena*.

[27] In the Norse poem *Hávamál* Odin lists a number of powerful runes, one of which is designed to turn a curse back on the curser (verse 151).

The farmer tells Egil that in an attempt to cure her he had the son of a neighbour carve runes and place them in her bed. Egil finds these runes in her bed scratched on a whalebone. He scrapes the runes off the bone and throws it in the fire. He then replaces them with his own runes and the young woman recovers (*Egil's Saga* 73).[28] Egil recites a verse as follows:

Skalat maðr rúnar rísta,	None should write runes
nema ráða vel kunni,	Who can't read what he carves.
þat verðr mörgum manni,	A mystery mistaken
es of myrkvan staf villisk;	Can bring men to misery.
sák á telgðu talkni	I saw cut on the curved bone
tíu launstafi ristna,	Ten secret characters,
þat hefr lauka lindi	These gave the young girl
langs ofrtrega fengit.	her grinding pain.

Egil assumes that the farmer's neighbour was not malicious, only incompetent. His accidental curse is overcome by physically destroying the runes and replacing them with efficacious ones.

In the Graeco-Roman world a wheel device was used in casting spells. The Greeks called it a *rhombus* and the Romans a *turbo*. The sorcerer pronounced the spell and span the wheel. A long thread was attached to the wheel and as the wheel span, the thread was taken up and became wound around the wheel. The more thread was wound around the wheel, the more the target supposedly fell under the spell of the sorcerer. In Epode 17 Horace begs Canidia, portrayed as a sorceress, to stop the spell she is casting over him and reverse the spinning wheel so that he might be free of her

---

[28] Chapter 72 in the translation by Pálsson and Edwards (1976), which is the one used here.

enchantment (*citumque retro solve, solve turbinem*).[29] There are other variants of this belief that if a given procedure produces one effect, reversing the procedure will produce the opposite effect. The Wayagga of Mount Kilmanjaro think that if someone has stepped over another person's body, they should at once turn back and leap over the body in the reverse direction, thus undoing the first action; if they fail to do so, the stepped-over person will soon die (Frazer 1911b: 289).[30] Another variant is for a procedure carried out in the reverse direction to turn good to evil.

A belief in an iconic relationship between the direction of action and its intended effect applies to language. Gager, writing about the curse tablets of the Mediterranean world during the period of the Roman empire, notes the practice of scrambling names or writing them backwards with the intention of producing an analogous effect on the intended victim (Gager 1992: 5, 91):

> Special forms of writing include either scrambling the names of the targets or writing them, and sometimes the full text of the spell, backwards... Such techniques clearly express a symbolic meaning, ... that the fate of the targets should turn backward or be scrambled, just like their written names.

The curse tablets also contain examples of alternate left-to-right and right-to-left (boustrophedon) writing long after this was the

[29] Anthon 1850: 136.
[30] When I was at school during World War II some boys were caught goose stepping, giving the Nazi salute, and shouting 'Heil Hitler!' They were sentenced to standing to attention and reciting 'God save the king' twenty times. Looking back I can see that this was an appropriate remedy. Standing to attention counteracted the goose stepping and every God-save-the-king was worth one Heil Hitler.

norm, and of upside-down writing, letters written backwards, and individual words written backwards. One tablet contains the statement, 'Just as these words are cold and right-to-left [*eparistera*], so too may the words of Crates be cold and backwards' (Ogden 1999: 30).

In Jewish folklore there are strong, dumb, human-like creatures known as *golem*. Some humans were thought to have the power to create a golem by shaping a figure out of clay and using the name of God to give it life, in particular by writing the name of God on a piece of paper and placing it in the mouth of the figure.[31] To reverse the process, one removed the piece of paper. In another version one shaped the *golem* from clay and walked around it reciting a combination of letters from the alphabet and the secret name of God. To kill the golem, one had to walk around it in the opposite direction and recite the words of creation backwards. In yet another version one wrote the letters aleph, mem, tāw (אמת) on the golem to bring it to life and then erased the first letter א to kill the golem (Hebrew is written right to left, remember). The letters אמת spell *emet* 'truth', but מת spells *met* 'dead' (Winslade 2000: 85). Modern-day science fiction and fantasy sometimes feature golem-type figures known as *androids*.

Belief in the potency of a reversal of direction was linked to other beliefs about the favourability or otherwise of particular directions. As we saw earlier, it was considered propitious to carry out various ceremonies, journeys, and voyages in the same

[31] The notion of the golem has appeared in modern literature and television, including Primo Levi's *Lilít*, Umberto Eco's *Foucault's Pendulum*, an episode of *The Simpsons*, and an episode of *The X Files*.

direction as the sun. In the northern hemisphere for a person looking south the sun appears to move from left to right or clockwise and this was a propitious direction in which to move around an altar or similar. The opposite direction, i.e. anticlockwise or counter-clockwise (*wythersŷnes* 'widdershins'), was considered unpropitious or as having the power to bring about a reverse effect. In one traditional Germanic story a girl chasing a ball inadvertently walks widdershins around a church and disappears. She is taken away to the Dark Tower by the King of Elfland and has to be rescued by her younger brother, Childe Rowland.[32]

One custom reported in Burchard of Worms (*c.*950–1025) is a procedure for getting rid of an unwanted husband. The wife has to strip, cover herself in honey, and roll in grain, which is then milled backwards to produce poisonous bread (Jolly 2002: 18). Milling is normally done in a clockwise direction, so the procedure involving milling widdershins. In this case the reversal of direction does not reverse some previous magic, but aims to bring about an evil result, namely the death of the husband.

In chapter 79 of *Grettir's Saga* Thorbjorn Angle employs the services of his foster mother, Thurid (Thurithr), to help him overcome his enemy, Grettir. Thurid is well versed in sorcery and she curses Grettir by inscribing runes on the smooth surface of a large tree stump found by the sea. She fills the runes with her

---

[32] The story of Childe Rowland is referred to in *King Lear* at the end of Act III, Scene 4.

> Childe Rowland to the dark tower came,
> His word was still,—Fie, foh and fum,
> I smell the blood of an English man.

blood, recites a spell, and walks backwards around the stump against the direction of the sun. The stump floats away against the tide to Drangey Island where it is brought to Grettir, who tries to chop it only to find that the axe glances off and cuts his thigh. Eventually the curse enables Thorbjorn to kill Grettir. In this instance Thurid walks around the stump backwards and against the direction of the sun to intensify the evil, just as Shakespeare's witches in *Macbeth* pile up supposed evil elements to make their brew more potent.

Over the centuries in Christian communities there have from time to time been those who conducted or attended black masses.[33] These are versions of the mass dedicated to Satan and they involve a principle of opposites. The crucifix is inverted, the candles are black instead of white, and some 'sinful' actions are included. In some versions a naked woman serves as the altar and the ceremony ends with intercourse. Significantly as far as language is concerned, the text of the mass, or at least part of it, is said to be recited in reverse. There are also other reversals such as substituting *Satan* for *God* and switching negatives and affirmatives so that part of the Lord's prayer would be read as, 'Lead us into temptation and deliver us not from evil' (Cavendish 1967: 335).

[33] Reports on witches' sabbaths (sabbats), black masses, and the like are not always accurate. Early testimony speaks of witches flying on broomsticks, sacrificial infanticide, and the presence of Satan. There are contemporary black masses (Moody 1993), but most modern witchcraft is a mixture of sorcery and animism involving fertility rites and healing magic. It is deliberately pagan in orientation and rejects Christianity and satanism (Russell 1993).

Another notion involving opposites is the idea that the true name of the devil is the true name of God spelt backwards. One version is *Havayoth*, which has been adopted as the name of a gothic metal band formed in Sweden. They have an album entitled *His Creation Reversed* and in one number we hear, 'I am ... damned to earth, I will lead the world astray'. Rock groups often adopt names associated with something 'bad', whether it be wicked or merely naughty.

One curious example of reversing the effect of a claim on the supernatural was to say a mass for the dead naming a living person in the hope that this would bring about that person's death. The practice was condemned at the 694 Council of Toledo, but was still practised as late as the sixteenth century (Cavendish 1967: 327).

7

WORDS TO AVOID

There is a superstition in avoiding superstition.

FRANCIS BACON (1561–1626)

The previous chapter dealt with using words and formulas that were deemed powerful. This chapter deals with avoiding such words. Some form of avoidance involving language is universal. It may concern certain words, phrases, or topics, or it may be a matter of refraining from speech altogether in some contexts. Linguistic self-censorship often arises out of respect. If we find ourselves chatting with the queen, we are not likely to refer to the mouth as the *cake-hole* or the eyes as the *mince pies* since these are slang terms with informal or lower-class associations. Failure to avoid inappropriate terms in a conversation with the queen would probably not have serious consequences, but in many societies taboos on unsuitable behaviour are stronger and a plea of ignorance or accidental transgression is no excuse. In extreme cases an autocratic ruler might impose the death penalty on someone who showed disrespect. Equally, most societies are fearful of provoking the wroth of deities or spirits through impertinent or proscribed language.

Usually the grounds for classifying language as disrespectful have to do with register, association, or connotation, as with the examples of *cake-hole* and *mince pies* above, but taboos on the use of names sometimes have a different basis. In traditional societies there is widespread belief in a natural connection between a word and its referent, and a name is considered part of one's being. In the following pages a number of name taboos are illustrated. While some are motivated by respect, the more interesting ones stem from the belief that the name is part of a person.

Names of Humans

Taboos on using personal names are reported in a wide variety of cultures. The details vary from language to language, but it is common for people to be reluctant to reveal their own real names. In many small-scale societies names are not much used. Instead, people are often addressed or referred to by kin terms such as 'son' or 'father's sister'. In some societies people have two names, a 'real' name, which they keep secret, and an extra name or nickname which is disclosed to outsiders. In other societies people will turn to a third party to announce their name when someone asks, because there is a taboo on uttering one's own name (Frazer 1911b: 244–6). Among the Andaman Islanders people avoid the name of a baby before and after birth, of an initiand into adulthood, of a bride or bridegroom around the time of the wedding, and of a dead person for the period of mourning, i.e. at all stages of the life course involving important changes of status (Radcliffe-Brown 1965: 79–80). In many cultures people refrain from mentioning their real name for fear that malevolent spirits will harm them or someone will use their name in sorcery. Australian Aborigines commonly regarded names as equally integral to their identities as body parts, and therefore capable of being used in sorcery. Curr (1886, vol. 1: 46) reports that in some tribes men gave up their name at initiation into manhood to prevent it being exploited in this way.

In some languages there is grammatical evidence that a name is treated like a part of the body.[1] In Acholi (Western Nilotic, Uganda), for instance, possession is indicated by the particle *pa* (Bavin 1996: 845–7):

(a) bongo   pa latin
    clothes of child
    'the child's clothes'

This particle is not used for parts of wholes, where the relationship is shown simply by juxtaposition, as in (b). The relationship of a name to the 'owner' of a name is shown in the same way (c):

(b) jang   yat
    branch tree
    'branch of a tree'

(c) nying   latin
    name   child
    'child's name'

---

[1] In many Australian languages names are treated like body parts and other parts of wholes. Florey (2005: 67) mentions that some Central Moluccan languages do the same.

The notion that knowledge of someone's name gives you power over that person is a recurrent one in folklore. Consider the following myth of the Ancient Egyptians:

> The Sun God, Ra, becomes old and begins to dribble. The goddess Isis, who was the daughter of Geb, god of the earth, and Nut, the goddess of the sky, mixes some of Ra's spittle with dirt and creates a snake, which she leaves in Ra's path. Ra is bitten and although he is all-powerful, he cannot cure himself since the snake has been made from his own spittle. Isis offers to cure him, but she claims the cure will work only if Ra reveals to her his true name. Ra tells her his name and Isis cures him, but he cannot recover his power, and from then on Isis is the more powerful.[2]

There are a number of interesting aspects of this myth. First of all, although Ra is all-powerful, he cannot cure himself because he has been bitten by a snake made from a substance from his own body.[3] Secondly, the secret to his power is his real name. The parallelism between a body part or bodily effluvia on the one hand and a name on the other is clear: both have power over the person.

Moving from myth to history we find further evidence of a belief among the Egyptians that a person can be harmed through mistreatment of their name:

---

[2] The story can be found in numerous sources, including Frazer 1911b: 387–9.

[3] Omnipotence is a barrier to drama, so heroes tend to have their weak points. Achilles had his heel; Baldur was vulnerable to mistletoe; Sigurd/Siegfried was invulnerable from having bathed in the blood of a dragon he had slain except for a spot on his back where a linden leaf had fallen; Superman loses his power in the presence of kryptonite.

An example of the coalescence of a symbol and the thing it stands for is the treating of a person's name as an essential part of him—as it were, in a way, identical with him. We have a number of pottery bowls which Egyptian kings of the Middle Kingdom had inscribed with the names of hostile tribes in Palestine, Libya and Nubia; the names of their rulers; and the names of certain rebellious Egyptians. These bowls were solemnly smashed at a ritual, possibly at the funeral of the king's predecessor; and the object of this ritual was explicitly stated. It was that all these enemies, obviously out of the pharoah's reach, should die. But if we call the ritual act of the breaking of the bowls symbolical, we miss the point. The Egyptians felt that *real* harm was done to their enemies by the destruction of their names.   (Frankfort et al. 1949: 21–2)

For the Ancient Egyptians entry into paradise was a trial involving a long succession of naming. They believed that in order to attain life in the world beyond the grave one had to know the names of the gods, the entry gates, and the gatekeepers and attendants. The last part of the journey was by boat and required knowledge of the names of the parts of the boat, the rivers, and the river banks (Budge 1899: 157–81).

Among the Ancient Egyptians and later among the Arabs of North Africa there was a belief that being able to name spirits gave one power over them (Budge 1899: 157; Frazer 1911b: 389f.). Gods or jinns who revealed their name had to submit to the will of the one who knew it. The importance of this knowledge for the efficacy of a charm or curse is clear in the following inscription on an amulet of uncertain date, but probably from early in the Christian era, found in Mesopotamia. The text refers to a lilith—a sexually voracious female demon. By the second century AD a belief arose that these unwelcome succubae could be separated from their human lovers by a divorce decree.[4] There is also a reference to Rabbi Yehoshua bar Perahya, who lived in the first century BC and was revered as a magus (Gager 1992: 229–31).

> By your name I make this amulet... I overcome all demons... whether I know their names or do not know them. And in case I do not know the names, they were already explained to me at the seven days of creation. What was not revealed to me at the seven days of creation was disclosed to me in the deed of divorce that came to me here from across the sea, written and sent to Rabbi Yehoshua bar Perahya. Just as there was a lilith who strangled human beings—and Rabbi Yehoshua bar Perahya sent a ban against her, though she did not accept it because he did not know her name—her name was written in the deed of divorce and a proclamation was made against her in heaven, so you [the demons] are... overcome under the feet of Marnaqa son of Qala [the client].

Although the author of this text shows he [sic] believes in the importance of knowing the names of the spirits that he wishes to bind, it seems he does not in fact know them. Another curse from the same period addresses a spirit by name and then adds 'or if you wish to be addressed by any other name', apparently in an attempt to hedge its bets (Ogden 1999: 45).

The power of naming is a common theme of European folklore. In one set of stories a young woman has a problem, which is solved by a gnome with magical powers. In return the gnome demands the woman's firstborn child unless she can guess his name. She manages to find it out so he is unable to claim the baby and disappears. One of

[4] The short story 'Lilít' by Primo Levi features a creation myth about the origin of Lilith.

the better-known examples is the story of *Rumpelstiltskin* (German *Rumpelstiltzchen*), originally published in the folk tales collected by the brothers Grimm (Grimm [1812] 2002).

> In *Rumpelstiltskin* a man boasts that his daughter can spin straw into gold. On hearing this the king locks her in a tower with straw and a spinning wheel and commands her to produce gold or she will be killed. She is saved by the appearance of a dwarf with the power to spin the straw into gold, but in return he demands her first-born child. Impressed with the young woman's ability the king marries her, but when her first child is born, the dwarf returns to claim the baby. However, he agrees to give up his claim if the queen can guess his name. This seems an impossible task, but the queen's servant goes off and spies on the dwarf and overhears him reciting a verse which ends with 'Rumpelstiltskin is my name'. When the dwarf returns, the queen is able to tell him his name and the gnome is powerless to enforce his claim.

This story exists in dozens of versions and the gnome appears with various names. In Britain the name is *Tom Tit Tot*, *Terrytip*, *Trit-a-Trot*, and *Whuppity Stoorie*, in Sweden it is *Tittel Ture*, in Hungary *Winterkobl*, and in Norway *Skaane*. In an early French version published in 1696 the gnome is *Ricdin-Ricdon* and there is an interesting variation. *Ricdin-Ricdon* actually reveals his name to the young woman, but she forgets it. As a result of the gnome's help in spinning, she finds favour at court and is taught to read, and she tries writing letters in an effort to recall the name, which is forever on the tip of her tongue, elusively out of reach. In the end the prince tells her what it is.[5]

---

[5] The original is by Marie-Jeanne Lhéritier and is published in *Ouvres meslées* (1696). There is a translation in Zipes 1991.

The power of the name also features in the medieval stories of the knight of the swan, which Wagner used in his opera *Lohengrin*.

> In the opera Elsa is accused by Telramund of having murdered her brother. The king decides that the truth of the accusation is to be determined by combat between Telramund and anyone who will champion Elsa. A knight appears in a boat drawn by a swan. He agrees to fight for Elsa and be her protector providing she never asks him his name. The knight defeats Telramund and marries Elsa, but Telramund's wife, Ortrud, sows doubt in Elsa's mind about the knight's origin and induces her to ask his name. Elsa asks the question and he is compelled to answer. Before the assembled court he reveals that he is Lohengrin, the son of Parsifal, a knight of the Holy Grail. However, since his name has been revealed, he must return to the Holy Grail.

In the Bible there are a number of references to names being kept secret. In Genesis 32:29, when Jacob asks the angel who has wrestled with him during the night what his name is, the angel only replies, 'Wherefore is it that thou dost ask after my name?' In the Book of Judges an angel appears to Manoah and his wife to tell them they are to have a son (who will be the hero Samson) and when Manoah asks the angel his name, the angel replies, 'Why asketh thou thus after my name, seeing it is secret?' (Judges 13:18). In Revelation 19:11–12 it is said of the rider of the white horse, 'His eyes were as a flame of fire, and on his head were many crowns; and he had a name written, that no man knew, but he himself'.

Among the curse tablets described in the previous chapter are some which explicitly state that the target's name has been deliberately damaged as in an attempt to harm him. One has a nail hole pierced through the name and bears the words, 'I nail his name, that is, himself' (Cavendish 1967: 43).[6] In others the name of the intended victim is written in reverse or jumbled. The purpose is not concealment, because in some such cases the name appears elsewhere in the text of the curse in normal form. It seems distortion of the name is intended to have an analogous ill effect on the victim. This is confirmed by one tablet which asks that the target's words and deeds be jumbled as his name has been jumbled (Ogden 1999: 299–30).

Names were also used to identify images that were subjected to magic. A form of love magic practised in Europe in the Middle Ages involved writing the names of various demons on the image of an unresponsive beloved. This was supposed to result in the demons tormenting the beloved until he or she submitted. 'The demons symbolically represented on the image are to be really present in the woman' (Kieckhefer 1989: 162). If a magician wanted to gain favour with a person in authority, he would make an image of himself and an image of the dignitary and write names on the images to identify them. The images were bound together, with the image of the dignitary bowing before that of the magician.

Among the Manambu of New Guinea all personal names are the names of totemic ancestral beings and each sub-clan jealously guards its stock of ancestral names. If a neighbouring sub-clan attempts to use one of them, a dispute ensues. People are unwilling to have their name written down since it could then be taken away, along with the life force of its owner (Harrison 1990: 60).

---

[6] The use of the masculine pronoun in this paragraph is deliberate. The victims of attempted sorcery were almost all male.

The same belief is reported from the Tolampoo of Sulawesi (Celebes) (Frazer 1911b: 319).

Among the Cherokees when prayers for the sick had no apparent effect, the patient was given a new name (Frazer 1911b: 318–19). Among the Jews the name of a dangerously ill person was often changed. The new name was the first one on a page of the Bible opened at random.[7]

> The underlying principle in changing the name of one who is ill is the assumption that the former name, under which the divine decree [causing the illness] was issued, becomes non-existent, and that, when a new name is given him, he becomes another person, in regard to whom the decree has no force. In a later period the original name was retained and another added to it, usually one signifying the recovery of the patient. The most popular additional names were *Hayyim* (life), *Shalom* (peace), *Raphael* (God heals), *Azriel* (God helps), or some other name, selected from the Bible.[8]

The names of evildoers were avoided, since these were regarded as curses. This can be seen, for instance, in Isaiah's prophecy that the names of the wicked shall be a curse and that the chosen will be given a new name to avoid the curse (Isaiah 65: 15).

A widespread taboo concerns the name of a dead person. This may be based on a fear of offending the spirit of the dead person or a fear that the spirit will remain in the locality and be malevolent, though respect may play a part too. In Ponape (now Pohnpei, one

---

[7] See also page 160 on bibliomancy.

[8] Quoted from the entry *SHINNUY HA-SHEM* in the *JewishEncyclo-pedia.com* by Wilhelm Bacher and Judah David Eisenstein.

of the Federated States of Micronesia) a man called Puik died. His name was also the word for pig, so pigs were referred to for some time as 'the animal that digs' (Frazer 1911b: 362). Among the Australian Aborigines there is a taboo on using the name of a recently deceased person (Berndt 1964: 389). He or she is said to be 'no name'. Among the people of the Warrnambool language group of southeastern Australia a dead person was referred to during a period of mourning as *muruka* 'dead person'. If their name was one that was also a common noun, then the common noun was replaced; so, for example, if a man called *wilan* 'black cockatoo' died, the black cockatoo was temporarily renamed *waang* 'crow'. The names of near relatives of the deceased were avoided during mourning. If a man's father died, the man was called *parapitj* 'male orphan' and if a woman's father died, the woman was called *parapiya* 'female orphan' (Dawson 1881: 42). Among the Manambu of New Guinea a bereaved person is given a new name to ward off the spirit of the person whose death they are mourning (Harrison 1990: 61). In some parts of the world anyone with the same name as the deceased takes on a new name, but among the Masai (east Africa) the deceased is given a new name, which can be freely used (Frazer 1911b: 354).

As we saw above, in the ancient Near East those seeking to enlist the power of supernatural beings sought to find out their names, but it is also true that names of deities were often treated with respect and subject to avoidance. Among the Jews YHWH (יהוה), the name of God, was avoided. Although there was no rule in the Torah prohibiting its use, such was the respect with which it was treated that the practice arose of not uttering it at all and eventually it was spoken only by the high priest in the Holy of Holies on Yom

Kippur.[9] At the beginning of Chapter 5 I mentioned that vowels were not written in the original Hebrew of the Bible. The vowels were introduced in the form of subscript pointing by the Masoretes ('bearers of tradition') around the seventh century AD, by which time the pronunciation of the vowels of the name of God had been lost.[10] The name YHWH was given the vowels of *Adonai* 'My Lord', one of the other names used for God. The name YHWH was often written in abbreviated form as YH or YHW. In Hebrew the letters of the alphabet also serve as numerals (as is illustrated in Figure 23 above) and 15 and 16 would normally be YH and YW respectively, but since these combinations are fragments of YHWH, they are avoided by using (טו) ṬW (9 + 6) and (טז) ṬZ (9 + 7). Avoidance of writing God's name led to writing the name as two yods (יי), generally with a stroke between them, or as dāleth (ד), the first consonant of *Adonai*. YHWH was also referred to as *Ha-Shem* 'the Name'. Other names for God appear in the Bible, including *Elohim* (actually a plural form), which is the name generally used in Genesis, and *El Shaddai* 'God Almighty'. All these names are treated with respect and some Jews today refrain from writing *God*, but instead write *G-d* or *G'd*.[11]

Christians use the names *God* and *Jesus Christ* freely in serious contexts. Such names are also used profanely by Christians and others and in such contexts there are deformations in various languages that smack of avoidance. In English euphemistic

---

[9] The Holy of Holies corresponds to the sanctuary in Christian churches. Yom Kippur is the Day of Atonement.

[10] The Temple was destroyed by the Romans in 70 AD.

[11] Roth 1966; Werbolowsky and Wigoder 1997. The practice can be seen in Web postings.

deformations of *God* abound, such as *gad, egad, gosh, golly*, and *by Godfrey*. The last, which has the preposition *by*, gives a clue to the origin of a lot of this profanity. Traditionally in making a formal oath one called God as witness or staked something precious. So one might say, 'I swear by God that what I say is true' or 'I swear on my mother's life what I say is true'. The implied penalty for untruthfulness was divine retribution directed at oneself or one's mother. Similar formulae in informal contexts are intended to emphasize one's sincerity and may be reduced to *by God* or deformed to *by golly*, etc. Euphemistic variants of *Jesus* include *Jeez, Jiminy, Gee wiz*, and *Jeepers*. For *Christ* there is *Crikey* and *Cripes*, and for *Jesus Christ* there is *Jiminy Cricket(s), Jeepers Creepers*, and *Judas Priest*.[12] For *Lord* there is *Law, (Oh) Lor*, and *Lawdy*. In general *Jesus* is not used as a given name, but it is so used in Spanish.

Over the centuries there has been a taboo on using the name of the devil or Satan, since he was considered just as real as God and a powerful, malevolent spirit whom it was best not to antagonize. In English we have an expression, 'Speak of the devil and he'll appear'. Originally this was a warning not to say *Satan* or *the devil* for fear of provoking an apparition or unwelcome attention. Nowadays the expression is used lightly, usually in the shortened form 'Speak of the devil', by people conversing about a third party when that third party appears within sight or earshot. Nicknames for the devil have proliferated, presumably to avoid using the real name. Some of the better-known euphemisms are *the*

---

[12] The phrase *Judas Priest* was adopted as a name by an English heavy metal group.

Arch-Fiend, the Evil One, the Prince of Darkness, His Sable Majesty, the Old Enemy (French *le mauvais ennemi*), and *Old Nick*. There is also *The Deuce!* and *What the Deuce!*, but these are presumably no longer thought of as terms for the devil.

It is not uncommon for there to be a taboo on using the name of a monarch or highly respected person. Frazer (1911b: 376–7) reports that this is true among the Zulus. Names may be common nouns, and a common noun used as the name of a chief is subject to the taboo. One Dwandwe chief was called *Langa*, which was the word for 'sun', so the Dwandwe substituted the word *gala* for the sun. In China there was a taboo on pronouncing the name of the emperor or any word homophonous with the emperor's name. The taboo extended to the characters used to write the emperor's name. This was problematic where the emperor's name contained common characters and Emperor Xuan of the Han dynasty, whose given name *Bingyi* contained two very common characters, changed his name to *Xun*, which was written with a far less common character, to make it easier for his people to avoid using his name. One could avoid writing characters used in the emperor's name by substituting a synonymous character or omitting a stroke, usually the final stroke. In 1777 Wang Xihou wrote the name of Emperor Qianlong in his dictionary without leaving out any stroke. He and his family were executed and their property confiscated.[13]

[13] See the Wikipedia entry on the naming taboo. During the time I was revising the manuscript of this book, a report appeared in the press of a man being jailed for three years for including a derogatory reference to a member of the Thai royal family in a novel. He was subsequently granted a royal pardon.

In-Laws

In many parts of the world there are strict rules governing conduct towards in-laws.[14] They may involve avoidance of any contact or direct communication; the use of a special vocabulary in speaking to an in-law or in the presence of an in-law; or not mentioning the name of an in-law. The purpose of such codes may be to minimize any conflict between loyalty to relations by marriage and loyalty to kin, but they are often treated as having been laid down by venerated ancestors or supernatural beings, and they are not treated lightly. Among the Dusun of Borneo it is considered bad luck to utter the name of a mother-in-law or father-in-law (Williams 1963b: 173, riddle 170), and Australian Aborigines are affected by a deep sense of shame or disgust if there is even an accidental transgression of a taboo relating to in-laws. There is a report of a man becoming very distressed because his mother-in-law's shadow had fallen on him (Fison in Fison and Howitt 1880: 103). The shadow is often regarded as part of a person akin to a body part and treated like a body part grammatically.[15]

Among speakers of Kambaata, an East Cushitic language spoken in Ethiopia, women traditionally practised a form of respect towards their mother-in-law, father-in-law, and in some cases the parents of

[14] We do not have any such taboo, but the mother-in-law remains the butt of male jokes. The French for father-in-law is *beau-père* 'fine/beautiful father', for mother-in-law *belle mère* 'fine/beautiful mother', and so on with other in-laws. These terms appear to be euphemistic.

[15] In the New Testament it is claimed that even the shadow of Peter falling on a sick person could effect a cure (Acts 5:15–16).

the father-in-law. This respect behaviour was called **ballishsháta** and it involved some avoidance of social contact, mainly with the father-in-law, and avoiding the names of the parents-in-law and any word beginning with the same syllable as their names (Treis 2005). On her wedding day the bride was given a laxative to void her stomach and bowels, and was then taught a small vocabulary of *ballishsháta* words, receiving a sip of drink or a morsel of food with each word learnt. She was also taught how to find substitute words to avoid using words with the tabooed initial syllables. These words could be found using the following principles. In each example the everyday word is given first and the *ballishsháta* word to the right.

(a) a word that is semantically similar
    afóo   mouth   *yaburú*   lips

(b) derivation, e.g. using *-aanchú*, which is like the *-er* in English forming agent nouns
    harruuchchú donkey   *iyy-aanchú* one who carries

(c) a periphrasis
    hizóo   brother   *ama'íbeetú* son of my mother

(d) using an antonym
    usur-   tie   *gaffar-*   untie
    uurr   stand up   *afuu'll*   sit down

As a last resort a woman can use the root *soomm-*, which means 'unspeakable'. Some women applied the restrictions to function words, though others applied them to lexical words only.

Among the Southern Bantu peoples such as the Zulu and Xhosa married women traditionally had to practise **hlonipa**, avoidance behaviour in relation to male in-laws, especially the father-in-law, and sometimes to the mother-in-law. With respect to language it involved avoiding the in-law's name, and what is remarkable,

avoiding any syllable contained in the name (Herbert 1990a, b).
For instance, a certain Xhosa woman with senior male in-laws
called *Dike*, *Ntlokwana*, and *Saki* and a mother-in-law called *Nina*
could not utter the syllables *di*, *ke*, *ntlo*, *kwa*, *na*, *sa*, *ki*, *ni*, and *na*.
In order to comply with this restriction a woman could substitute a
different consonant:

> unina utsitsa your mother
> idikazi ishikazi unmarried woman

It is well known that Bantu languages have noun classes, each of
which is marked by a prefix. One strategy for avoiding a potentially
offending syllable is to move a word from one noun class to
another. For instance, the word *sana* 'baby' is in class 11, for
which the class prefix is *u-*, yielding *usana*, but in class 9 the prefix
is *in-*. When this prefix is put in front of a root beginning with *s*, it
induces an affricated stop t^s, so that *sana* becomes *int^{s}ana*. In this
way the syllable *sa* can be avoided.

Another strategy is to simply to drop a consonant:

> umlenze um'enze leg
> -hleke 'eke laugh

All these strategies for avoiding a particular syllable involve consonants, never vowels. Herbert notes that the substituted consonants are often clicks.[16] Since clicks were a distinctive feature of the

---

[16] Clicks are used in English, but not as parts of words. The *tsk tsk*
sound used to express disapproval is a type of click. The back of the tongue
is pressed against the soft palate and the tip of the tongue is pressed against
the teeth. As the middle of the tongue is lowered, a low pressure pocket is
formed and as the tip of the tongue is moved from the teeth, the inrushing

Khoisan languages, Herbert suggests that these languages provided a pool of consonants not found in Bantu languages and therefore a sure-fire means of avoiding the taboo syllables. Clicks have now spread to Southern Bantu languages in general, and Herbert suggests that the practice of using Khoisan words to provide safe consonants may be responsible for this. Herbert's explanation is highly plausible, since borrowing from Khoisan languages into Bantu consists almost entirely of consonants. Each married woman would have had different in-laws and therefore different syllables to avoid, but since the number of syllable onsets in traditional Bantu languages is not high, many onsets would have been taboo for a large majority of women. Some women must have adopted ready-made hlonipa forms so that they became regular for women and then for the speech community at large.

Hlonipa does not involve just phonological means of avoiding taboo syllables. There were lexical strategies that included using archaic words or borrowed words such as *ukupaya* from English 'pay'. There was also substitution of semantically similar words:

intasa	brushwood	iinkuni	firewood
iswekile	sugar	intlabathi	sand
ninzi	many	inkitha	great number

Among the Kalapalo of Central Brazil, and more widely in the area, there is mutual respect between in-laws involving avoidance of eye contact, of working together in close proximity, and of

air produces a click. Another type of click is used to express encouragement (usually accompanied by a thumbs-up sign), and yet another to tell horses to 'giddy-up'.

walking in front of a mother-in-law or father-in-law. Communication with an in-law is indirect, through an intermediary. Kinship terms or other indirect expressions are substituted for the names of one's in-laws. For instance, one man referred to an in-law named *Tafitse* 'Macaw' as 'the one with the blue tail feathers' (Basso 2007: 171).

Among the Australian Aborigines there is a widespread taboo on having any dealings with in-laws. The taboo is stronger for men and is strongest between a man and his mother-in-law or potential mothers-in-law. The system of kinship is classificatory, so that a man can have a mother-in-law (the mother of his wife) and other women such as the sister of his mother-in-law who are also mothers-in-law (Berndt 1964: 82, 132). Dawson (1881: 29), writing about the people of the Warrnambool area in Victoria, notes, 'should he meet them [mothers-in-law] on a path, they immediately leave it, clap their hands, cover up their heads with their rugs, walk in a stooping position and speak in whispers till he has gone past'. In some areas a man and his mother-in-law may not have direct dealings. If something such as food is to be conveyed from one to the other it must be passed via a third person or left on the ground for the other party to pick up (see, for instance, Meggitt 1962: 153 on the Warlpiri). Among the Kamilaroi of New South Wales a man and his mother-in-law can only converse by facing away from one another and shouting as if they were some distance apart. Among the Kurnai of Gippsland no direct speech is allowed and any verbal exchange must be through a third person (Fison and Howitt 1880: 103, 203).

Among the Guugu-Yimidhirr of northeast Queensland a man must not speak to his mother-in-law and he must use a special respect register to speak to his brothers-in-law or father-in-law. In the following example the everyday version is given in the first line and the in-law version in the second (Haviland 1979a: 368, see also 1979b).

> Ngayu mayi   buda-nhu.
> Ngayu gudhubay bambanga-nhu
> I   food   eat-PURPOSIVE
> 'I want to eat food.'

Respect forms of language are common in Australia. They are often referred to as 'mother-in-law languages' since they were mostly used when a mother-in-law was within earshot. These respect forms of language have the same phonology, morphology, and syntax as the everyday language, but a separate lexicon. Note in the example above that the pronoun *ngayu* 'I' and the purposive inflection *-nhu* are retained in the in-law version. The vocabulary of mother-in-law languages is much smaller than that of the everyday language and a word in the mother-in-law language will often correspond with a number of words in the everyday language. For instance, where there would be different words for different kinds of spear or boomerang in the everyday language, there would be only one general term in the mother-in-law language. In Dyirbal the mother-in-law language has equivalents for all the words in the everyday lexicon (Dixon 1972: 32–4), but in other languages such as Bunuba not all the words in the everyday language have a mother-in-law equivalent and some everyday words have to be used (Rumsey 1982).

The vocabulary of these respect forms of language often contains words from the everyday vocabulary of other dialects or languages, a phenomenon which is reminiscent of our euphemistic use of French words such as *derrière*.

Among the Gurindji vagueness is common in the respect language, as is avoidance of imperatives and even of the second person pronoun. The apologetic interjection *wartirri* 'sorry!' is also frequent. All these characteristics are illustrated in the following example, where (a) is the everyday version and (b) the respect (*pirntika*) version (McConvell 1982: 96).

(a) Yanta kayirra.
    go   north
    'Go north!'

(b) Wartirri   nganta-lu   luwa-wu   kuya-partak.
    sorry   perhaps-they DO-FUTURE   thus-way
    'Oh dear! perhaps they will DO that way (pointing north)'

The verb *luwa* normally means 'to hit with a missile', but in the respect language it is a generic verb standing in for all verbs, rather like English 'do', and is glossed as DO.

Other Avoidance

Taboos on the names of creatures are very widespread, particularly predators and dangerous animals. In the cooler regions of the northern hemisphere the inherited names of the bear, the wolf, and the fox, which are threats to humans, livestock, or domesticated animals, are often avoided. The bear is often referred to by such terms as 'uncle', 'grandfather', or 'old man', and it is commonplace to note that the Indo-European root for 'bear', which is reflected in Sanskrit *rkšah*, Greek *arktos*, and Latin *ursus* (hence Italian *orso*, French *ours*, etc.), has been replaced in a number of languages by terms having what Ullmann (1957: 184) calls 'an unmistakably euphemistic and propitiatory ring' such as Lithuanian *lokys* 'licker', Russian *medvéd* 'honey-eater', and Middle Welsh *melfochyn* 'honey-pig'. English 'bear' originally meant 'brown'. The wolf is referred to by descriptive phrases such as 'grey legs' or 'the silent one' and the fox is 'the long tail' or 'the one that goes in the forest' (Frazer 1911b: 396–8).

Another animal regarded as an enemy in Europe is the weasel, a small carnivorous mammal of the Mustela genus, which includes stoats, some species of mink, polecats, and ferrets. The weasel preyed on domesticated birds like barnyard fowl and small animals such as rabbits and, as with the fox, acquired a reputation for villainous cunning. In Kenneth Grahame's *The Wind in the Willows* the weasels are the villains and *weasel words* are misleading words. Across Europe the weasel bears a number of euphemistic names, mostly on the theme of 'young woman': Danish *kjönne* 'beautiful' and *bruden* 'bride', French *belette* 'little pretty one', Humgarian *menyét* 'nice little girl', Italian *donnola* 'little lady', Portuguese *doninha* 'little lady', and Rumanian *nevasta* 'bride' (Ullmann 1957: 190; Guérios 1956: 152–5).

In the following Old English charm designed to woo bees to take up residence in some desired location the bees are addressed by a euphemistic kenning, *sigewif* 'victory woman/women'. According to Flom the charm would have been thought ineffective if the normal word had been used (Flom 1930: 340).

> Forweorp ofer greot, þonne hi swirman, and cweð:
> Sitte ge, sigewif,   sigað to eorþan!
> Næfre ge wilde   to wuda fleogan.
> Beo ge swa gemindige   mines godes,
> swa bið manna gehwilc   metes and eþeles.

Throw gravel over them when they swarm and say:
Sit ye, victory-women   sink to earth!
Never be wild   to woods to fly
Be ye mindful   of my good
As is every man   of food and land.

The names for snakes are often subject to taboo, as are the names of the larger members of the cat family. In Africa the lion is referred to by such titles as 'the owner of the land' or 'the great beast' (reminiscent of our 'lord of the jungle'). In India the tiger is referred to as a dog or jackal, and in Southeast Asia as 'the grandfather' or 'the grandfather of the forest' (Frazer 1911b: 400–4). The tiger's name is avoided altogether by anyone venturing into its habitat.

Naming taboos may apply to plants and even minerals. In Malaysia and Indonesia it is common for those who go into the forest to collect camphor to use special vocabulary known as *bahasa kapur* 'camphor language' in place of their everyday language, because camphor has a spirit which must not be disturbed. In many parts of the world the name of something that is hunted or gathered is taboo for the duration of the quest.

Among the Kharwars of southern India the names of animals such as the pig, jackal, and monkey are taboo only in the morning. In parts of Germany there was a taboo on the name of the wolf for the twelve days of Christmas. In Scotland a number of alternative words had to be used at sea, so *a sgian* 'knife' became *a ghiar* 'the sharp one' and *sionnach* 'fox' became *madadh ruadh* 'the red dog'.

Some taboos apply only among women. Tariana women were not allowed to see *piri*, a sacred flute, and words similar to *piri* were replaced in their presence. Some place names that contained *piri* had two forms, one containing *piri* and a second version that women could use (Aikhenvald 2003: 619).

There are also taboos on certain numbers in those cultures that have numbers. We have a remnant of this with 13, which is considered an unlucky number by some, and many hotels and other public buildings do not use 13 in numbering floors and rooms. In Chinese culture the number 4 is sometimes considered unlucky because of the near homophony between *sì* 'four' and *sǐ* 'death' (Mandarin example). In the ancient world of the Near East and Mediterranean any definite number was a problem in that it gave scope for sorcery. In the poem *Vivamus, mea Lesbia* (v) the Roman poet Catullus asks his lover to give him a thousand kisses, then a hundred, then another thousand, and so on. He concludes with, 'We will lose count of the number, so that we do not know what it is, lest an evil person will be able to cast a spell knowing what the number of our kisses is.' In another poem, *Quaeris quot* (vii), he says he will be satisfied when their kisses are as numerous as the stars or the grains of sand in the Libyan desert, so that the inquisitive cannot count them nor evil tongue bewitch.

The survey of avoidance in this chapter is by no means exhaustive. Many cultures manifest avoidance in connection with sex and bodily functions, and there is a wide range of other types which we do not have space to cover here. Some further examples are given under the heading of euphemism in Chapter 9.

8

JARGON, SLANG, ARGOT, AND 'SECRET LANGUAGES'

> The one stream of poetry which is continually flowing is slang. Every day a nameless poet weaves some fairy tracery of popular language.
>
> **G.K. CHESTERTON, *THE DEFENDANT*, CHAPTER 13: A DEFENCE OF SLANG**

In a small-scale society it is usually pretty much true that all speakers have a complete vocabulary of their language. There may be some specialized, secret, ritual language, but other than that speakers usually know the words for most of the plants and animals in their environment and for all the artefacts and cultural practices. There is little or no differentiation by occupation. Apart from some division along gender lines the whole community is involved in the same hunting, planting, gathering, tool making, preparation of food, and cooking. The same applies to leisure activities. Games, singing, dancing, telling stories, reciting poetry, asking riddles, and various forms of word play are communal activities.

In a large-scale society, on the other hand, people are distinguished by class, occupation, and recreational interests. In western society there are hundreds of occupations and leisure pursuits, many with an extensive specialized vocabulary or **jargon**. Individual speakers will know the vocabulary they need for their own work and leisure, but this will be only a fraction of the total vocabulary of the language.

Where a language is spoken in more than one location, dialect differences will appear. In modern large-scale societies this differentiation is more apparent in the colloquial language, especially **slang**, which is relatively immune to standardizing influences and tends to be promoted as a marker of local identity, though it is true that there is national slang and at least one variety of international slang disseminated from America via the media.

Groups who are oppressed, imprisoned, or isolated from the community at large and those whose activities are under scrutiny by the authorities tend to develop an extensive in-group variety of language known as **argot**. The anonymous author of *The Vulgarities of Speech Corrected*, published in 1826, wrote that slang 'is chiefly what was invented, and is still used, like the cipher of diplomatists, for the purposes of secrecy, and as a means of eluding officers' (McKnight 1928: 507). The writer is referring to what is here called argot, this term not being in general use in the early nineteenth century. An argot is colloquial and has the character of slang, but some of its vocabulary is technically jargon in that it is specialized and has no standard equivalents.[1]

---

[1] Argot is a marker of a social class, typically low social class. In some societies social stratification is quite marked with special forms for addressing people of high social status. In Javanese, for instance, there are three forms of the language: *ngoko, madya,* and *krama,* which differ in vocabulary. In general

All of these specialized varieties present a source of potential obscurity to anyone who knows only formal, mainstream language.

Jargon

As we have seen, then, large-scale societies are not homogeneous. People have different occupations and recreational pursuits. If you are involved in building work, you will be familiar with terms such as *beam*, *joist*, *stud*, and *truss*. If you are interested in tennis, you will know terms such as *advantage*, *baseline*, *deuce*, *let*, and *love*. These specialized terms are **jargon**. They are a necessary part of the language. You need to know them if you are going to talk about certain activities. The difference between mainstream vocabulary and jargon is ill defined. Consider the terminology of food preparation. There is a continuum from *boil*, *fry*, *poach*, *roast*, and *stew*, which are generally known, through lesser-known terms such as *parboil* and *simmer* to more esoteric terms like *al dente*, *blanch*, *macerate*, *marinate*, and *roux*, which are part of the jargon of food preparation. It is much the same with gardening, where terms like *trowel*, *spade*, *prune*, and perhaps *mulch* are generally known, as are some common names of plants such as *rose* and *carnation*, but there are hundreds of lesser-known plant names, including learned Greek and Latin botanical names.

people use *ngoko* at home and among friends, and in addressing people of lower social standing; and *krama*, the high form, in addressing people of high status in formal situations. They can use *madya*, the middle form, in ambivalent contexts or where they are unsure about what is appropriate (Errington 1988). In Thailand there is a special form of the language that must be used in talking to members of the royal family. This high style is replete with 'big words' of Pali and Khmer origin (Khanittanan 2005).

While a receptionist or salesperson probably uses few terms not in general use, some occupations have large jargons. Armed services jargon is replete with abbreviations such as *ADC* 'aide-de-camp', *RSM* 'regimental sergeant-major', and *WILCO* 'will comply'. The law has an extensive jargon of terms such as *plaintiff*, *defendant*, and *contempt* (of court), and it includes Latin phrases such as *habeas corpus* 'Produce the body (of the arrested person)', *sine die* '(to be adjourned) without a day (being fixed)', and *decree nisi*, a decree which comes into force after a stipulated period unless (*nisi*) an objection has been lodged. Medicine and pharmacy also have an extensive jargon, a small proportion of which is familiar outside the profession to health-conscious amateurs, hypochondriacs, and viewers of relevant television programmes. More secret is the system of Latin terms doctors use in communicating with pharmacists, terms such as *mane* 'in the morning', *a.c.* (*ante cibum*) 'before meals', *nocte* 'in the evening', and *p.c.* (*post cibum*) 'after meals'.

Each sport has its own jargon and people who follow a number of sports need to master a corresponding number of jargons. To list just a few examples, baseball, basketball, billiards, bowling, boxing, car racing, cricket, cycling, football, golf, hockey, horse racing, motor racing, tennis, volley ball, and wrestling all have jargons consisting of scores of terms, in some cases hundreds or even thousands.[2] Closely related to jargon is **register**, the style associated with a certain

---

[2] Andy Pawley of the ANU informs me that one glossary of baseball terminology runs to 5,000 entries and his own collection of cricket terms runs to over 2,000 without being complete. A quick survey of some glossaries of technical terms reveals the following figures: architecture 4,500, cooking 22,000, gardening 6,000, medicine/nursing 44,000, music 3,000, nautical 8,000, sewing 800, and stocks and investment 2,300.

occupation, activity, or medium. An auctioneer, for instance, will use stock expressions such as, 'What am I bid for this?', 'Any advance on £500?', 'Against you, madam/sir', and 'Going, going, gone'.

In general there is no choice between using jargon and non-specialist terms, but some speakers do use jargon to outsiders either inadvertently or through a desire to impress. Certain types of learned jargon and register seem to arise from a feeling that a serious subject needs 'big' words. Consider the following paragraph in a publication from a leading geographical society:

> The examples given suggest that the multiformity of environmental apprehension and the exclusivity of abstract semantic conceptions constitute a crucial distinction. Semantic responses to qualities, environmental or other, tend to abstract each individual quality as though it were to be considered in isolation, with nothing else impinging. But in actual environmental experience, our judgements of attributes are constantly affected by the entire milieu, and the connectivities such observations suggest reveal this multiform complexity. Semantic response is generally a consequence of reductive categorization, environmental response or synthesizing holism.

This is quoted in *The Jargon of the Professions* by Hudson, who suggests the authors 'should be locked up without food or water until they can produce an acceptable translation'(1978: 87). I think the passage simply means that in experiencing the environment we need to look at it as a whole rather than at particular properties, though I am at a loss to decode the first sentence.[3]

---

[3] I am unable to paraphrase the following example from an administrative memo. I wonder how many of the recipients felt the same. The problem is a mixture of jargon and poor syntax.

> Care is taken to avoid creating new categories of high staff turnover schools in regional areas not within defined categories

When it comes to learned jargon English presents a problem that is by no means common to all languages. English has borrowed most of its learned vocabulary from Greek and Latin and the make-up of these words is not always clear to the average person. Take stamp collecting. We call a person who collects stamps a *stamp collector*, a term which is perfectly transparent, but there is also *philatelist*, which is not at all transparent. The term *paediatrician* is not transparent, and is often thought to relate to feet in light of words such as *pedestrian*, especially with the American spelling *pediatrician*. In fact it means a doctor who specializes in children. In German it is *Kinderarzt*, literally 'children-doctor', a compound, the make-up of which is perfectly plain to any speaker of German. Although German has borrowed a few words from Greek and Latin, it forms most of its learned words by compounding simple roots and using its own prefixes and suffixes.

Slang

In speaking and writing we have a choice between being formal or informal. For example, *I received your letter* is formal but *I got your letter* is informal or colloquial. Words and phrases that would be deemed colloquial include *no problem* and *see you later*. Overlapping with the term 'colloquial' is the term 'slang'. The difference is not clear-cut but is one of degree; we might start by saying that slang means 'very colloquial'. The verb *to vomit* is standard, *to sick up* is informal or colloquial, and expressions such as *to spray paint*

of remoteness in determination of hard-to-staff schools developed under the total recruitment strategy.

or *to have a technicolour yawn* are slang. While 'colloquial' has positive or neutral connotations, the word 'slang' is often used negatively. Many people do not see slang words as respectable or legitimate. If someone tries to use *nix* in Scrabble, particularly if they want to use the 'x' on a triple-score square, they are likely to be told that *nix* is not a 'real word'. Writers of yesteryear who have bemoaned the use of slang include those once prominent guardians of the English language, H.W. and F.G. Fowler, whose book *The King's English* was originally published in 1906 and reprinted in several editions: ' . . . as style is the great antiseptic, so slang is the great corrupting matter; it is perishable itself, and infects what is round it—the catchwords that delight one generation stink in the nostrils of the next' (1931: 61). Greenough and Kittredge (1931: 55) say that 'slang is commonly made by the use of harsh, violent or ludicrous metaphors, obscure analogies, meaningless words, and expressions derived from the less known and less esteemed vocations or customs'.

Slang is covered here for a number of related reasons, some of which are touched on in the above quotations. One, slang is inventive, abounds in metaphor and allusion, and is often more demanding or more opaque than the standard language. Two, since slang is inventive, there is a good deal of turnover, with fresh slang replacing existing slang. Three, slang tends to be local and restricted to an area or a social group.

The Inventiveness of Slang

A number of writers on language remark approvingly on the inventiveness of slang. Even the conservative H.W. Fowler, writing at a later date than the quotation above, described slang as 'the diction that results from the favourite game among the young and lively of playing with words and renaming things and actions; some invent new words, or mutilate or misapply the old, for the pleasure of novelty, and others catch up such words for the pleasure of being in fashion' (Fowler 1926: 308).

Some slang words have different roots from their mainstream counterparts and there is no particular motivation for the choice. The once-popular London slang term *nim* 'to take', for instance, is a reflex of the Old English verb *niman*, whereas the standard equivalent *take* comes from the Old Norse of the Viking invaders and settlers. It could equally have happened that *nim* became the mainstream word and *take* became slang or dialectal. However, the great majority of slang terms are motivated in the sense that they are composed by compounding or affixation and tend to be descriptive. An old slang term for *clerk* is the compound *ink spiller*, which has obvious origins. *Bread basket* derives from the fact that the stomach is a repository for bread, and *coffin nail* for 'cigarette' refers to the medical opinion that smoking shortens one's lifespan. Similar again are suffixed terms like *kisser* for 'mouth' or the obsolete *prancer* for 'horse'. There are also colloquial-forming suffixes such as those found in *brekkie*, *brekker*, and *brekkers* 'breakfast', which change the connotations, as do abbreviations as in *prof*, *staph*, *strep*, *tute*, *ex div*, and *tlc*.

Alliteration is frequently used to create catchy slang expressions such as *bible basher*, *greedy guts*, and *thunder thighs*, and rhyme is a fertile source, as in *barber starver* 'a man who lets his hair grow long', *bum chum* 'male homosexual', *chick flick* 'a movie aimed at female audiences', *fake bake* 'suntan achieved by lamp or bottle', *mop chop* 'haircut', *pooper scooper* 'a tool for picking up dog mess', *rugger bugger* 'macho young man', and *tin grin* 'orthodontal braces'.

Metaphor plays a large part in slang. A few generations ago the motor car provided a popular source of metaphor with expressions such as *to be in overdrive, to blow a gasket, to be (really) motoring (along)*, and *to be sparking on all four (cylinders)*. More recently electricity provided a number of examples, including *AC/DC, to light up, to press the right switches, to be switched on*, and *to turn someone on* or *off*. Various sports have contributed metaphors. From boxing we have *below the belt, knockout*, and *throw in the towel*, from cricket *sticky wicket, clean bowled*, and *hit for six*.

Striking similes include *to be flat out like a lizard drinking* (said of someone having to work hard), *to charge like a wounded bull* (of someone demanding high prices), and *to have more push than a revolving door* (of someone forceful or pushy). Expressions like these involve two different senses of the key words, one literal and the other metaphorical. Some similes are based on paradox, for instance *runs in the family like wooden legs* or *sweating like a pig* (pigs don't sweat). Colourful exaggeration, a regular feature of light-hearted conversation, is lexicalized in *timber merchant*, a British slang term for 'match seller'.[4]

Slang expressions tend to be self-consciously inventive, but some are rather forced and probably too clever to achieve wide circulation or longevity. In his *Dictionary of the Vulgar Tongue* (1785, 1811) Grose gives *Athanasian wench* for a woman of easy

[4] A match seller is usually an out-of-work man registering a protest or legally begging rather than someone hoping to make money by the sale of matches.

virtue. It is based on the first words of the Latin version of the Athanasian Creed, namely *Quicumque vult* 'Whoever wishes', a prayer included in the *Book of Common Prayer* with these Latin words as its title. Partridge (1960: 34) gives *gone to the Diet of Worms* for 'to be dead'. In South African English de Klerk (2006) records *act like jeans and fade* 'go away' and *blow some zeds* 'sleep'—an expression which presumably relates to the representation of sleep in comic strips.

Another method of forming colloquial if not slang terms is deliberate malformation, as in *picture-askew* for 'picturesque' and *trick cyclist* for 'psychiatrist'. The French phrase *faux pas* has sometimes been pronounced as *fox's paw* or *fox paw* since the eighteenth century. These deformations are of the folk etymology type in that an exotic original is associated with familiar words. Another slang mechanism is the formation of pseudo-learned words, as in *obstropolous* (and its abbreviation *stroppy*) for *obstreperous*, and *rumbumptious* for *rambunctious*. Slang often contains malapropisms such as *What are you incinerating?* for *What are you insinuating?* These probably start off as deliberate attempts at humour, but it is uncertain whether all users are conscious of the substitution.

Slang is by definition informal, but it is also often irreverent, as with *(cat)gut scraper* for 'violinist', *scandal broth* for 'tea', and *louse trap* or *flea rake* for 'comb'. An eighteenth-century hotel in Covent Garden that gloried in the name *The Golden Lion* was dubbed by locals *The Yellow Cat*, and *The Eagle and Child* in Oxford has been *The Bird and Baby* for some hundreds of years. A streak of dysphemism is evidenced in terms like *floating coffin* 'unseaworthy boat', while the eighteenth-century expression *fart catcher* for an attendant who walks a few paces behind his master is a clear attempt at crudery. Similarly, *cock-rag* has a crude transparency which is lacking in the anthropologist's 'phallocrypt'. Unpleasant slang is prolific and includes terms such as *brown nose* or *brown tongue* for a sycophant (or 'crawler'), *fly cemetery* (currant cake), *frog spawn* (sago), *snot block* (vanilla slice), *snot rag* (handkerchief), and *nun's fart* (cream puff).[5]

There is also a deliberate insensitivity in the use of light-hearted, off-hand descriptions of serious conditions. A diseased penis is said to have *knob rot* and death is treated lightly in expressions such as *kick the bucket* or *fall off the perch*, or *lead poisoning* for someone who has been shot. In the same vein are obsolete phrases for death by hanging such as *hempen fever, hearty choke*, and *wry mouth*. These jocular expressions for death are similar to the impulse towards comedy in the face of tragedy. Slang and humour often go hand in hand.

Is Slang Ephemeral?

Some dictionaries include 'ephemeral' in their definition of slang, and Greenough and Kittredge (1931: 73) claim that 'Slang words ... are evanescent, counting their duration by days instead of decades, and becoming obsolete even while one is speaking them. Hence slang is ill-adapted to serve as a medium of intercourse.' While it is true that most slang is short-lived, many slang words endure for centuries. To *lift* 'to steal' (cf. *shoplifter, shoplifting*) has been around since the sixteenth century, the police have been called *pigs* since the late seventeenth century, and

---

[5] Compare French *pet de nonne*.

booze, which was borrowed into Middle English from Middle Dutch *būsen* 'to drink', has been current as a noun as well as a verb ever since, and has spawned other slang expressions such as *boozer* 'pub' or 'heavy drinker', *booze-up* 'drinking spree', and *booze artist* 'heavy drinker'. The terms Grose lists in his *Dictionary of the Vulgar Tongue* (1785, 1811) include many that are still current: *bum fodder* 'toilet paper', *claret* 'blood', *clink* 'jail', *clod hopper* 'country bumpkin', *crocodile tears* 'insincere tears', *duds* 'clothes', *elbow grease* 'hard work', *flabby*, *French leave*, *gob*, *guts*, *hick*, *to hump* 'copulate with', *nix*, *in queer street* 'bankrupt', *riff raff*, *to pump* (somebody for information). Others such as *physog* (from *physiognomy*) 'face' and *to plant* 'hide' (intransitive and transitive) lasted into the twentieth century, but are perhaps obsolete now.

Words may change their status over time. Some words that began their life in English as slang achieved respectability. These include *bamboozle*, *banter*, *bigot*, *bus* (an abbreviation of the Latin *omnibus* 'for all'), *carouse* (from the German *(trinken) gar aus* 'drink right out'), *frisk*, *hoax* (from the pseudo-Latin phrase *hocus pocus*), *mob* (an abbreviation of the Latin phrase *mobile vulgus* 'the fickle common people'), *shabby*, *sham*, and *tandem* (a Latin adverb meaning 'at length'). In the nineteenth century *tandem* was a colloquial term for a vehicle pulled by two horses one behind the other. It was later applied to 'a bicycle built for two', but since it is the only term for such a bicycle in this context it counts as a technical term rather than slang.[6] Some of the phrases listed above

---

[6] The phrase 'a bicycle built for two' comes from the popular song 'Daisy, Daisy', which resurfaces in Chapter 10.

started as educated slang. Other words have moved up the social scale, including *pal*, which came into English slang from Romani (Romany), the language of the Gypsies, and today is standard, albeit colloquial.

Local Slang

It has been characteristic of slang over the centuries to be socially and geographically restricted—i.e. confined to particular areas, particular strata in society, and particular interest groups. At one extreme slang may be peculiar to a particular factory, university, or school, even to particular forms within a school. At the other extreme it may cover a whole country, as with New Zealand slang or South African slang. To the extent that it is restricted it is unsuitable for formal purposes, which often involves communication with the language community at large.

Part of the attraction of slang lies in its esoteric character. It is a good marker of identity, a language of the in-group and of solidarity. Groups of slang users from particular areas, including particular countries, are usually proud of their slang. They consider it smart and colourful and use it self-consciously, with the more imaginative speakers contributing new terms. It is interesting to note the large number of publications dedicated to listing slang terms; many of these are put together by amateurs who are motivated by interest if not pride in the variety of slang they are recording.

Nowadays American slang is propagated via pop music, films, and television. It permeates the English-speaking world and spreads into other languages. In German, for instance, one can *ausflippen* 'flip out' or *abchecken* 'check out (something or someone)'. Such widespread slang can still serve as a marker of identity. As particular terms are spread, they are largely picked up by the young, and a knowledge of the latest American slang can mark you as 'with it' or 'cool'. This is particularly true of the current slang of young African Americans. As Eble reports, 'The fashionable value of the style invented by African American youth in urban ghettos has given international cachet to hip-hop slang such as *dawg*, *floss*, *holla back*, *pimp*, *playa*, *props*, and *word*. Thanks to the new means of communication, youth around the world who have never met or spoken to an African American jockey for social status among their peers by using the slang popularized by hip-hop' (Eble 2006: 414).[7]

The Slang Lexicon

It is commonplace in linguistics to point out that languages differ not only in grammar and lexicon, but also in the set of concepts for which they have words. Each language encapsulates a particular world view, in fact a language can encapsulate different world views at different times and more than one view at a particular time. With respect to change over time consider the now obsolete view of marriage reflected in terms such as *to be jilted*, *breach of promise*, *old maid*, and *to be (left) on the shelf*. More relevant here

---

[7] Eble gives other examples of international slang. Devotees of the television series *Buffy, the Vampire Slayer* (1997–2003) use a distinctive vocabulary in communicating through e-mail, chat rooms, Web sites, and magazines (Adams 2003). Players of the role-playing game *Shadowrun* form a worldwide community and have a Web site for their own slang, which includes *sidewalk outline* for 'a recently deceased person', a reference to the chalk outline of a body at a murder scene.

are the differences of conceptualization between the standard language and its colloquial varieties. Although in many instances slang provides informal alternatives for standard words, as with *saw-bones* for 'surgeon', in some cases it expresses a different set of concepts. Consider the words *pecs*, *abs*, and *glutes*, which came into vogue in the 1990s. They are derived from *pectoral muscles*, *abdominal muscles*, and *gluteal muscles*, terms which play practically no part in the standard language. The abbreviated forms arose in the context of advertising which exploited the sex appeal of the semi-naked male body. They represent new concepts. Errol Flynn and Clark Gable did not have pecs, abs, and glutes.

While slang by no means offers equivalents for every word in the standard lexicon, for some referents it is rich in synonyms. Partridge (1960: 29) remarks that 'the less "reputable" an action or object, the more synonyms'. Writing of French slang Guiraud (1985: 43) notes that there are words for denigration, jubilation, satiety, boredom, and irritation, but not for compassion, tolerance, generosity, altruism, or tenderness. A survey of English slang over the centuries reveals that around a thousand slang terms for *penis* and *vagina* are or have been used somewhere in the English-speaking world at one time or another, with words for sexual acts, excretion, and bodily effluvia also rating highly.[8] Terms of approval (*swell*, *awesome*, *great*, *groovy*, *unreal*) are common, but generally short-lived, as are terms of disapproval. Alcohol, money, and drugs give rise to numerous slang terms, along with terms for physical characteristics (*carrot-top*, *titch*, *shorty*, *lofty*) and physical deficiencies (*spaso/spaz*). There is a welter of terms for mental

---

[8] See Fryer 1964: 69–85 for some figures and numerous examples.

deficiency or insanity: *barmy, bats (in the belfry), cracked, crackers, crackpot, cranky, dippy, dotty, loopy, lost his/her marbles, mad as a hatter, nuts, nutty as a fruitcake, potty, a screw loose, a shingle short, two bob short in the pound, two sandwiches short of a picnic,* and for a stupid person: *blockhead, bonehead, dill, dope, donkey, drip, drongo, dunderhead,* and *nong.* Of a person showing signs of senile dementia it is likely to be said *the lights are on but no one's at home.*

There are more colloquial terms for a woman as a provider of sex, whether in a professional or amateur capacity, than for any other referent. There are expressions such as *a bike, a bit of a goer, been around a bit, been around the block a few times, ho, moll/mole, no better than she should be, tart, slut,* and *an easy lay.* This proliferation is reflected in the language in general, with terms such as *harlot, strumpet, trollop,* and *whore,* or the old-fashioned *woman of easy virtue.*[9] It is interesting to note that the double standard that condemns women's sexual activity while lauding men's is not only seen in the large number of terms for promiscuous women, but in the fact that some words have negative connotations when applied to women, but not so negative when applied to men. A *fast* woman is a promiscuous one, but a *fast* man is a good sprinter, and if he is a *fast worker,* then he is good at attracting females. A *loose* woman is promiscuous, but a *loose* man, at least in Australian football, is one who has evaded his opponents and is in a position to receive the ball unopposed. A *fallen woman* is one who has turned to prostitution, but a *fallen soldier* is one who has died for his country.

---

[9] Significantly *strumpet, trollop,* and *whore* all have, or have had, colloquial variants: *strum, troll,* and the currently popular *ho.*

There are numerous imperatives advising someone to depart: *bugger off, buzz off, hop it, make yourself scarce, nick off, piss off, rack off, scat, vamoose.* Closely related are other dismissive imperatives such as *Get stuffed!, Go to blazes!,* and *Go to hell!* Slang is also rich in exclamatory words and phrases like *Beauty!, What the blazes?!, Stiff cheese!, Blow me down!,* and *My oath!*

Argots and 'Secret Languages'

The tendency for slang to be geographically local or associated with a particular group of people is epitomized in **argot**. This is a body of non-standard vocabulary used by a group bound by common interest, isolation, or their opposition to authority. The word 'argot' is traditionally associated with those who live outside the law: burglars, cardsharps, confidence tricksters (grifters), highwaymen, pickpockets, racketeers, swindlers, thieves, and the like, and is sometimes referred to as 'thieves' slang'. But argots have also been in use among other groups who tend to be itinerant: beggars, entertainers, Gypsies, circus folk, vagrants, and travelling tradesmen such as chimney sweeps, knife sharpeners, masons, tinkers, and window cleaners. Those who supply goods or services without having a shop are traditional users of an argot, people such as street vendors or market stall-holders. Prostitutes, drug dealers, and gays have their own argots, as do prisoners and schoolchildren. Argot is included in what Halliday calls **anti-language**, which he describes as a special form of language used to maintain social structure by anti-society, a society within a larger society set up as an alternative, in some cases a hostile alternative' (Halliday 1976: 570).

In most argots the bulk of the distinctive vocabulary is derived by the usual word-building processes, though some argots use their own peculiar suffixes (see p. 237). Some vocabulary is borrowed. Yiddish, a Germanic language used in some Jewish communities, and Romani, the language of the Gypsies, have both been a source of vocabulary for various European argots, a not unexpected development since Jews and Gypsies tended to be denied access to mainstream occupations. Part of the motivation for argot is to maintain in-group solidarity, and part is to provide a secret code that will not be understood by targets of criminal activity or the authorities. Some of this secrecy is achieved via a special vocabulary, and some by means of systematic phonological distortion of the Pig Latin type. This is covered under 'Secret languages' below. In some circumstances the use of a language not known to the authorities provides a ready-made in-group tongue. In geographical areas which experience invasion, the indigenous vernaculars serve as in-group languages. English had this status for over two hundred years after the Norman French invasion of 1066, which introduced a French-speaking ruling class, but for most of its history English has been an invading language, particularly from the seventeenth century onwards.

Since argots are often found among those engaged in illicit or illegal activities, it is not surprising that there are numerous terms for authorities (*the old bill, coppers, pigs*), for evading authorities (*to scarper, to do a runner, to be on the lam*), and for types of crime and criminal, means of carrying out crime, penalties, and prisons. Some argot terms have no equivalent in the standard language and while having the flavour of slang, they qualify as jargon. These include *angler*, an old term for a thief who steals using a hook on the end of a long stick, a *snowdropper*, someone who steals washing from clotheslines, and the modern *shoulder-surfing*, which is observing someone's pin number at an ATM for future use. Some of the argot passes into mainstream usage when an activity comes to the attention of a wider public, as has happened with *pimp* and more recently *supergrass*.

Gay argot has a number of terms for which there is no simple equivalent in the standard language. These include the terms *bean queen* (a male homosexual in the USA who likes partners from south of the border), *chicken queen* (likes young partners), *curry queen* (likes South Asian partners), and *rice queen* (likes East Asian partners). A *green queen* is active in parks and *cottaging* is gay activity in public toilets.[10]

Argot in England

One of the argots we know most about is the argot of thieves and vagabonds in the London area from the sixteenth century on, from sources such as Harman (1567). This argot was generally called 'cant', but the term 'cant' was also used for jargon and its associated register, so that people would talk about lawyer's cant (Gotti 1999). Like slang in general it had an elaborate vocabulary for anything connected with sex, and as expected a large vocabulary of terms for criminals and criminal activity. In Grose's *A Dictionary of the Vulgar Tongue* (1785, 1811) there are about four thousand entries, of which over three hundred are for types of malefactor and types of crime. The criminals include *badgers* (who rob and murder near rivers), *boung nippers* (cutpurses), *cloak twitchers* (who snatch cloaks

---

[10] *Cottaging* takes its name from the fact that public toilets in public parks in Britain were built to look like cottages, a kind of architectural euphemism.

from passers by), *cracksmen* (burglars), *forks* (pickpockets), *glazyers* (burglars who break windows or remove panes), *jarkmen* (counterfeiters), *jumpers* (burglars who enter by a window), *rushers* (who rush in when the door of a house is opened), and *scourers* (roaming bucks who break windows, assault passers by, etc.). The tools of the trade include *cracking tools* such as the *betty* or *jemmy*, the latter still in current usage. There is a set of terms for those involved in confidence tricks with card games. The person who first approached the mark (the *cousin* or *coney*) was the *setter* or *taker-up*. He was joined by the *verser* and the two of them play the part of sophisticated gentlemen who gain the mark's confidence. They and the mark are joined by the *barnard* or *barnacle*, who appears to be drunk or stupid or both. The mark is induced to play cards against the barnard, who invariably wins. Someone employed to start a diversion if necessary was a *rutter*. There are about a hundred terms for a promiscuous woman and another hundred for a man who is stupid, gullible, or a *greenhorn* (to quote one of the words in Grose that is still current today, particularly in US English).

As with slang in general, some of this argot consisted of different roots from those in the standard language, such as *nab* 'head', *fambles* 'hands', and *cank* 'dumb', but the greater part of the vocabulary is descriptive in the sense that it is a compound or affixed root picking out a characteristic of a referent or a metaphorical description. A streak of humour runs through the traditional argot. Prisons were often described as *schools*, as in the contemporary *College of Correction*, and the hulks used to accommodate prisoners were the *floating academies*. Brothels were *convents* or *nunneries*, the prostitutes who worked in them were *nuns*, and the madam was an *abbess*.

In the English argot compounding was prominent. For instance, some body parts were formed from a descriptive participle and *chete/cheat* 'thing': *crashing chetes* 'teeth', *hearing chetes* 'ears', *smelling chete* 'nose', and *prattling chete* or *prating chete* 'tongue'. Similar formations were used for farm animals: *bleting chete* 'lamb', *cackling chete* 'chicken', *grunting chete* 'pig', *lowing chete* 'cow', and *quacking chete* 'duck'. There were compounds with *law* 'activity' or 'way': *cheating law* 'cheating at cards or dice', *curbing law* 'stealing by means of a hook on a stick', *figging law* 'pickpocketing', *lifting law* 'stealing of parcels', *prigging law* 'horse stealing', and *sacking law* 'prostitution'. *Ken* 'house' or 'premises', a word borrowed from Romani, the language of the Gypsies, was also used a lot in compounds: *croppin-ken* 'privy, toilet', *flash ken* 'house that harbours thieves', *quyerkyn* 'prison' (*quyer* [queer] = 'bad'), *smuggling ken* and *snoozing ken* 'brothel', *staulinge ken* 'receiver's, fence's', and *touting-ken* 'alehouse, tavern'.[11]

A number of body parts were named by taking a characteristic or function and adding the *-er* noun-forming suffix: *grinders* 'teeth', *heavers* 'breasts', *panter* 'heart', and *smiter* 'bottom'. *Hands* were called *pickers and stealers*, a phrase that occurs in *Hamlet*.[12] The same suffix appeared in *lifters* 'crutches', *prauncer* (*prancer*) 'horse', *spreader* 'butter', and *stampers* 'shoes'. It is also in *peepers*, which at one time meant 'mirror' but later 'eyes', a usage

---

[11] The examples are from various sources, but most can be found in Gotti 1999.

[12] Act III, Scene 2:

ROSENCRANTZ My lord, you once did love me.
HAMLET   So I do still, by these pickers and stealers.

that continued into the twentieth century in expressions such as *park your peepers on the pony* 'have a look at the horse'.

The plural marker is used as a derivational suffix in words such as *dindins, cuddles, preggers*. It is also combined with *man* to give the suffix *-mans*, which is used to derive nouns from adjectives. Examples include *crackmans* 'hedges', *darkmans* 'night', *greenmans* 'fields', *harmans* 'stocks', *lightmans* 'day', and *ruffmans* 'forest, woods, bushes'.

Where borrowing was concerned, the oldest stratum was from Latin, but there were also borrowings from French, Italian, and, as we have seen, Romani and Yiddish. The apparently Italian borrowings are likely to have come from Lingua Franca, the Romance-based pidgin of the Mediterranean, probably introduced by seamen. The term *cant* itself is from Latin/Italian *cantare* 'to sing' and may result from the tendency of beggars in the past to chant their pleas.

bene	good (Latin/Italian *bene*) as in *bene cofe* 'a good fellow', also *benely* 'well'
bone	good (Latin/Southern Italian *bonus/bona* or French *bon(ne)*)
case, carser	house, building (Latin/Italian *casa*)
cassam	cheese (Latin *caseus*, acc. *caseum*)
to couch	to lie down (French *coucher*)
cull	man, also *rum-cull* 'mate' (Romani *chal*)
fogel	handkerchief (German/Yiddish *Vogel* 'bird')
grannam	corn (Latin *granum*)
ken	house (Romani *ken*)
mort	woman (Romani *mort*)
ogle	eye (Dutch, *Oogelijn*, a little eye)
pannam	bread (Latin *panis*, acc. *panem*)
togeman	cloak (Latin *toga* + man)

Back Slang

In Britain there has been a form of secret language called **back slang** since at least the early nineteenth century. It is reported to have been in use in England among food vendors such as butchers and greengrocers, and among street sellers, those who sold goods from barrows or stalls, especially the costermongers who sold fruit, vegetables, and 'fish' ('seafood' in current terminology). Back slang allowed dodgy vendors to converse in front of unwary customers, but it must have been known to at least some of the regular clientele. It is essentially a system of enciphering words by taking the written forms and pronouncing them backwards. It resembles the play languages or secret languages described later in this chapter, which involve systematic phonological alteration of words, but is based on English spelling and is therefore a lot less systematic than most other 'secret languages'. The fact that it is based on spelling is interesting in that most of the street sellers were illiterate, but some could read and there was a class of patterers—vendors who excelled in patter or clever spiel—many of whom had various degrees of education. Although back slang was essentially a means of encipherment and could be used on an ad hoc basis, a back slang lexicon developed and this extended far beyond the needs of the costers. Early reports are from London (Hotten 1864, 1874; Mayhew 1851), but it is not certain whether back slang was peculiar to that area or just that we happen to have reports from the capital.

The basic principle of back slang is that each word is pronounced backwards:

fish	→	shif
look	→	cool
market	→	tekram
no good	→	on doog
yes	→	say

Although back slang was spoken, it was based on the written language, and the sequence of letters is reversed except for a few digraphs that represent a single phoneme like *sh* in *fish* (see above). This reversing leads to problems in a language like English with its highly irregular relationship between sound and spelling and its constraints on which sounds can appear in various positions in a syllable.[13] For instance, reversing a word like *hat* raises a problem since /h/ cannot occur at the end of a syllable, so *ch* or *tch* was usually substituted, but in some cases *sh*.

hat	→	tatch
half	→	flatch (note the silent 'l' makes an appearance)
have	→	vatch
home	→	eemosh

Where the reversal would produce a consonant cluster outside the normal range for English an unstressed vowel (i.e. /ə/) could be inserted:

---

[13] There is also a Javanese version of back slang. In Javanese there is a close correspondence between phonology and orthography, so there are none of the problems that arise in English, and one cannot easily distinguish whether the back slang is based on speech or writing.

    bocah iku dolanan asu.
    hacob uki nanalod usa
    'The boy is playing with the dog'

back slang	→	kecab genals
cold	→	deloc
lamb	→	bemal
long	→	genol
old	→	delo
penny	→	yennep

Another possibility was to pronounce the name of a letter, so that, for instance, the final *l* in girl was pronounced *el*.

girl	→	elrig
knife	→	eefink
lamb	→	beemal (alternative to *bemal*)
old	→	deelo (alternative to *delo*)
pork	→	kayrop

Adherence to the spelling produces odd relationships in pronunciation between the original and the back slang version:

apple	→	elpa (also helpa)
bone	→	enob, eenob
cow	→	woc
door	→	rude
one	→	eno (*doogeno* 'a good one', *dabeno* 'a bad one')
pot of beer	→	top o' reeb
thirteen	→	neetrith
two	→	owt
week	→	kew

The plural 's' is usually excluded from the reversal, as in the following examples:

greens	→	neergs
turnip tops	→	pinurt pots

However, the 's' is retained where the referent normally occurs in pairs or groups:

balls	→	slab
cherries	→	siretch[14]
nuts	→	stun

The unusual relation between the singular and plural of *woman* is handled by using *namow* (or *nemow*) for 'woman' and adding *s* to form a plural *namows*.

There appears to have been some variation in how much speech was enciphered. In some instances back slang was only used for a few key words, as in 'I've been doing bloody *dab* (bad) with my *tol* (lot) 'n' ha'n't made a *yennep* (penny), s'elp me'. In other cases all lexical words were enciphered, but function words were left intact, though in the third example below, *at* becomes *ta*.

doing badly	→	doing dab
Look at him	→	Cool 'im
Look at the old woman	→	Cool ta delo nemow

Two words have moved from back slang into wider currency. *Yob*, a back slang version of *boy*, is a well-known colloquialism for 'undesirable young man', and *ecaf* 'face' and its abbreviated form *eek* has some currency in British slang, including Polari (see p. 225). Otherwise back slang seems to be dying, as are many other forms of secret communication. Oddly the principle lives on in joke

[14] *Cherries* is interesting. The back slang retains the *s* as in *siretch*. The word came into Old English as *ciris* via Latin, ultimately from Greek *kerasos*. Since cherries normally occur in the groups, the final *-s* was taken to be a plural marker. The makers of back slang seem to have reversed the process by taking the sibilant to be an integral part of the stem. It appears that the fact that cherries occur in groups has had two different outcomes. First it led to the final sibilant being taken as a plural marker and then it led to the plural marker being taken as part of the stem.

names for properties and businesses, such as *renroc* 'corner' and *emoh ruo* 'our home' (also the name of a 1985 satirical film).

Rhyming Slang

A form of in-group communication that has been traditional among Cockneys since the nineteenth century is **rhyming slang** (Hotten 1874). Rhyming slang is not confined to Cockneys and there are sporadic reports of its use from various parts of the English-speaking world. A certain social stigma has been attached to it, and it is sometimes associated with the criminal classes, but in fact it is used across a wide social spectrum, mainly by males. Basically it consists of a rhyming phrase substituted for a word so that, for instance, 'eyes' becomes *mince pies*, 'mouth' becomes *north and south*, and 'nose' becomes *I suppose*.

Rhyming slang has something of a secret code about it, since the referent is not always clear to the uninitiated. It becomes more cryptic when the rhyming element is omitted. In the television series *Minder* dodgy used-car saleman Arthur Daley used to talk about getting on the *dog*. The *dog* is the *dog and bone*, that is, the phone. In the following exchange from the episode *Poetic Justice, innit?* he is acting as foreman of a jury.

UPPERCLASS FEMALE JUROR	The man's clearly guilty. You only have to look at his face.
ARTHUR DALEY	Madam, with respect. A man's boat is hardly the foundation on which to base a conviction.
INDIAN JUROR	What is boat? I do not understand.
ARTHUR DALEY	Boat race, madam.

Arthur assumes that supplying the missing rhyme from the rhyming slang phrase *boat race* is sufficient. He fails to explain that it refers to face, though this can be guessed from the context.

A particularly obscure term is *oliver* as in, 'Do you oliver?' meaning 'Do you understand?' *Oliver* is short for Oliver Cromwell, which in the traditional pronunciation was *crummel* or *crumble*, the rhyme for 'to tumble' in the sense of 'to understand' (Matthews 1938: 133).[15]

When we talk about someone *rabbiting on*, we are using a word derived from rhyming slang. *Rabbit* is short for *rabbit and pork*, rhyming slang for 'talk' (originally for the noun and later for the verb). If someone is *rabbiting on*, they are talking at length. Other examples of expressions that started life as rhyming slang but have come into more general use include *brass tacks* for 'facts', *chew the fat* for 'chat', and *Dutch treat*, which was originally rhyming slang for 'eat' but has come to mean a meal in a café or restaurant where two or more persons pay their own share, i.e. 'they go Dutch'.

Here are a few lines heavily laden with rhyming slang terms. The key can be found below.

> When 'e come 'ome from the rubbidy, I could see 'e was Brahms. 'e'd been on the ol' Aristotle. 'is I-suppose was red an 'is mince pies was glazed an' 'e couldn't 'ardly climb the apples.

[15] The current pronunciation of *Cromwell* is a spelling pronunciation. The [w] sound at the beginning of an unstressed syllable was generally lost, as it still is in *Norwich*, *Dulwich*, etc., but it has been restored on the basis of the spelling in words like *midwife*, *housewife*, etc.

Some terms have had different meanings at different times. *Rory o'More* was once rhyming slang for 'floor', but came to refer to 'door', and also 'whore', according to Partridge (1960: 274–5). Conversely some referents have been allotted different rhymes at different times. In the nineteenth century 'mouth' was *east and south*, but has long been replaced by *north and south*.

Local variants of rhyming slang occur in various parts of the world. In Australia 'Give us a look' is *Give us a Captain Cook* or just *Give us a Captain*, 'trouble' is *froth and bubble*, and a prostitute is a *mallee root*.[16]

	Rhyming Slang	Reduced Form
alone	Pat Malone	pat, as in 'on your pat'
arse	Khyber Pass	Khyber
balls	cobbler's awls	cobblers, as in 'a load of cobblers'
bottle	Aristotle	
eyes	mince pies	minces
face	boat race, Chevy Chase	
facts	brass tacks	
fart	raspberry tart	raspberry
feet	plates o' meat	plates
go	Scapa Flow	scapa [It. *scappare* 'to flee']
hair	Barnet Fair	barnet

[16] A mallee root is the root of a type of eucalypt tree known as a malee, or a piece of firewood chopped from such a root. *Root* is also slang for intercourse or a provider of intercourse.

hat	tit for tat	titfer
Jew	five-to-two	
look	Captain Cook, butcher's hook	captain, butcher's
mate	China (plate)	china
missus	cheese and kisses	
mouth	north and south	
nose	I suppose	
nun	currant bun	
piles	Chalfont St Giles	chalfonts
pinch (steal)	half-inch	
pissed (drunk)	Brahms and Liszt, Schindler's List	
poof	iron hoof, cow's hoof	iron
pub	rub-a-dub, rubbity-dub	rubbidy
sleep	Bo Peep	
snake	Joe Blake	
stairs	apples and pears	
thief	tea leaf	
tits	brace and bits	braces
titties	Bristol cities	bristols
Yank	septic tank, army tank	septic

Parlyaree and Polari

An argot developed among itinerant entertainers in Britain as early as the seventeenth century called **Parlyaree** or **Parlary** (variously spelt), which is thought to be from Italian *parlare* 'to speak'. The entertainers in question included jugglers, clowns, fire eaters, trapeze artists, singers, monkey trainers, various musicians including organ grinders, puppeteers, and, until the nineteenth century, almost all actors, since there was little permanent urban theatre before that time. These performers travelled around performing in shows or busking at fairs or markets and on the streets. The argot contains a number of Italian words. *Varda* 'see' is likely to be from northern Italian *vardar* (from *guardare*), and *homa* 'man' and *bona* 'good' may reflect southern Italian forms which lack the diphthong that developed in standard Italian *uomo* and *buono/buona*. Other Italian words include *dona* [donna] 'female', *feielia* [figlia] 'child', and phrases such as the following (Mayhew 1851: 449–50):

How are you getting on?
Ultra cateva [oltre cattiva = very bad]

Questra homa a vardring the slum, scarper it.
Quest'uomo sta vedendo the slum, scapa (it)
This man is looking at the slum, beat it!

As with the Italian element in British argot generally, Hancock (1984b) suggests that some of these words may have been brought in by returning seamen from Lingua Franca, the Romance-based pidgin of the Mediterranean ports, though he recognizes that many entered the argot in the nineteenth century from the prominence of Italian immigrants among itinerant entertainers. In a more recent paper Hajek (2002) suggests that most of the Italian words in what he calls *Parlaree* were introduced by these Italian immigrants, and he suggests that the evidence for earlier borrowings from Lingua Franca is weak.

Polari is a British argot of gay culture that grew out of Parlyaree. This development is natural enough considering that male homosexual activity was illegal, so there was need of a secret language to conceal such activity from outsiders, especially the undercover police. Given that gays are often to be found among performers, it is not surprising that they mainained a version of the itinerant performer argot. Polari came into wider view when it was featured in the BBC radio programme *Round the Horne* (1964–9). An 'outing' of this kind is not beneficial to an argot, but after male homosexuality between consenting adults was legalized in Britain in 1967 and the Gay Rights movement became active around the same time, the need for a secret form of language somewhat diminished and Polari vocabulary came into more general use.

Like its predecessor, Polari is a small set of distinct lexical items, many of which are of Italian origin, including *buvare* 'drink' (verb and noun), *capella/capello* 'hat', *dinarly* 'money', *manjarie* and *jarrie* 'food/eat', and *parlare pipe* 'telephone'. Jewish theatre was established in the East End of London in the late nineteenth century and Yiddish contributed words such as *meese/mies* 'plain, ugly', *meshigener/meshugener* 'mad, crazy', and *shyker* 'wig' [Yiddish *sheitel/shaitel*]. This is part of a more general contribution of Yiddish to colloquial English, a contribution that includes *gelt* 'money', *shlep* 'to have to carry a burden or to have to travel on a burdensome journey', and *shtum/shtoom* 'quiet', 'dumb', especially in the phrase 'to keep shtum'. English words used in a special sense included *blue* 'homosexual', *chicken* 'young male', *cottage* 'public toilet', *crimper* 'hairdresser', *dish* 'buttocks', *fruit* 'homosexual', *trade* 'sex', *tootsie trade* 'passive role in homosexual sex'. There was some rhyming slang such as *vera (Lynn)* 'gin' and some back slang such as *riah* 'hair' and *ecaf* 'face' and its abbreviated derivative *eek* as in *How bona to vada your eek* 'How nice to see your face'.

A number of words once confined to Polari have moved into general use, including *butch*, *mince*, *naff* (*off*), and *queen*. In the nineteenth century *varda* 'see, look at' passed into general slang.

'Secret Languages'

In many languages there are special forms that are nominally secret. Almost all of these employ some systematic means of phonological distortion such as transposing syllables or inserting extra syllables. These forms of language are designed to restrict communication to an in-group and exclude others. They are mostly used by older children and early teenagers as much for fun as for real secrecy, and they are sometimes referred to as play languages, but they are also used somewhat less systematically in various non-English-based argots.[17] Play languages were once popular among young English speakers, but they have fallen from use over the last few decades.

The best-known play language is Pig Latin, which involves transposition. There are a number of varieties. In most of them any consonants that precede the first vowel of a word are moved to the end of the word and are followed by *-ay*. If there is no such consonant or consonant cluster—that is, if the word begins with a vowel—then *-way*, *-yay*, or *-ay* is added at the end of the word. Here is an example where *-way* is used.

> I will now give you an example of Pig Latin.
> Iway illway ownay ivegay ouyay anway exampleway ofway
> Igpay Atinlay

[17] Laycock 1972 coins the label *ludling* from Latin *ludus* 'game' and *lingua* 'tongue, language'.

In a word like 'typical' where 'y' represents a vowel, the Pig Latin form is *ypicaltay*. In some versions the transpositions apply only to content words.[18]

Pig Latin is used for fun or so that kids can talk in front of outsiders (e.g. their parents or other children) without being understood, except by each other. Outsiders are likely to cotton on after a bit of exposure, but Pig Latin still serves to mark the in-group from the out-group.

Pig Latin has been featured in a number of films and television programmes. In the animated film *The Lion King* there is the following exchange featuring Simba, the lion cub, Zazu, a hornbill, and Banzai, one of three threatening hyenas:

SIMBA   But, Zazu, you said they [the hyenas] are nothing but slobbery, mangy, stupid poachers.
ZAZU   Ixnay on the upidstay.
BANZAI   Who you callin' 'upidstay'?

Expressions of the pattern *Ixnay on the so-and-so* have some currency in American English. *Ixnay* is the Pig Latin form of *nix* (from Yiddish *nichts* 'nothing') and is a general negative covering 'no', 'not', 'don't', and 'nothing'.

Transposing syllables is common in secret languages. Among the Bantu peoples of Angola and Zambia the children have a secret

---

[18] Movement of the first syllable to the end of the word is also found in *Arepecunmakke*, one of several play languages used among the Kuna of Panama and Colombia (Sherzer 1982: 177).

| osi 'pineapple' | → | sio |
| ipya 'eye' | → | yaip |

language in which the last two syllables of a word are reversed, as in the following Luchazi example (White 1955: 96):

Nayi   nakuswinga   vantsi
Yina   nakungaswi   ntsiva
'She has gone to catch fish with a sweeping basket.'

The Zande of the Democratic Republic of the Congo, the Central African Republic, and the Sudan used a play language at court which also involved transposing syllables, so that *vuse* 'belly' became *sevu* and *parakondo* 'egg' became *rapandoko* (Evans-Pritchard 1954). It was especially popular with the 'many sons of the many wives of a prince [who] had few duties and could devote their leisure to pastimes'.

Teenage speakers of Pitjantjatjara in the Areyonga community in central Australia use a special form of language among themselves, which they call 'short way language'. Words are formed by dropping the initial syllable, as in the following example (Langlois 2006):

kutjara   tjara   'two'
rapita   pita   'rabbit'
pukurlarinyi   kurlarinyi   'be happy'
kuula   laa   'school'

The process is simple but the disguise effective. Consider, for example, *pita* 'rabbit', which bears no obvious resemblance to *rapita*, a word borrowed from English. Similarly with *kuula* 'school', a word borrowed from English without the initial *s* since Pitjantjatjara and Australian languages generally do not have initial consonant clusters with *s*. In this example *la* is lengthened to *laa* to meet the minimum requirement for a word. In the short term the 'short way language' is secret, though anyone familiar with Pitjantjatjara would soon realize how it works. The practice of dropping an initial syllable is not a common historical development in languages, but curiously dropping an initial consonant or even an initial syllable is a recurrent feature of historical development in various parts of Australia. For instance, the word for 'two' given as the first example above appears as *athira* or *thira* in some of the Arandic languages of central Australia.[19]

A common principle for disguising words is to introduce new material into each syllable. Either a vowel–consonant sequence is introduced before the vowel of a syllable or a consonant–vowel sequence after the vowel. A syllable *go*, for instance, could have a sequence like *am* introduced before the vowel to produce *gamo* or a sequence *ma* introduced after the vowel to produce *goma*. Either way consonants are separated by vowels to produce sequences that are relatively easy to pronounce. In *Eggy Peggy* the sequence *egg* is introduced before the vowel of each syllable. Examples can be found in Nancy Mitford's *Love in a Cold Climate*.

> Don't you dare tell the teacher.
> Deggont yeggou deggare teggell thegge teggeacher.

In Javanais, a disguised form of French, the syllable *av* is infixed after the initial consonant or consonant cluster of the word so that

[19] In Javanese, one of several play languages deletes all but the first syllable of words, but retains the initial consonant of the second syllable (Sherzer 1982: 184).

aku arep lungo → ak ar lung

beau 'fine' becomes *baveau, non* 'not' becomes *navon,* and *jardin* 'garden' becomes *javardin* (Jennings 1965).

In those secret languages that insert a consonant–vowel sequence after the vowel of each syllable, the vowel is usually an echo of the vowel of the syllable, as in the following Japanese example (Farb 1974: 106):

> Anohito-wa sore-o watashi-ni kureru-deshoo.
> Akanokohikitoko-waka sokoreke-oko wakatakashiki-niki kuk-urekeruku-dekeshokooko.

Kuna has two secret languages of this type. In the first the insertion is *pp* plus a repeat of the vowel of the syllable (Sherzer 1982: 179):

> pia 'where'   → pippiappa
> perkʷaple   → pepperkʷappapleppe

In the second the inserted consonant is *r*:

> pe 'you'   → pere
> tanikki 'he's coming' → taranirikkiri

In Javanese there are secret languages using the same principle with *f* and *p* as the inserted consonants, plus a more complicated one where the inserted consonant is *s*, and this *s* is also used as the final consonant of the initial syllable, replacing the final consonant where there is one (Sherzer 1982: 184):

> aku arep tuke klambi...
> askusu asresep tuskese klasbi...
> 'I want to buy clothes...'

In some play languages a syllable is added after each word. There is very little disguise about such systems. In the first example below-*na* is added, and in the second -*gree* is added (see, for instance, Wentworth and Flexner 1960).

> Can you keep a secret?
> Canna youna keepna ana secretna?
> Cangree yougree keepgree agree secretgree?

Equally unsecret are systems where something is added at the beginning of a word. In *Skimono Jive sk* is said to be added before each word, but in practice an unstressed *e* is often needed to facilitate pronunciation:

> I've had a skinful and so have you.
> Skive sk(e)had ska sk(e)skinful skand sk(e)so sk(e)have sk(e)you.

A little more secret is *Nyōbō kotoba*, a secret language that developed in Japan among women of the court in the Muromachi era and then spread to other women. It involves prefixing words with the polite prefix *o-* and removing the final syllable of disyllabic words or the last two syllables of longer words. The word *kawame-shi* 'rice with red beans' becomes *okawa*. In some instances a suffix -*moji* is added. The word *sushi*, for instance, is truncated to *su-*, prefixed by *o-* and suffixed by -*moji* to produce *osumoji*.

Among the Lardil people of Mornington Island and the Yang-kaal people of Forsyth Island in the Gulf of Carpentaria men were taught a special form of ritual language called **Damin** when they underwent advanced initiation. Although it was taught in the context of initiation, it was used in the community and could be overheard by women and children. It consisted of a small vocabulary of generic words to be substituted for everyday words, so that it is rather like the mother-in-law languages mentioned in the previous chapter. However, a curious feature of Damin words is that some contained unusual speech sounds, including a voiceless *l*-sound made by sucking air in, rather like a sound we make when someone tells us about a gruesome injury. There were also nasalized clicks (Hale 1973: 401–58). As we saw on p. 187, clicks do not occur in the normal register of any languages other than the Khoisan languages of southern Africa and some neighbouring Bantu languages.

People aiming to be sarcastic or ironic often say the reverse of what you might expect, so it is not surprising to find that antonymy plays a part in disguising language. Among the Hanunóo of the Philippines antonymic expressions are introduced sporadically. So, for instance, one might say *da:qut qay waydiq* 'very bad indeed' instead of *mayad waydiq* 'very good' or *Hayga pinabi : lug nimu kanmu bayqun?* 'Why did you make your basket round?' instead of *Hayga qinaŋa : bang kanmu bayquŋ?* 'Why is your basket flatsided?' (Conklin 1964: 296). The Warlpiri of central Australia have a play language based on antonymy where, for instance, 'I go north' becomes 'You go south' (Hale 1971).

Non-English-Based Argots

Argots are reported from a number of languages and generally involve esoteric vocabulary and/or systematic distortion of words. In a typical argot words are drawn largely from the mainstream language of the community, but an alternative possibility is an argot based on a minority language. About a thousand years ago Gypsies began migrating from India across Europe, some reaching Britain in the late Middle Ages. They had their own language, Romani, which developed different dialects influenced by the languages of the countries in which Gypsies found themselves. Over the centuries Romani tended to be eroded and replaced by the languages of host countries. In Britain Romani lasted until the twentieth century, mainly in Wales, but most Gypsies came to speak Anglo-Romani, which is essentially English interlarded with some hundreds of Romani words so that it is like a code (Price 1984: 232–40). While most of the distinctive Anglo-Romani vocabulary consists of old Romani words, there are also new formations such as *sasti-groi* 'iron horse' for locomotive (Hancock 1984a: 378).

There was an analogous erosion of Romani in Spain, where the language is called Caló. Compare the following sentences, which share three Romani roots (Geipel 1995: 124).

ANGLO-ROMANI	Let's jal ta pee mull.
CALÓ	Chalemos ta piyar mol.
	'Let's go and drink wine.'

The secrecy afforded by this Romani vocabulary is fostered and members are discouraged from revealing Romani words to non-Gypsies.

In Ireland masons had an argot called Bearla Lagair (also Berlagar na saer) containing many Irish words. The masons in question were stone workers, not Freemasons, but the way they maintained secrecy is reminiscent of the latter (Sinclair 1909: 354).

This masons' talk is a secret language spoken only by stone-masons, they all claim. Apprentices obtained from a master-mason first papers, second papers, and finally a third paper, called an 'indenture', and an increase in wages with each paper. No apprentice was entitled to his indenture until he could speak the Bearla Lagair. They were forbidden to teach it to any one not a mason, even to a member of their own family. No stone-mason would work on any job except with members of the order. This language identified them. They also had secret signs, methods of handling their trowels, squares, and other tools, ways of pointing, and laying and smoothing mortar, which indicated a member, without a word being spoken.

There is another Irish-based argot known as Shelta, traditionally used by itinerants in Ireland, Great Britain, and North America. It is essentially English with a large number of distinct words, mostly from Irish plus a few borrowed from Romani and English cant. A few Shelta constructions have Irish syntax, such as *Have you the feen's dorah nyocked?* 'Have you the man's bread taken?' (Hancock 1984b, Hancock 1986). Shelta differs from Bearla Lagair in that it incorporates several of the phonological distortions mentioned in the previous section (Sinclair 1909: 359). For instance, the first syllable, or the only syllable of a monosyllabic word, may be reversed so that *mhac* 'son' becomes *cam*, and *cailín* 'girl' becomes *lackeen. Cailín* has come into English as a word for a young Irish woman and as a proper name. The colloquial words *bloke* and *moniker* come from Shelta.

We now turn to argots based on the majority language of their communities. Lunfardo is a Spanish-based argot that sprang up around Buenos Aires at the turn of the twentieth century, perhaps in prisons. The word *lunfardo* is from non-standard Italian *lombardo* and means 'criminal'. In Lunfardo the initial syllable of a word is moved to the end of the word, so *tango* becomes *gotán* and *café con leche* 'café au lait' becomes *féca con chele*. Note that the function word *con* 'with' is not affected. Speakers of Lunfardo do not convert every word, they merely intersperse their speech with 'reversals'. Lunfardo also borrows from Italian, French, Portuguese, and the indigenous language Guaraní. Secret languages similar to Lunfardo are found throughout South America.[20]

Another argot in which syllables are moved is Šatrovački. This originally developed among criminals in what used to be called Yugoslavia, but has spread into more general use. It is based on what used to be called Serbo-Croatian. Examples include the following and show the initial syllable being moved to the end of the word: *Ganci* (for *Cigan*) 'Gypsy', *Rijama* (*Marija*) 'Marija', *Binsr* (*Srbin*) 'Serbian', and *Rajvosa* (*Sarajevo*).[21]

The French have an argot called Verlan, which originated among the criminal classes. It also involves moving the initial syllable to the end of the word so that *café* 'coffee' becomes *féca*, *cigarette* becomes *garetci* (also abbreviated to *garo*), and *Bonjour, ça va?* 'Good day, how are you?' becomes *Jourbon, va ça?* In fact the name *Verlan* or *Verlen* is derived from *l'envers* 'backwards'. With a monosyllabic word, the initial and final consonants switch positions, as in *ouf* (*fou*) 'mad', *sub* (*bus*) 'bus', and *luc* (*cul*) 'arse'. The 'silent e' is used, so 'la classe' becomes *la secla*. As one would expect, the spelling is not fixed so this word could be spelt *cecla* or *seucla* or *ceucla*. This movement of syllables is only a supplement to the argot vocabulary; for instance, one may use the slang word *mec* 'bloke' or use consonant reversal to encode this word as *quem*.

---

[20] In Rio de Janeiro and São Paolo there is a Portuguese secret language called *Gualin*, the name being derived from *lingua* 'language'.
[21] Examples are from the Wikipedia entry for *Šatrovački*.

In Louchébem, a French argot dating back to the butchers of Villette in the nineteenth century, the initial consonant or consonant cluster is replaced by *l* and moved to the end of the word and a suffix is added. The name Louchébem is formed from *boucher* 'butcher' by this process, using the suffix *-em*: *b-oucher* > *loucher-b-em* > *loucherbem* or *Louchébem*.

vingt 'twenty'	→	linvé
prince 'prince'	→	linspré
beau 'fine'	→	leaubiche
fou 'mad'	→	loufoque

The last form on this list, *loufoque*, has passed into general French slang.

A common process in French slang is to add a suffix to a truncated form of a word, as with English *garb-o* from *garbage collector* (Guiraud 1985).

fort	fortiche	'strong'
poisson	poiscal	'fish'
pernod	perniflard	'pernod'
directeur	dirlot	'director'

Other suffixes that have become popular recently include *-if* (*rasoir* 'razor' → *rasif*), *-ingue* (*sale* 'dirty' → *salingue*), and *-aga* (*pernod* → *pernaga*).

Sign Argot

An alternative to speech and writing is the use of hand signs. We are all familiar with signs such as a raised palm to indicate *stop*, the thumb pointing over the shoulder used in hitch-hiking, an index finger raised to pursed lips to request silence, and so on. Fully developed sign languages include British Sign Language and Ameslan (American Sign Language), used by the deaf, and there are other elaborate signing systems. In some societies signs are used in hunting or in situations where respect is required, as in mourning. These are overt systems, but secret signs are used among some of the groups described above as users of argot. Religious communities who practise silence are reported to have signs. Documented examples from the Middle Ages include signs for food, clothing, religious terminology, ranks, and occupations (Bruce 2007). Most of the signs correspond to nouns and most, if not all, have an iconic origin. The use of signs was introduced to restrict mundane conversation and to promote decorum and religious contemplation, but, as Bruce notes, signs served as a lingua franca in monasteries where there were monks from different language backgrounds who were not fluent in Latin. The signs were not known to outsiders and thus served to maintain a sense of solidarity (Bruce 2007: 79, 96).

One deliberate method of secret signs used in the Renaissance was to touch parts of the body to spell out a word. Various body parts were associated with letters of the alphabet by their initials, so the system was essentially a substitution cipher. To signal *Fuge!* 'Flee' one would touch in succession the forehead (*frons*), the stomach (*uenter*), the knee (*genu*) or throat (*guttur*), and the epiglottis (*epiglossa*) (Shumaker 1982: 108). This sounds straightforward, but distinguishing the throat and epiglottis under conditions requiring secrecy would have been tricky.

Another system involving touching parts of the body is the traditional system of hand signals known as **tic-tac**, which was used to transmit betting odds. In Britain it was used by employees of bookmakers to convey prices over a distance—for instance, from the main betting ring to the minor ones. In Australia it is illegal, but was once used to signal odds to the cheaper enclosures or to illegal bookmakers outside the course. To indicate odds of 9/4, for instance, the hands touch the head. To indicate 10/1 the fists are held in front of the body, in some variants with the right thumb raised, the idea being that this gives a rough approximation to the figure 10. In Britain the argot for odds consists of some rhyming slang such as *Burlington Bertie* or *scruffy and dirty* (100/30), some back slang, for instance *net* (10/1) and *rouf* (4/1), plus a number of terms related to the tic-tac signals. For example, 5/4 is a *wrist* because the tic-tac signal is to place the right hand on the left wrist and 6/4 is an *ear'ole* because the tic-tac signal is to raise the right hand to the left ear. Tic-tac has been rendered practically obsolete by the proliferation of mobile phones.

Internet Argot

The invention of the internet has given rise to an extensive argot among those communicating by email, instant messaging, and other social media. There are a number of rebus-type substitutions for syllables such as B4 'before', C 'see', M8 'mate, U 'you', abbreviations such as LOL 'laughing out loud', and emoticons such as :-) for 'smile' and :-(for 'sad' (if they are not transparent, turn them 90 degrees clockwise). Similar abbreviations are used in texting by mobile phone.

Leet or **Leetspeak** is an internet argot involving deliberate misspellings such as *teh* for 'the' (which requires auto-correct to be switched off), and substituting numerals and other keyboard characters for some letters. *Leet*, for instance, can be written 1337 with figures for letters, and 'porn(ography)' can be misspelt as *pron* or as *pron* with *o* for *o*. The word *Leet* comes from *elite* and originally referred to an in-group of hackers who shared access to material such as pirated software and instructions on how to manufacture drugs and explosives.

Inserting non-alphabetic characters into words is not confined to Leet users. It is used by anyone trying to bypass a security filter designed to stop the flow of junkmail and Spam. Internet advertisements for Viagra are often irregular in their spelling. This kind of substitution is also used as gimmick in advertising. For example, singer Marilyn Manson, who takes his name from Marilyn Monroe and Charles Manson, spells his name MAR1LYN MAN50N on the cover of *Mechanical Animals*.

There is some distinctive morphology in Leet. The suffic *-xor* (also *-xxor* and *-zor*) is used in place of *-er* to form agent nouns, so that 'hacker' can be spelt *haxxor*. Curiously these derived nouns can be used as verbs as in *U have been haxxored* 'You have been hacked (into)' or *That suxorz* for 'That sucks'.

Leet also features a kind of rebus in the use of & 'ampersand' as a substitute for *-and* or *-anned* as in S& 'sand' and B& 'band' or 'banned'.

Computer jargon is prominent in internet argot, but there are also a few non-English words such as German *ist* 'is', *Krieg* 'war', and *über* 'over'. This last is now in general use and is employed in compound adjectives such as *übergood* 'very good' or as a stand-alone superlative *U R uber* (the umlaut is optional) 'You are great'.

9

THE EVERYDAY OBLIQUE

My English text is chaste, and all licentious passages
are left in the decent obscurity of a learned language.

GIBBON, *AUTOBIOGRAPHY*

Knowledge of grammar and lexicon is not sufficient for successful communication in a language. For various reasons people do not always speak plainly and directly. Requests or criticisms may be phrased indirectly out of politeness, and the wish to avoid giving offence may lead people to refrain from using certain types of language. In other contexts people express themselves obliquely to protect their dignity or feelings. Would-be lovers often broach the subject of a liaison indirectly to gauge the likelihood of success, rather than risking the embarrassment of refusal. People also indulge in indirect strategies for fun. They are sometimes deliberately obscure as a way of teasing, or they say the opposite of what is expected because they are being ironic, sarcastic, or playfully abusive.

In some societies various indirect modes of discourse are highly favoured. Among the Kiriwana of the Trobriand Islands, for instance, oblique speech is the norm and direct expression of criticism or difference of opinion is avoided. Tropes such as metaphor, metonymy, analogy, and litotes are used, especially in political debate and romantic overtures (Weiner 1984: 176–7). Some sub-Saharan African cultures also prefer elaborate circumlocution to simple, plain speech. Peek (1981: 23) writes, 'Brevity of speech also tends to be poorly regarded. While we are enjoined to "get to the point", such quick and direct speech is often the sign of a poor speaker in Africa'. He also notes that, 'In settling disputes, the Limba stress the importance of "going round for long in parables" in order to "cool" the hearts of those involved and re-establish social harmony'. Elinor Keenan (1974: 140–1) has similar things to say about the Malagasy:

> To speak indirectly is to speak with skill. Men and women alike consider indirect speech to be more difficult to produce than direct speech. Most villagers can tell you that one who speaks well *manolana teny* (twists words). In *kabary* [formal style], a good speechmaker *miolaka* (winds in and out). The meaning of the utterance becomes clear gradually as the speaker alludes to the intent in a number of ways.

Phrases such as 'twist words' and 'wind in and out' seem derogatory to us, as we strongly disfavour long-windedness in most situations. However, while we eschew 'long-term' indirectness, we use various 'short-term' forms that are indirect or obscure. By 'short-term' I mean confined to the word, phrase, or sentence. Some of these means are described in the following sections and include euphemism, sarcasm, and irony.

Among the Hanunóo of the Philippines there are several techniques for secret forms of language of the type illustrated in the previous chapter.[1] These are learnt by children, but are mostly used in courting, especially when young men serenade young women and visit them by night. A valued suitor must have a number of social skills including the ability to play the musical instruments used in serenading, to commit to memory a large repertoire of verses, and to 'master the art of facile, rapid conversation, in which the highest value is placed on the most indirect method of statement' (Conklin 1964: 297). Among the Hanunóo, and more generally in the Philippines, riddles are also used in erotic overtures (Burns 1976: 143), a practice also reported from the Efik in Nigeria (Simmons 1958: 124).

Among the Wana of central Sulawesi in Indonesia a two-line verse form called *kiyori* is used, mostly by men, for a variety of purposes ranging from compliments to expression of political attitudes. Typical *kiyori* verses are oblique. They are full of metaphor and cultural references. As Atkinson writes (1984: 60), 'Ambiguity is a premium in *kiyori* use because it serves as a means to avoid opposition and conflict, while at the same time conveying an impression of cleverness and profound insight'. A *kiyori* poem

---

[1] These techniques include transposing the consonant and vowel of the initial syllable with the consonant and vowel of the final syllable, as in *balaynun* 'domesticated', which becomes *nulayban*, or adding a prefix *qay-* to forms of each word reduced to just consonant-vowel-consonant, so that *bu:ŋa* becomes *qaybuŋ*. Another is to add a suffix to just the first consonant and vowel of each word, so that *rignuk* 'tame' becomes *rinsiŋ* or *rinsuwayb*, and *qusah* 'one' becomes *qunsiŋ* or *qunsuwayb*. Note the suffix supplies a coda to the first syllable (Conklin 1964: 295).

consists of two lines and the vowel pattern of the final two syllables in each half-line must be the same. The following example is oblique not only in expression, but also in that the man presenting it attributes it to a dead aunt who gave him the poem in a dream. When the woman was near death her husband had, under pressure from the government, considered giving up the traditional Wana religion in favour of Islam or Christianity. The aunt is saying that she nearly missed out on the traditional Wana funeral. The first half-line may refer to the grave or to a mainstream religion. *Jampu kamumu* is the invisibility between earth and heaven. The last line refers to the path of mythical heroes (Atkinson 1984: 55).

Yowu da rapsinjuyu	The hole that is to be shared.
liu ri jampu kamumu	Passing beyond the purple veil of invisibility
sangkodi taamo kululu	I almost no longer followed
jaya ri wali ngkatuntu	the path of the magical story.

Politeness and the Like

When we want to make a request or pass criticism, we often express ourselves obliquely out of diplomacy. Requests may be phrased as statements or questions. Comments such as 'It's a bit stuffy in here' or 'Those bushes along the drive could do with a bit of clipping back' are meant to prompt action on the part of an addressee or to indicate that the speaker is about to take action. According to Keenan (1974: 136) it is common among the Malagasy for requests to be made indirectly in the form of a statement from which listeners are expected to infer a request:

Young boys suddenly speak of a journey to be made that evening and describe the blackness of the night and their lack of candles. Women will chatter about the poor quality of Malagasy soap in relation to European soap in my presence. Men will moan over the shortage of funds for a particular project. The host or listener is expected to pick up these cues and satisfy the request.

These examples have parallels in our society. A non-driver about to leave an evening social gathering might ask if anyone is going in his or her direction in the hope of 'botting a lift', or might ask the host what time the local bus goes in the hope that the host will arrange a lift.

An indirect stratagem for making requests is to involve a third party as a kind of catalyst. A woman with a pram on a bus might want someone to help her in getting off. There is a big man nearby and a not-so-big woman. Shy about asking the man, she asks the woman to help her, hoping the man will overhear and offer to assist.

Direct criticism can be avoided in various ways. Someone who habitually leaves coffee stains, used teabags, or unwashed cups around the sink in the staff room is likely to hear the comment, 'Some people clean up after they've had a drink' addressed to no one in particular. Couples often express criticism of one another by using *someone* or *some people* as the agent. For instance, he says, 'We are out of sugar' and she replies, 'Someone must have forgotten to put it on the shopping list'. These vague agents are also used in talking to a third party. Suppose I am talking to a couple and I find they are moving to another city and I ask why. One of them replies, 'Some people want to be near their relatives'. Vague agents are fairly standard in addressing children or commenting on their behaviour to a third party: 'Someone's wet their nappy, haven't they?', 'Someone's showing off'. Criticism is often made to an uncomprehending third party such as a baby or a pet in the presence of the real addressee: 'Someone we know got out of the wrong side of the bed, didn't he?'

Another possibility is to ask questions such as, 'How did that door manage to come open?' or pseudo-questions such as 'I wonder how this dirty glass got here'. A third option is to be disingenuous. Suppose you find your partner has swept fallen leaves over your pansies; rather than upbraid the culprit you remark, 'The wind must have blown those leaves onto the garden'.

Humour and word play provide a further strategy for avoiding conflict. Malapropisms may be used for lighthearted effect, as in 'I hope you're not casting nasturtiums' for 'I hope you're not casting aspersions'. Deliberate mispronunciations such as 'That's obvious' for 'That's obvious' may serve a similar purpose.

Deliberate Obscurity

Languages often contain idiomatic expressions that appear to make little or no sense, such as 'It runs in the family like wooden legs' or 'Boys will be boys'. Proverbs are not always transparent, and in English we often quote only part of them, as in 'pots and kettles' or 'too many cooks', which adds a layer of obscurity. Learning a language involves learning a stock of such expressions and how they are used. It also entails mastering obscure indirect expressions that involve an implication on the part of the speaker and require an inference from the addressee. For instance, if someone takes up a position where they block your view, you might use an old expression (recorded in Grose 1811), 'Is your father a glazier?' This was quite obscure to me as a child. It implies that the addressee thinks he or she is made of glass and is see-through. Another old expression that is still current is 'Were you born in a barn?', generally addressed to someone who has failed to close a door.

Rhetorical questions of this kind are common in lieu of greetings. In the days when men were expected to have short hair, a man or boy with longer than average hair would often be greeted with, 'When are you going to get your violin?' because long hair was associated with musicians and artists. (In 'Portrait of a Lady' T.S. Eliot writes about going 'to hear the latest Pole / transmit the Preludes, through his hair and fingertips'.) An indirect expression that has survived the years is to ask a man wearing a bandage, 'How's the other guy?' Here are some other examples. The exact phrasing varies, but these are standard themes.

- A woman appears with a cut or abrasions: 'Has your husband been beating you again?'
- Someone seems more expensively dressed than usual: 'Did you win the lottery?'
- Someone turns up in an outfit you think looks cheap: 'Are the Salvos [Salvation Army] having a sale?'

Some speakers go out of their way *not* to be understood. A good example occurs in Ian Rankin's novel *Black and Blue* (1997: 28). Hard-bitten detective Rebus is confronted by a television reporter with a camera who is keen to record a statement about an ongoing case. Rebus says to the reporter, 'You'll think you're in childbirth'. 'Sorry?' queries the confused reporter, to which Rebus replies, 'When the surgeons are taking that camera out of your arse'.

A number of reports from Nigeria mention the use of proverb-like riddles as a form of greeting (e.g. Simmons 1958: 124 on the Efik). The following example is from the Anang (Messenger 1960: 226). One young man greets another thus:

A single vine does not fill a forest.

And the other replies:

A single coin falls without a sound [no jingling].

These utterances are two parts of a standard proverb-type riddle. Messenger reports having heard this exchange in a context where it referred obliquely to an event of a few days before where one of the young men had argued unsuccessfully before the elders against a decision by the village head to place him on the tax roll. The basic notion is that one is ineffectual on one's own against many.

In some situations indirect language is practically obligatory. If a referee at a football match fails to award a penalty you think your side deserves, you might shout, 'Did you swallow your whistle?' Similarly a jockey who makes his run too late on the favourite might be heckled with remarks such as, 'Do your sleeping at home'. It would be unthinkable for people in the crowd to ask, 'Why did you make your run so late?', though entirely appropriate for an owner or trainer.

Another form of oblique speech is understatement. It is probably more common in English than in many other European languages and also more prevalent in older people, and, in my opinion, among men. The male role model in films, the Hollywood hero, is certainly laconic. Suppose I set my friend Harry up with a date who has film-star looks and a sparkling personality.

I ask him what he thinks of her. He is most unlikely to say, 'I think she's wonderful', partly because that would be stating the obvious and partly because it wouldn't be sophisticated or 'cool'. He is more likely to say something like, 'She's all right', 'She'll do', or even, 'Could do worse, I suppose'.

Humour

Obscurity plays an obvious part in jokes involving riddles and silly questions: 'What do you get if you cross Big Ben with the Leaning Tower of Pisa?' (the time and the inclination) or 'What's the difference between ignorance and apathy?' (I don't know and I don't care). In fact almost all verbal humour involves double meaning in the form of either a pun or a structural ambiguity. Typically a situation is contrived in which one interpretation fits the context but another, funnier one is also possible. Consider a conversation about the problems of marriage where one speaker remarks, 'Monogamy leaves a lot to be desired'. This can be taken to mean that the institution of marriage is unsatisfactory, but there is a 'smart' interpretation, namely that having just one partner leaves a lot of other persons to be lusted after.

It is a feature of language that phrases and sentences can be ambiguous. On the basis of a dictionary sample I estimate that English provides about four thousand pairs of words that sound the same (homophones) and four thousand examples of words with clear multiple meanings (polysemy). An individual speaker will know some thousands of proper names not in the dictionary, so we can think of an average speaker having about ten thousand possibilities of punning. On top of this a language like English provides scope for structural ambiguity since there are very few grammatical suffixes. A sentence like *Driving across the plains the zebras made a strange sight* relies on common sense rather than grammatical affixes to determine the intended meaning.

Indirect or allusive references are common in humour when (as is so often the case) it comes to sex. This is partly to reduce possible offence and make a joke acceptable to a wider audience, and partly to enhance the humour. Oblique references to sex often possess a cleverness that would be missing from direct reference. Faced with a threat to his brain Woody Allen cries, 'Oh, no, not my brain. That's my second favourite organ'. Someone says that sex isn't dirty. Woody replies, 'It is when you're doing it right'.

Euphemism

Chapter 7 showed that some topics and some particular words are subject to taboo in various societies. Some words are taboo because their use might antagonize a spirit or some other supernatural being, or because speakers have such respect for a god or monarch that they do not want the name profaned. More often words become taboo because of properties of the referent. Words for excrement and other bodily effluvia fall into this category. Taboo leads to avoidance of certain topics or the use of euphemisms, a phenomenon that is probably universal (Brown and Levinson 1987: 216; Allan and Burridge 1991: vii). Euphemism is literally 'speaking well' and it involves replacing a word or expression with an alternative.

Not all euphemism is an attempt to avoid a taboo; some euphemisms, particularly those found in advertising, are a way of presenting something in a favourable light.[2] Consider the term *life insurance*. It is really death insurance, but it sounds more positive to call it insurance that stretches over the course of one's life, rather than insurance that is paid out on one's death. As I write this, I flip through the real estate magazine from my local paper. Average suburban 'homes' are 'treasured gems in brilliant locations' with 'inspired floor plans' and 'grand proportions'. All are 'immaculately presented'. Housing estates in parched paddocks on the fringes of the city are given names such as *Fountain Lakes, Caroline Springs*, and *Water Gardens*. A feature of euphemism is the substitution of big words or phrases for simple ones, as with *negative outcome* for *failure* and *negative outcome potential* for *risk*. The military have a number of technical-sounding expressions that cloak death and destruction. Successful bombing has been described as *pacification of the enemy infrastructure*. Here it is not only *pacification* that is a euphemism, but *infrastructure* also.

Taboo and euphemism entail an extra layer of difficulty for the language learner, because in areas subject to taboo words frequently change their status and there is frequent replacement. Race is an area where replacement is common; even the term *race* itself tends to be replaced by *ethnicity*. The noun *native* has fallen out of fashion, along with terms such as *picaninny* for 'native child' and *squaw* and analogous terms for 'native woman'. In Australia the *native* people of the nineteenth century became the *Aboriginal* people of the twentieth century and are currently *Indigenous*. In the United States people of African descent were

[2] I do not propose to deal with this area in detail as it has been well covered in several books, e.g. Allan and Burridge 1991 and 2006.

referred to as *Negroes* until the middle of the twentieth century, and then acquired a succession of official names such as *Afro-Americans* and the current *African Americans*. *Coloured people* have become *people of colour*.

An area where taboo is common and some kind of avoidance is probably universal is death. Although in English there is no proscription on using the words *to die* and *death*, we tend to use euphemisms such as to *pass away*, *pass on*, or *go to rest* or religious euphemisms that assume an afterlife: *met his/her maker, passed over, gone upstairs, gathered to his/her ancestors*. As can be seen from this example, taboo can lead to a proliferation of euphemisms. Criminals rarely speak of killing someone; they have people *rubbed out* and *wasted*. Governments have their enemies *taken out* or *terminated*. Until recently one talked of having an animal *put down*, that is, 'killed', but now the term *euthanized* is taking its place.

In all societies there are restrictions on reference to sex and bodily functions, though the nature of the restrictions varies a lot from one culture to another. The strength and scope of a taboo can vary over time. To speakers of contemporary English it comes as a surprise to find the mildly vulgar word *piss* in the Authorized Version of the Bible (1611): *Hath he not sent me to the men which sit on the wall, that they may eat their own dung, and drink their own piss with you?* (2 Kings 18:27). This word was once respectable, but suffered derogation from association with its referent, though it lives on as a respectable term in the abbreviation *pee*.

In western culture a number of strategies are used in avoiding direct reference to sex and bodily functions. The complete avoidance strategy is illustrated by someone at a social gathering enquiring about the location of a toilet by asking, 'Where's the…?', leaving the question unfinished. While this is a trivial example, it is alarming to recall that up until a generation or so ago even 'doctor's books' were incomplete with respect to the uro-genital system and its functions and some showed pictures of naked humans with the genitals omitted.

Something akin to complete avoidance can be found in expressions for the pubic area such as *down there* and *her you-know-what*, and expressions for nakedness such as *in the altogether* and *as God made her/him*.[3] There is similar avoidance in *to expose oneself* (compare 'He exposed himself to public criticism'), *to interfere with* (an under-age person), *doing it*, *doing the deed* (having sexual intercourse), and *getting a bit* (of sex). Other euphemistic devices include vagueness (*plumbing, waterworks*), phonetic alteration (*shit → shite, shute*), use of a synonym including one borrowed from another dialect or language (Latin *faeces*), an archaism (*swive*), a nursery word (*wee-wees*), an abbreviation (*BO* for *body odour*), or a periphrasis (*passing water*).

Pregnancy was subject to taboo a few generations ago and there were a number of substitutes for 'pregnant' such as *to be in the family way, to be in a delicate condition*, and *to be expecting*, the last one still being current. Menstruation was under a strong taboo until recently and still cannot be spoken of directly in many situations. The same applies to menopause. In the Bible when Abraham's wife, Sarah, hears a prophecy that she is going to have a son, she laughs, because, as the Authorized Version delicately puts

[3] A naked person is also said to be *in his/her birthday suit*. For years this struck me as strange since in my experience people did not disrobe on their birthday, but of course the reference is to *birthday* in its literal sense not in the more common sense of 'anniversary of one's birth'.

it, 'Abraham and Sarah were old and well stricken with age, and it had ceased to be with Sarah after the manner of women' (Genesis 18:11).

The taboo nature of certain word forms can lead to their avoidance even when they carry different meanings. The word *ejaculation* was in common use until the mid-twentieth century for 'a brief, exclamatory utterance'. Up till then ejaculation in the physical sense was not mentioned in polite conversation and never in the media, but as the taboo relaxed and references to ejaculation of semen became possible, the linguistic *ejaculation* fell into disuse. Much the same happened with *erection* in the sense of structure, which was common enough until erection of the penis became mentionable. A similar phenomenon can be observed with words that sound similar to taboo words. *Mensuration* was a standard term when I was in primary school, but as menstruation became mentionable, *mensuration* disappeared. Other words which are avoided because they resemble taboo words include *rection* (*erection*), *regina*, as in 'Victoria Regina' and 'Elizabeth Regina' (*vagina*), *masticate* (*masturbate*), and *tampion* (*tampon*). Admittedly there is not much cause for most of us, who don't own a rifle, to use *tampion*, but there are people who hesitate to mention a certain city in Florida that bears a similar name.[4]

Squeamishness about using certain expressions can interfere with the flow of information. As is well known from attempts to ban books such as *Lady Chatterley's Lover* as late as 1960,

---

[4] Fryer (1964: 85) gives a number of other examples, including *circumscribe* (circumcise), *privet* (privy), *sects* (sex), *titter* (tits), and *vowels* (bowels).

censorship of explicit sexual material was the norm until fairly recently. Reference books such as encyclopaedias often omitted mention of sexual functions and activities, and sexually transmissible diseases, while dictionaries omitted certain words altogether or replaced certain letters of taboo words with asterisks. In Grose's *Dictionary of the Vulgar Tongue* (1785/1811) the following entry can be found:

> C**T. The χοννος of the Greek, and the *cunnus* of the Latin dictionaries; a nasty name for a nasty thing: un con Miege.

A number of entries in Grose's dictionary refer to the vulva/vagina. One such is *bottomless pit*, which is defined as 'the monosyllable'. The entry for *monosyllable* is 'a woman's commodity'.

The entry quoted above also illustrates another feature of euphemism, namely the use of foreign languages, in this case Greek, Latin, and French. Anthropological works of yesteryear often described sexual matters in Latin, and Latin is still used in some quarters as a source of euphemism. I notice that the list of ingredients of some beauty products includes *aqua*, and a woman told me that a doctor described her baby's birthmark as a *naevus*. A man interviewed on television recounted that he went to the doctor with what he called an 'itchy arse'. The doctor examined him and said that he had *pruritus ani*. As the interviewee commented, this was vacuous. All the doctor had done was give the Latin name for what he knew he had in the first place.[5]

---

[5] The practice of doctors' use of obscure Latin in front of patients is lampooned in Molière's *Le Malade imaginaire* (1673).

Until a generation or so ago it was normal practice to refer to physical and mental shortcomings directly, and, as we saw in the section on slang, there was an extensive vocabulary to describe these perceived deficiencies. Recently official parlance has introduced euphemisms for these conditions. A person who would have been described as *handicapped* came to be described as *disabled* and, more recently, *differently abled*. School children at the lower end of the ability spectrum were sometimes called *special children*, a particularly confusing euphemism. Some euphemisms, such as *vertically challenged* for 'short' and *socially challenged* for a recluse, seem to backfire. People often use them jokingly and sometimes confusion arises as to whether a term is being used seriously or humorously, or even whether it is a parody rather than a genuine example.

Euphemism and various forms of indirection play a part in negotiation. When the fraud squad or the tax inspectors call, the person under investigation might mention that he has had a tip on a horse running on the following Saturday and that he will put something on for the investigators. He can't name the horse. If word got around, the price would tumble. The unspecified horse invariably wins and on his next visit the authorities are offered their share of the winnings. Sexual advances are often made obliquely, sometimes with compliments about physical appearance or assumed properties, sometimes by working expressions such as *It needs a screw* or *I could do with a stiff one* into the conversation to see if the other party picks up on a sexual insinuation.

A curious example of something akin to euphemism can be found in the way betting information in Australia is given over the radio or television. It has always been illegal to disseminate betting information from a licensed venue such as a racecourse, although it is becoming difficult to maintain this restriction with the avail-ability of mobile phones. However, no radio broadcaster has been charged over relaying odds using terms such as the following:

1/1 'flip of the coin odds' or 'one of theirs for one of yours'
4/1 'each-way odds'
8/1 'double each-way odds'
10/1 'double-figure odds' or 'just into double figures'

These terms can be supplemented by addition and subtraction so that 3/1 is 'a point under each-way odds' and 5/1 is a 'a point over each-way odds'. Although a broadcaster would be penalized for using figures, descriptive phrases that carry the same information have never incurred a penalty.

Abusive Language

Another form of indirect language is to use nominally abusive language to a friend. It is pretty much standard for males to say 'You silly bugger' or 'You mean bastard' to one another without being offensive, or even use 'sonuvabitch', which theoretically is maximally offensive but is weakened by convention, a weakening that is captured in the spelling. Consider the following dialogue overheard at the bar ('the nineteenth hole') of a country golf links when one man—we'll call him Tom—spots a friend, whom we'll call Bill. Bill is a grim, unsmiling man who would pass for a gangster in a Humphrey Bogart film. When we consider the whole exchange, we can see that they are friends, but you wouldn't know it from Bill's first two turns.

TOM Hey, Bill!

BILL People you meet when you haven't got a gun.

TOM I thought I might see you here.

BILL What are you doing here? Are the pubs fuckin' closed?

TOM I just thought I'd get a bit of exercise for a change.

BILL Come on. I'll buy you a beer.

Abusive exchanges are used by Turkish boys from around the age of eight to the age of fourteen. The exchange begins with an insult such as calling someone the equivalent of English *prick* or claiming they play a passive role in homosexual sex. It may escalate to alleging prodigious promiscuity on the part of the other boy's mother or sisters or threatening to split him, his mother, or his sisters with one's giant penis. These threats and allegations are not to be taken literally, though they are meant to be insulting and provocative. A boy who suffers such a verbal assault is expected to reply with a rhyming line (Dundes, Leach, and Özkök 1972), and this can lead to an exchange of rhyming banter, although there is also the danger that the taunts can lead to violence (Glazer 1976: 88). In the first example below A calls B a bear. This is not a sexually oriented insult, but a bear is considered a big, clumsy, stupid animal, and B replies 'May a violin bow enter your anus', the violin bow being notable for its length and the fact it is moved back and forth.

A. Ayi
   bear

B. San-a   girsin   keman   yayi
   you-to enter   violin   bow
   'May a violin bow go up you.'

In the second example A calls B a cucumber, a cucumber being a traditional insult because of its phallic shape. B suggests where the cucumber might be placed.

A. Hiyar
   cucumber

B. Göt-ün-e   uyar
   arse-your-to fit
   'It fits your arse.'

Some insults have conventional rhyming replies, but Turkish youths are expected to be able to extemporize and carry on duels with a series of exchanges.

Among African-American males nearing the age of puberty and in early teens there is a tradition of trading insults largely aimed at one's opponent's mother. This is known as 'playing' or 'sounding', and is also referred to in the literature as 'the dozens' or 'playing the dozens'. Typical assertions are that the speaker has had sex with his adversary's mother, as in the first example below, or that the mother is promiscuous, as in the other examples (Abrahams 1962).

> I fucked your mother in a horse and wagon
> She said, 'Scuse me, mister, my pussy's draggin'.

> At least my mother ain't no cake, everybody get a piece.
> At least my mother ain't no doorknob, everybody gets a turn.
> Your mother's like a railroad track, laid all over the country.

Other themes are the obesity, age, stupidity, or ugliness of the other boy's mother. These have developed into a genre of humorous abuse circulated via books and Web sites.

Among Australian Aborigines obscene banter is expected behaviour between certain kin, most often between grandparent and grandchild of the same sex. The banter often involves jibes about alleged deficiencies in the genital area (Thomson 1935; Haviland 1979a, b; McConvell 1982).

Speaking in Opposites

A number of idiomatic expressions have a meaning that is more or less the opposite of their literal meaning. Consider, for instance, 'You don't say so!' and 'You can say that again'. Idioms apart, there are common strategies for interaction that involve saying exactly the opposite of what we mean. Suppose you ask me to nominate who will win Wimbledon and my selection is eliminated in the first round. You might say to me, 'What a great judge you turned out to be!' Obviously you are criticizing my poor judgement in this instance and the context makes that clear. This is an example of **sarcasm**—saying the opposite of what you mean in an attempt to mock. To appreciate how this works consider the possibility of making a direct statement such as 'Your favourite didn't do very well'. This is to state the obvious. You can't do that without appearing naïve, but you can quite reasonably use sarcasm. It is conventional to do so and therefore not particularly offensive.

Examples of what I am calling sarcasm are often referred to as irony (see, for example, Brown and Levinson 1987: 221–2). **Irony** is used in a number of senses. Some would say it is ironical if the inventor of the guillotine is the first person to be executed by it. In fictional contexts irony involves a character being unaware of something that is obvious to another character in a story or to the audience. This is sometimes called dramatic irony. The story of King Oedipus provides a classic example. Oedipus hears a prophecy that he is destined to kill his father and marry his mother, so he leaves the people he believes to be his parents and goes to another kingdom. However, he does not realize that he has been reared apart from his real parents and, in an attempt to avoid his fate, enters his parents' kingdom and fulfils the prophecy.

The contrast between ignorance and knowledge is the essential feature of irony. If we apply the notion to verbal irony, then irony is accidental, whereas sarcasm is deliberate. An example I remember from my student days is of a man who was criticized for his accent, particularly for pronouncing *fine* as 'foine'. He replied indignantly, 'Oi never say *foine*'. But he repeated the alleged error in his pronunciation of the diphthong in 'I', thus giving the lie to his protestation of innocence. There is also the story of a bishop who told his flock, 'In the eyes of God we are all equal from me right down to the lowest of you'. Many malapropisms involve irony in that the speaker says something he or she didn't intend. In a Miss World contest the competitors had to say one line about their home country. The US contestant described her country as the land of 'opportunism'.

In practice irony is used in a way that overlaps with sarcasm, and this is understandable when one considers that there is a continuum from outright sneering to a kind of conventional use of opposites not directed at anyone in particular. If someone clumsily drops the dinner plates and they smash, you might say, 'Congratulations!' If you hear that the airline staff have walked off the job just when you are about to fly off for a holiday in the Bahamas, you might exclaim, 'Lovely!' The former is directed against the perpetrator and probably qualifies as sarcasm; the latter is an expression of dismay not aimed directly at the perpetrators. It is not obviously sarcasm and falls into the category of irony in the wider sense.

The English lexicon contains certain established sarcastic or ironic formulas. For instance, there is a standard expression to use when giving someone a small sum of money, namely, 'Don't spend it all at once'. If somebody seems to be in an unnecessary hurry, you say, 'Where's the fire?' Obviously there is no fire. You are chiding the over-anxious person and trying to get them to proceed more slowly. If somebody arrives or returns sooner than expected, you can say, 'What kept you?' A common way of indicating that you think someone is complaining too much over a minor condition is to say, 'Nothing worse!' In many situations no ready-made expression is available, but sarcasm may feel appropriate. For instance, a boy cuts his finger and makes a lot of fuss about it so someone says, 'Do you want me to call an ambulance?'

An addressee is supposed to pick up on sarcasm or irony from the discrepancy between an event and a comment, but sometimes this misfires. Suppose a woman from a group of acquaintances gets up and sings 'Amazing Grace'. A member of the group who is critical of the performance remarks to another, 'What a fantastic singer she is!' The addressee might be uncertain about the quality of the singing and in doubt as to whether to take the statement at face value. Recently it has become popular among younger speakers to say the opposite of what is meant and then after a pause add, 'Not'. So someone with a poor opinion of the singer might say, 'What a fantastic singer she is! . . . Not!'

A good example of irony can be found in Aldous Huxley's short story 'The Portrait'. A nouveau-riche man approaches Mr Bigger, an art dealer, with a view to purchasing some paintings for his recently acquired 'Manor House'. Mr Bigger makes a comment that is sarcastic, if you like, or ironical, and then there is further irony in that the original irony is not picked up.

> 'In a house of this style,' he was saying, 'and with a position like mine to keep up, one must have a few pictures. Old Masters, you know; Rembrandts and What-his-names.'
>
> 'Of course,' said Mr Bigger, 'an Old Master is a symbol of social superiority.'
>
> 'That's just it,' cried the other beaming, 'you have said just what I wanted to say.'
>
> Mr Bigger bowed and smiled. It was delightful to find someone who took one's little ironies as sober seriousness.

A lot of speaking in opposites is meant to be joking. If I am pouring myself a brandy, just as my disapproving daughter comes by, I might remark, 'Purely medicinal'. This kind of slightly humorous antonymy is common in epithets. A heavy drinker might be described as a *teetotaller*, a frigid woman as a *nympho*, and an unintelligent person as an *Einstein*.

Oxymora and Other Contradictions

The **oxymoron** is a traditional rhetorical device in which the modifier in a construction appears to contradict the modified, and the listener or reader has to try and resolve the anomaly. In a typical example an adjective appears to contradict a noun, as in *democratic tyrant*. English contains a number of lexicalized examples such as *bitter sweet*, *deafening silence*, *hasten slowly*, and perhaps *timeless moment*, which has some currency in the media. There is an unwitting irony in some phrases used in advertising and the media such as *essential luxury* and *instant classic*, but most oxymora are deliberate attempts at irony. Sometimes the irony is only apparent when a phrase is listed with other oxymora. For instance, there does not usually seem to be anything incongruous about the term *political science*, but when it is given in a list of oxymora, one can see a certain irony. Other examples often presented in an ironic sense include *business ethics*, *honest politician*, and *government efficiency*.

10

ELUSIVE ALLUSIONS

Bitter constraint, and sad occasion dear

MILTON, *LYCIDAS* 6

By sweet enforcement and remembrance dear

KEATS, *ODE TO PSYCHE* 2

Literary Allusions

An **allusion** is an incidental or passing reference. If I say, 'Jim is so mean he makes Scrooge look like a spendthrift', I am making a statement about Jim but alluding to Scrooge in the course of making it. Allusions are not confined to language; they can be found in music and the visual arts. Many allusions are to figures from myth, history, or literature, to places, customs, or events.

Another type of allusion occurs when literary works (and other creative productions) relate to earlier works. Julia Kristeva, in her 1969 essay, 'Word, Dialogue, and Novel', termed this 'intertextuality'. It can range from similarities of plot and character, to allusion, quotation, and parody. Vladimir Nabokov's novel *Despair* is rich in allusion to characters and events in earlier works, particularly Fyodor Dostoevsky's *Crime and Punishment*, and the poems of T.S. Eliot are full of allusions to a great range of European literature. His seventeen-page poem *The Waste Land* is supplemented by seven pages of notes on the allusions.

Allusions can also be internal to a work. The use of musical themes in operas associated with characters and ideas, particularly in Wagner's operas, are of this type. For instance, in *Lohengrin*, as we saw in Chapter 7, the knight who appears to save Elsa forbids her to ask his name. Later, when Ortrud dares Elsa to ask the knight to reveal his name, she uses a variation on the same melody the knight used when he announced the ban.

Allusions to names are normally recognizable even if one cannot identify the referent. If we read that someone has made the greatest comeback since Lazarus, we know from the context that Lazarus is someone the writer expects readers to recognize. More interesting is the covert textual allusion where the wording of an earlier text is worked seamlessly into the present text. Picking up on the allusion is not essential to understanding the text, and that is the whole point and the reason why literary allusions are covered in this book. They are esoteric. They communicate to an in-group who derive satisfaction from picking up the allusion, while others may read the text without realizing there are allusions lurking in it.

Allusion differs from quotation in that a quotation is usually marked. Speakers often announce they are quoting, and writers use quotation marks, but they don't always do this, and the difference between allusion and quotation is sometimes blurred. Good examples of allusion and quotation and the blurring of the distinction between them can be found in *Willy Wonka and the Chocolate Factory*, the film version of Roald Dahl's *Charlie and the Chocolate Factory*. This is a film aimed at children, yet the speech of Willy Wonka, the proprietor of the chocolate factory, is peppered with passages from texts, some well known, others obscure. For instance, Willy Wonka says, 'A thing of beauty is a joy forever', which is a well-known line from Keats (first line of *Endymion*), and 'Round the world and home again, That's the sailor's way', which is from the poem 'Homeward Bound' by the not very well-known poet William Allingham (1828–1889). There is no indication as to which of Willy's utterances are from previous texts as he conducts his guests around his chocolate factory, though it is obvious that his speech is not everyday language but is full of rhymes and rhetorical flourishes. There is little chance of children recognizing the quotations; they are a kind of secret communication between the writer of the screenplay and some members of the adult audience. It is characteristic of films aimed at children that they contain language and allusions aimed at adults. The whole plot of *The Lion King* is an allusion to *Hamlet*, and it contains learned words like *affianced* and clever puns. In *Madagascar* four animals, bred in captivity, escape from the Central Park Zoo and are washed ashore in Africa. Finding themselves in nature for the first time one of them thinks they are in the San Diego Zoo, an ironic allusion likely to be lost on children, who are unlikely to know that that particular zoo is famous for keeping animals in natural surroundings.

One of the most esoteric allusions in literature, and one that falls within the domain of linguistics, can be found in the 1968 science fiction film *2001: A Space Odyssey* written by Arthur Clarke and Stanley Kubrik. When HAL, the computer controlling the space mission, starts to malfunction, astronaut Dave Bowman begins to dismantle its cognitive functions and it regresses. Its last speech is a rendition of the popular song 'Daisy, Daisy, give me your answer do'. In 1962 this song was the first text used at the Bell Laboratories to demonstrate speech synthesis, and it was later used in other phonetics laboratories. Audience members who know this might pick up the suggestion that the song was one of the first texts taught to HAL; when his cognitive powers are progressively removed, he is left with his first text, just as humans suffering from dementia retain best what was learnt first.

Allusions in most literature are straightforward references to persons, places, or events, but the corresponding allusions in Germanic alliterative verse are often indirect. A feature of Germanic alliterative verse is the use of a descriptive phrase or compound to replace a regular word or name. As we saw in Chapter 3, these phrases are called **kennings**. For instance, the sea was often referred to as the *whale-road* or *swan-road*, and a warrior was a *feeder of ravens* since ravens fed on the bodies of the slain. In the Old Norse Skaldic verse these kennings are more esoteric and often make reference to Norse mythology. For example, Odin was sometimes called *the hanged god*, a reference to his having hanged himself from the tree Yggdrasill for nine days and nights in order to gain wisdom and power (*Hávamál* 138–9), and mistletoe was referred to as *Baldur's bane*, a reference to the story that all plants and animals swore never to harm Baldur, save the mistletoe.

The wrist was referred to as the *wolf's joint*, a reference to the fact that Fenrir the wolf bit off Tyr's hand.

Some traditional allusions have largely lost their original associations and have become part of the language, so that one can use them without knowing their significance. Take *Achilles' heel*, for instance. It refers to the story of Achilles' mother, Thetis, dipping her son in the river Styx to make him invulnerable. She held him by the heel so this area remained vulnerable. A *Trojan horse*, which lives on in the name of computer viruses, refers to the wooden horse 'pregnant with armed men' that the Trojans let into their besieged city with fatal consequences (Virgil, *Aeneid*, Book II). Some allusions lie buried in words and phrases like *gargantuan*, *Herculean*, *quixotic*, *sisyphean*, *tantalize*, and *titanic*. Some appear in set phrases such as *since Adam was a boy* and *to the right of Genghis Khan*.

An allusion can be made to an event or a practice. In T.S. Eliot's *Murder in the Cathedral* a messenger is asked about the ongoing friction between Becket, the archbishop of Canterbury, and Henry II with the words, 'But again, is it war or peace?' The messenger replies, 'Peace, but not the kiss of peace'. The reference is to the *osculum pacis* 'the kiss of peace' practised as a greeting among Christians and incorporated into the mass until the fourteenth century. It was also known as the *osculum sanctum* 'holy kiss', the term used in the Vulgate translation of 2 Corinthians 13:12, where the Corinthians are enjoined to greet fellow Christians with such an embrace.[1]

---

[1] The exchange of kisses at mass was replaced in the fourteenth century by a pax board, an icon passed around and kissed. The exchange of greetings of peace among the celebrant and the congregation was reintroduced into the mass by Vatican II and in some non-Anglo cultures it involves kissing among family members and friends.

One of the main sources of literary allusion has been the Bible. In the Authorized Version of the Song of Deborah there is a verse which goes, *They fought from heaven; the stars in their courses fought against Sisera* (Judges 5:20). The phrase *the stars in their courses* has caught the imagination. It has been adopted as the title of several works on astronomy, including one by Sir James Jeans (1931) and one by Isaac Asimov (1971). In these cases the phrase simply supplies an apt title, but the same phrase was worked into the text of a speech given by Winston Churchill in 1941 at a time when Nazi Germany had occupied most of Europe, and Britain was under threat. He said, 'The stars in their courses proclaim the deliverance of mankind'.[2] To those familiar with the Bible it recalled a triumph of the Israelites and provided inspiration at a time when, to use another of Churchill's phrases, 'the long night of barbarism had descended over Europe unbroken even by a star of hope'.

Some biblical allusions have become standard references, so that we can refer to a *David and Goliath* contest, or say *the writing is on the wall*, or speak of *killing the fatted calf*. We can call someone a *Judas* or a *Doubting Thomas* or refer to someone as the *Prodigal Son* (Luke 15:11–32). When we talk of someone wearing only a fig leaf or eating forbidden fruit, we are indirectly referring to Adam and Eve, and if we say something is not set in stone, we are indirectly referring to Moses receiving the Ten Commandments on two tablets of stone (Exodus 32:15, 34:1–5). A more direct reference

[2] The speech was recorded in London and broadcast to the University of Rochester Commencement when Churchill was awarded an honorary degree of Doctor of Laws, June 16 1941.

> In Trollope's *Barchester Towers* two clergymen banter with biblical
> quotations by giving chapter and verse and leaving the text
> unspoken, as in the following anecdote.
>
> A vicar went out one Saturday to visit members of his parish. At
> one house it was obvious that someone was home, but nobody came
> to the door even though the vicar knocked several times. Finally, the
> vicar took out his card and wrote *Revelation 3:20* on the back of it,
> and stuck it in the door.
>
> *(Behold, I stand at the door and knock. If anyone hears my voice
> and opens the door, I will come in to him and dine with him and he
> with me.)*
>
> The next day, the card turned up on the collection plate. Below
> the vicar's message was the notation *Genesis 3:10.*
>
> *(I heard your voice in the garden, and I was afraid, because I was
> naked; and I hid myself.)*

occurs when someone unable to find accommodation at a hotel
reports that there is 'No room at the inn' (Luke 2:7). Expressions
such as being *all things to all men*, to *arise as one man*, *the blind
leading the blind*, *a man after one's own heart*, to escape by *the skin
of one's teeth*, and *signs of the times* can be found in the Bible and
probably owe their currency to their appearance in that once
much-read text, but they are too much a part of the language
and too little associated with particular persons or events to count
as allusions.

Along with the Bible the other main source of literary allusions
is Shakespeare. The opening words of Richard III, which incidentally contain a pun, have become a most hackneyed source of
allusion:

> Now is the winter of our discontent
> Made glorious summer by this son of York

A novel by John Steinbeck has the title *The Winter of Our Discontent* and journalists writing about any unpleasant winter have a tendency to trot out this phrase.[3]

In the 1980s there was a BBC television series called *To the Manor Born*. This combines a pun and an allusion since it is based on Hamlet's remark,

> though I am a native here,
> And to the manner born,—it is a custom
> More honour'd in the breach than the observance.

The expression *pound of flesh*, as in, 'He wants his pound of flesh', comes from Shakespeare's *Merchant of Venice* where Shylock tries to hold Antonio to a contract secured on a pound of Antonio's flesh. Many common expressions are found in Shakespeare, including *didn't sleep a wink*, *in my mind's eye*, *method in his/her madness*, and *to eat someone out of house and home*. Like the examples from the Bible given above, they probably owe their currency to their appearance in a much-read text, but they are not recognized as having come from a particular source.[4]

The Winter of Our Discontent and *To the Manor Born* represent the tip of an iceberg. Innumerable titles of books, plays, and films are allusive, as are names of various groups and organizations. The extent of Shakespeare's popularity when it comes to

[3] An advertisement for a sale of camping gear featured this clever variation: *Now is the discount of our winter tents.*

[4] 'I have not slept one wink' (*Cymbeline* III.4.103); 'In my mind's eye, Horatio' (*Hamlet* I.2.185); 'Though this be madness, yet there is method in it' (*Hamlet* II.2.211); 'He hath eaten me out of house and home' (*King Henry IV, Part 2*, II.1.82).

choosing an allusive title is epitomized by the large number of titles taken from Hamlet's 'To be or not to be' soliloquy. The italicized phrases in the following passage have all been used as titles of various kinds, some of which are identified below.

> *To be, or not to be*, that is the question:
> Whether 'tis nobler in the mind to suffer
> The *slings and arrows* of *outrageous fortune*
> Or to take arms against a *sea of troubles*,
> And by opposing end them. To die, to sleep—
> No more—and by a sleep to say we end
> The heartache, and the thousand natural shocks
> That flesh is heir to. 'tis a consummation
> Devoutly to be wish'd. To die, to sleep—
> To sleep—*perchance to dream*. Ay, there's the rub!
> For in that sleep of death *what dreams may come*,
> When we have shuffled off this *mortal coil*,
> Must give us pause—there's the respect
> That makes calamity of so long life.
> For who would bear the whips and scorns of time,
> The oppressor's wrong, the proud man's contumely,
> The pangs of disprized love, *the law's delay*,
> The insolence of office, and the spurns
> That patient merit of the unworthy takes,
> When he himself might his quietus make
> With a bare bodkin? Who would fardels bear,
> To grunt and sweat under a weary life,
> But that the dread of something after death
> *The undiscover'd country*, from whose bourn
> No traveller returns, puzzles the will,
> And makes us rather bear those ills we have
> Than fly to others that we know not of?

To Be or not to Be: 1942 film with Carole Lombard and Jack Benny
Slings and Arrows: Canadian TV series

Outrageous Fortune: film with Bette Midler and Shelly Long (1987), New Zealand TV series

Sea of Troubles: P.G. Wodehouse short story (1917)

Perchance to Dream: Ivor Novello stage musical (1945)

What Dreams May Come: novel by Richard Matheson (1978), and a film with Robin Williams (1998)

Mortal Coil: dream pop band headed by Ivo Watts-Russell, and supernatural role-playing game

The Law's Delay: non-fiction book by Sara Woods (1977)

The Undiscover'd Country: subtitle of *James Joyce: The Undiscover'd Country*, literary work by Bernard Benstock (1977)

The film *Chariots of Fire* (1981) takes its title from a poem by William Blake, which originally appeared in the preface to his epic *Milton* (1804), but is better known as the hymn 'Jerusalem'. It is quoted here in full as this short poem contains two phrases, namely *dark satanic mills* and *England's green and pleasant land*, which are in common use. However, for many they would not be recognized as allusions, or at least the source would not be known. For such speakers these phrases would be just part of the stock of idiomatic phrases in the lexicon, rather like *salt of the earth* or *all that glitters is not gold*.

> And did those feet in ancient time
> walk upon England's mountains green?
> And was the holy Lamb of God
> on England's pleasant pastures seen?
> And did the countenance divine
> shine forth upon our clouded hills?
> And was Jerusalem builded here
> among these dark satanic mills?
>
> Bring me my bow of burning gold!
> Bring me my arrows of desire!

Bring me my spear! O clouds, unfold!
Bring me my chariot of fire!
I will not cease from mental fight,
nor shall my sword sleep in my hand,
till we have built Jerusalem
in England's green and pleasant land.

The phrase *chariot of fire* is itself an allusion to a passage in the
Bible in which the prophet Elijah is taken up to heaven in a chariot
of fire: 'And it came to pass as they still went on and talked, that,
behold, there appeared a chariot of fire, and horses of fire, and
parted them both asunder; and Elijah went up by a whirlwind into
heaven' (2 Kings 2:11). The theme of the first stanza is also an
allusion, to the apocryphal story that Jesus Christ and Joseph of
Arimithea visited Glastonbury, which is in England's green and
pleasant land. This story figures in *The Da Vinci Code*.

Just as titles can be taken from texts, texts can incorporte titles as
allusions. In Ian Rankin's novel *Black and Blue* we find the
following exchange (1997: 459):

'And don't think a reprimand is going to be the end of the affair.'
'Not such much as the end of the affair,' Rebus told him, 'more
like the heart of the matter.'

'The end of the affair', meaning the end of the business in this
instance, is a common expression, but it happens to be the name of
a novel by Graham Greene. Rebus picks up on this and introduces
the title of another Greene novel, *The Heart of the Matter*.

Other popular literary sources of allusion include *Alice's Adventures in Wonderland, Oliver Twist, Peter Pan*, and *Treasure Island,*
though allusions to these works are to characters and situations as

well as text. *Alice* is the source of the notion of the 'unbirthday', and a disorganized event is often described as being like 'the Mad Hatter's tea party'. The hatter in *Alice* is often thought of as having given rise to the expression 'mad as a hatter', but this phrase was used earlier, in *Blackwood's Edinburgh Magazine*, January-June 1829, and has its origins in the idea that the mercury used in hatmaking affected the nervous systems of hatters. In Dickens's *Oliver Twist* young Oliver, sent to toil in a workhouse, has the temerity to ask for a second helping of gruel ('Please Sir, I want some more') – an incident which is often cited when someone asks for a second helping of food. J.M. Barrie's 1904 play *Peter Pan, or the boy who wouldn't grow up* has led to a male who is slow to mature sometimes being called a Peter Pan. It gave rise to *Wendy house*, an alternative name for what is otherwise known as a play house or cubby house, and to the term *Neverland* (or *Never Never Land*) for an imaginary paradise. This was also the name the late Michael Jackson gave to his ranch in California, which incorporated an entertainment park for children. Robert Louis Stevenson's *Treasure Island* is a source of indirect allusion in that it has inspired a genre of pirate adventure literature. The most recognizable character is the one-legged pirate Long John Silver. It would be difficult to find a costume-hire firm in the English-speaking world that could not supply a Long John Silver pirate outfit, complete with parrot, peg leg, and crutch. Some literary works generate specific verbal allusions, as with Joseph Heller's *Catch 22*, the source of 'a catch 22 situation'.

Although allusions are often esoteric, what is arcane for one group can be common knowledge for another. Not all literary allusions are to works having pretensions to high culture, despite a certain snobbery about the superior value of highbrow knowledge. Ambrose Bierce captures this narrow view in *The Devil's Dictionary* (see p. 88), where he defines *ignoramus* as 'A person unacquainted with certain kinds of knowledge familiar to yourself, and having certain other kinds that you know nothing about'. In the film *Die Hard 2* Bruce Willis goes to an airport desk to collect a fax. The young woman on the desk makes a pass, to which our hero replies, 'Just the *fax*, ma'am'. This is a play on the words 'Just the facts' frequently uttered in a deep monotone by Joe Friday, a detective in the TV series *Dragnet*. Popular culture abounds with allusions of various kinds. The group Aerosmith had a hit called 'Lord of the Thighs', playing on William Golding's 1954 novel *Lord of the Flies*. The film *The Usual Suspects* takes its title from a line in another film, namely Claude Rains's instruction 'Round up the usual suspects' in *Casablanca*.

Some modern allusions are not at all esoteric. If we say, 'He thinks he's Tarzan' or 'I'm not Superman', we are making an allusion that will be widely understood. The same applies if we call a very bright person *Einstein* or use the name *Sherlock* for someone who solves some little mystery. Some allusions are accidental, particularly where they involve words of songs. You remark, 'What a beautiful morning!' and someone starts singing the opening number from the musical *Oklahoma*, or someone ordering a beverage says, 'Tea for two', and somebody else starts singing, 'Tea for two, and two for tea...'.

One type of modern allusion is the catchphrase—a phrase that captures the attention of a wide audience and is widely repeated. Some catchphrases are derived from a genre. If I say 'It's bigger than both of us' (referring to love) I am repeating what is thought to be a cliché from romantic movies of yesteryear, or if I say 'They went thataway' I am repeating a catchphrase from an old Hollywood western. A more typical catchphrase has a definite source.

- A catchphrase that has caught on is *Show me the money*, which comes from the film *Jerry Maguire*. The words are spoken by football player Cuba Gooding Jr to his manager, Tom Cruise.

- Someone annoys you by repeating unwanted advice, so you say *Play it again, Sam*, which is widely believed to be a quotation from the movie *Casablanca* (it is actually a misquotation).

- You want to indicate that you can solve a problem easily or have done so, so you say *Elementary, my dear Watson*, a phrase used by Sherlock Holmes to Dr Watson in films and television dramatizations of the works of Sir Arthur Conan Doyle (though never in the original stories).

Presentations at conferences and essays in journals regularly use puns and allusions in their titles. The titles of articles in newspapers and magazines often attempt to be catchy or clever by incorporating a pun or an allusion. For example, an article about the armed robbery squad of the police force is headed *The Force is with them*, which plays on the words *May the force be with you* from the movie *Star Wars*. The title of the film *Desperately Seeking Susan* has become a template into which journalists substitute for *Susan* whatever they are writing about, so we get *Desperately Seeking Sienna*, *Desperately Seeking Solace*, etc.

The allusions built into headlines are often just attempts at verbal ingenuity, but the best allusions carry a message. When Shakespeare's Julius Caesar is being stabbed to death, he says *Et tu, Brute?* 'Even you, Brutus?', expressing surprise that his friend is one of the murderers. Several writers have worked variations on this quotation into their text. One newspaper reported the challenge to the leader of a political party with the heading, *Et tu Natasha?*—an allusion which suggested the challenger was being disloyal. A more arcane example I saw some years ago was the caption *O temptress! O mores!* for a review of an autobiography of a bed-hopping woman. The reviewer was playing on the Latin quotation *O tempora o mores* 'Oh times, oh customs', the sort of thing a conservative might say about the alleged moral laxity of younger generations. The allusion suggests horror, presumably mock-horror, at the shocking revelations in the book.

Colloquial language is full of allusion. As two prominent scholars put it, 'The very currency of slang depends on its allusions to things which are not supposed to be universally familiar or generally respectable' (Greenough and Kittredge 1931: 72). Rhyming slang incorporates allusions such as *Brahms and Liszt* for 'pissed' (i.e. drunk) and its updated version *Schindler's List* (from the film version of Thomas Keneally's book, *Schindler's Ark*). Allusion plays a part in humour too. Many jokes depend on the audience picking up on a reference. Among actors it is taboo to mention Shakespeare's *Macbeth* by name; it must be referred to as 'the Scottish play'. In a modern television adaption of the play by Peter Moffat, set in a hotel kitchen with Macbeth as a chef, a sous-chef is rebuked for mentioning a famous rival chef by name. He is told to call him 'the Scottish chef'.

One type of allusion is to mention the punchline of a joke. In the 1997 film version of *Lolita* there is a scene in which a widow (Melanie Griffith), her lodger (Jeremy Irons), and her young teenage daughter (Dominique Swain) are sitting around after dinner. The widow, wanting to be alone with the lodger, tries get rid of young Lolita by saying, 'Isn't it time we were in bed?' Lolita, irritated by being addressed as a child, replies, 'What's with the "we", paleface?' This is the punchline of a joke in which the Lone Ranger and his faithful Indian companion, Tonto, find themselves surrounded by hostile Indians. The Lone Ranger says to Tonto, 'We are in big trouble, Tonto'. Tonto replies, 'What's with the "we", paleface?'

In *Summer, the Second Pastoral* Alexander Pope incorporates four lines from the aria 'Where'er you walk' from Handel's opera *Semele*. This extreme form of allusion has its roots in classical literature. Aristophanes wrote verses consisting of lines from Homer and Aeschylus, and a number of authors writing in Latin composed works consisting entirely of lines from poets such as Virgil, Horace, or Ovid. This strange practice outlived the Roman empire and continued until at least the seventeenth century. Virgil was the most common source. These poems are called **centos**.

Here is one stanza from an English cento (quoted in Augarde 1984: 140):

> I only know she came and went,
> Like troutlets in a pool;
> She was a phantom of delight,
> And I was like a fool.

These four lines are taken respectively from Powell, Hood, Wordsworth, and Eastman.

Allusive Names

Names are allusive. Some given names and family names suggest a particular cultural background, and changing fashions mean that certain given names have connotations of particular age groups. Names such as *Homer* and *Cleo(patra)* allude to to historical figures, but not everyone is aware of the significance of mythological and historical names. We have boys called *Tarquin* (the early Roman king who raped Lucrece) and girls called *Lilith* (the sexually voracious succuba of Jewish folklore) and *Jezebel* (the wicked woman of the Bible, Kings 1 and 2). Some given names refer to celebrities, as with *Marilyn* and *Britney*, though the strength of the allusion depends on the distinctiveness of the name. There was an increase in *Elizabeths* following the birth of Princess Elizabeth later Queen Elizabeth II, but since *Elizabeth* is not an unusual name, there is little if any perceived allusion.

Given names of humans are taken seriously, but where fictional characters, registered animals, and properties are to be named, there is scope for in-group allusion. When I was a child, I read a comic strip in one of the local newspapers about two characters called Pip and Emma. To me they were just arbitrary names, but I subsequently learnt that *pip emma* was World War I signallers' slang for p.m. (compare *ack emma* for a.m.). Recently I came across a racehorse called *Turing*, and I wondered if the horse had been named after the ill-fated mathematical genius, Alan Turing. A check of the breeding revealed the sire was Bletchley Park, the site of Britain's code-breaking operations in World War II where Turing was a leading light.

Names in pop music often incorporate allusion and word play. The rock-and-roll singer Chubby Checker has a stage name that is based on the name of an earlier rhythm-and-blues performer, Fats Domino. The Latin rock-and-roll group Santana have an album called *Abraxas* after the Gnostic deity (see Chapter 5), and a number of bands choose names that have dark, sinister, or occult connotations. One example is *Black Sabbath*, who featured a song of the same name which made much use of the dissonant tritone, known as the devil's interval. The heavy metal band *Iron Maiden* takes its name from a medieval instrument of torture, and *Styx* takes its name from the river in Hades. Some names refer to non-mainstream sex. *Soft Machine* takes its name from a novel by William Burroughs, most of whose works contain lots of explicit gay sex, and *Steely Dan* refers to a large strap-on penis featured in another Burroughs novel, *The Naked Lunch*.

The choice of names for characters in fiction is often allusive and sometimes the names are thinly disguised. In the film *The Blair Witch Project* (1999) the witch of the title is called Elly Kedward, a thinly disguised form of Edward Kelley (1555–1597), who claimed to be a spirit medium and alchemist. He acquired a kind of vicarious fame by being the collaborator of John Dee, the celebrated mathematician, astronomer, and occultist. There are a number of references to Edward Kelley in the literature of the occult. For instance, in the 1987 film *Angel Heart*, based on the novel *Falling Angel* by William Hjortsberg, the devil, who calls himself Louis Cyphre (Lucifer), hires a private detective. The private detective eventually encounters a character involved in a ritual killing who goes under the names of Ethan Krusemark and Edward Kelley. In chapter 113 of Umberto Eco's *Foucault's Pendulum* Edward Kelley is summoned up at a séance. In this work Kelley is treated as an historical figure, but in *The Blair Witch Project* and *Angel Heart* his name is chosen in an occult context, a choice which is significant to those familiar with the occult but apparently arbitrary to anyone else.

Nicknames are allusive in that they pick up on a perceived characteristic. Those that are popular in the media are usually called **sobriquets** (or soubriquets). For example, the sobriquet *Satchmo* has been given to Louis Armstrong. It is based on 'satchel mouth' and refers to his embouchure. Arnold Schwarzenegger has been dubbed the *governator*, a reference to his role in the *Terminator* and his position as governor of California. Sobriquets are often used in the media as a form of elegant variation and the alternation between the real name and the nickname can be confusing for the uninitiated. Commonly encountered examples include *the Big Apple* (New York), *GOP* (Grand Old Party, i.e. the Republican Party in the US), and *the Old Lady of Threadneedle Street* (the Bank of England).

Parody and Satire

Parody and satire involve allusion. A parody is a mocking imitation of any form of artistic expression whether it be a literary form such as a poem, a story, a religious text, a non-fictional text, a novel, a film, or a play, or other forms such as paintings, ballet, or music, especially vocal music. Parody is most effective if the audience can match its distortions and incongruities point by point with the original. A parody may consist of a few lines of verse, as with many children's parodies of nursery rhymes, popular poems, and songs, or it can extend over a long passage or even a whole work. Satire may be based on creative work or the target may be a person or group associated with politics, religion, the arts or some other prominent sphere. Although a satire can be short, as with various comedy sketches, most satire is in the form of complete works such as a play, a film, or a novel.

The allusive dimension of parody and satire will not necessarily be detected by their whole audiences; some people may take them at face value. Most of the poems in *Alice's Adventures in Wonderland* are parodies and the originals would have been well known to Lewis Carroll's readership, but with the passage of time their familiarity has waned, with the exception of 'Twinkle, twinkle, little bat' in chapter seven, which is a parody of 'Twinkle, twinkle, little star'. The verses still seem entertaining, but the fact that most of them mock sententious poems is lost. In the following abbreviated examples Carroll's parody is given to the left and the original to the right.

In chapter two we find a parody of Isaac Watts's 'Against Idleness and Mischief':

How doth the little crocodile	How doth the little busy bee
Improve his shining tail,	Improve each shining hour,
And pour the waters of the Nile	And gather honey all the day
On every golden scale!	From every opening flower!

The poem 'You are old, Father William' in chapter five is a parody of a poem by Robert Southey (1774–1843) called 'The Old Man's Comforts and How He Gained Them'.

'You are old, father William,'	You are old, Father William,
the young man said,	the young man cried,
'And your hair has	The few locks which are
become very white;	left you are grey;
And yet you incessantly	You are hale, Father William,
stand on your head—	a hearty old man,
Do you think, at your age,	Now tell me the reason,
it is right?'	I pray.
'In my youth,' father William	In the days of my youth,
replied to his son,	Father William replied,

'I feared it might injure the
    brain;
But, now that I'm perfectly sure
    I have none,
Why, I do it again and again.'

I remember'd that
    youth would fly fast,
And abused not my health
    and my vigour at first,
That I never might
    need them at last.

In chapter six the Duchess recites a parody of a poem called 'Speak Gently' attributed to G.W. Langford:

Speak roughly to your little boy,
    And beat him when he sneezes:
He only does it to annoy,
    Because he knows it teases.

Speak gently to the little child!
    Its love be sure to gain;
Teach it in accents soft and mild;
    It may not long remain.

In chapter ten there is a parody of Isaac Watts's 'The Sluggard':

'Tis the voice of the Lobster;
    I heard him declare,
'You have baked me too brown,
    I must sugar my hair.'
As a duck with its eyelids, so
    he with his nose
Trims his belt and his buttons,
    and turns out his toes.

'Tis the voice of the sluggard;
    I heard him complain,
'You have wak'd me too soon,
    I must slumber again.
As the door on its hinges, so
    he on his bed,
Turns his sides and his shoulders
    and his heavy head.

This chapter also contains 'Will you walk a little faster? said a whiting to a snail', which echoes 'Will you walk into my parlour? said the spider to the fly', but does not follow the sense of the earlier rhyme.

Satire is usually deadpan, to borrow a theatrical term. It makes use of exaggeration and irony to show that it is satire. It is not uncommon for an audience to take satire seriously and miss the target. When the British television programme *The Office* was broadcast, many viewers took it at face value, at least for a period, since it appeared to be a serious drama until one noticed oddities piling up.

In 1729 Jonathan Swift published a pamphlet entitled 'A modest proposal for preventing the children of poor people in Ireland from being a burden to their parents or country, and for making them beneficial to the public'. He writes as a well-intentioned economist. The tone is learned and full of mathematical calculations. This leads the reader to take the piece seriously, and it is only the narrator's outrageous suggestion that the Irish sell their children as food (the last paragraph of the extract below) that unmasks the whole work as a clever piece of sustained irony.

> It is a melancholy object to those who walk through this great town or travel in the country, when they see the streets, the roads, and cabin doors, crowded with beggars of the female sex, followed by three, four, or six children, all in rags and importuning every passenger for an alms. [...]
>
> I think it is agreed by all parties that this prodigious number of children in the arms, or on the backs, or at the heels of their mothers, and frequently of their fathers, is in the present deplorable state of the kingdom a very great additional grievance; and, therefore, whoever could find out a fair, cheap, and easy method of making these children sound, useful members of the commonwealth, would deserve so well of the public as to have his statue set up for a preserver of the nation. [...]
>
> As to my own part, having turned my thoughts for many years upon this important subject, and maturely weighed the several schemes of other projectors, I have always found them grossly mistaken in the computation. It is true, a child just dropped from its dam may be supported by her milk for a solar year, with little other nourishment; at most not above the value of 2s., which the

mother may certainly get, or the value in scraps, by her lawful occupation of begging; and it is exactly at one year old that I propose to provide for them in such a manner as instead of being a charge upon their parents or the parish, or wanting food and raiment for the rest of their lives, they shall on the contrary contribute to the feeding, and partly to the clothing, of many thousands. [...]

I shall now therefore humbly propose my own thoughts, which I hope will not be liable to the least objection.

I have been assured by a very knowing American of my acquaintance in London, that a young healthy child well nursed is at a year old a most delicious, nourishing, and wholesome food, whether stewed, roasted, baked, or boiled; and I make no doubt that it will equally serve in a fricassee or a ragout.

The rest of Swift's essay discusses in great detail the advantages of using Irish children as a source of meat. There is an element of parody in that Swift is mocking reformist literature of his time, but without having any familiarity with these writings present-day readers can still see a bitter humour deriving from the use of learned language and a serious tone for an outrageous proposal.

Parodies of genres as opposed to parodies of particular works are not uncommon. Comedians often write sketches taking off the pompous style of politicians or the jargon of sports commentators. Here is a parody of the overblown, clichéd style often found in television documentaries (Blake 2007: 18):

Looking at this humble cottage behind me it is hard to believe that we are standing in front of the birthplace of a man who would change forever the way we live. After him life would never be the same again.

A well-known satirical work is *The Devil's Dictionary* published by San Francisco columnist, Ambrose Bierce, in 1911. Some of his entries are given below (some in abbreviated form). The work is based on the conventional dictionary, but dictionaries are not the target of the satire. Bierce uses the form of a dictionary to make satirical comments about a great variety of subjects.

DIAGNOSIS, *n.*   A physician's forecast of the disease by the patient's pulse and purse.

ESOTERIC, *adj.*   Very particularly abstruse and consummately occult. The ancient philosophies were of two kinds,—*exoteric*, those that the philosophers themselves could partly understand, and *esoteric*, those that nobody could understand. It is the latter that have most profoundly affected modern thought and found greatest acceptance in our time.

FAITH, *n.*   Belief without evidence in what is told by one who speaks without knowledge, of things without parallel.

GRAMMAR, *n.*   A system of pitfalls thoughtfully prepared for the feet for the self-made man, along the path by which he advances to distinction.

LOVE, *n.*   A temporary insanity curable by marriage or by removal of the patient from the influences under which he incurred the disorder.

QUEEN, *n.*   A woman by whom the realm is ruled when there is a king, and through whom it is ruled when there is not.

Allusive Brainteasers

The following titles are allusive, and readers might like to try their hand in identifying the sources. The answers are in the appendix.

Eyeless in Gaza
Novel by Aldous Huxley (1936)

Til Human Voices Wake Us
Film with Guy Pearce and Helena Bonham-Carter (2002)

A Price above Rubies
Film starring Renée Zellweger (1998)

Arms and the Man
Play by George Bernard Shaw (1894)

Far from the Madding Crowd
Novel by Thomas Hardy (1874) and film (1967)

Devices and Desires
Crime fiction by P.D. James (1989)

One Fine Day (1996)
Film with George Clooney and Michelle Pfeiffer

Here are some titles, mostly of articles from newspapers, which are allusive in that they are variations of a title or well-known phrase. Again, the answers are in the appendix.

'The empress strikes back'
Article about deposed empress of Iran, Farah Pahlavi, hoping to return to the throne

'Scent and scentuality'
Review of a book on aromatherapy

'The line in winter'
Article about rail travel in Europe in winter

'The woes of Kilmanjaro'
Article about environmental problems on and around Mount
  Kilmanjaro

'Climb every mountain'
Article about a mountain climber

'The ever so easy rider'
Article about a cycling tour of France

'Round the world in less than 80 days'
Voyage to antipodes by container ship

Beware of Greeks Bearing Guns
Film with John Bluthal and Zoe Carides (2000)

II

FINALE

This book describes ways in which people choose to be oblique in their use of language as a system of communication and situations in which they are constrained from indiscriminate direct communication. Four factors motivate oblique communication:

- a desire to tease or amuse
- practical security
- maintaining an identity
- fear of the power of words.

A desire to tease and amuse leads to word games, riddles, irony, and the use of colourful slang. The need for security prompts people to devise ciphers and codes, both the elaborate written ones used by governments, the military, and the financial world, and spoken systems like rhyming slang, back slang, and Pig Latin. The factors overlap. If we use some esoteric form of language such as an argot, we are maintaining our identity as a member of a subculture and operating a system that has some degree of security.

The most striking examples of deviating from straightforward communication are tied up with a belief in a real connection between a word, particularly a name, and its referent. This belief leads to a fear of the power of words and hence to strong taboos and restrictions on the use of language, particularly names thought to have power to provoke the supernatural.

The more spectacular examples of constraints on the use of language come from cultures remote from the modern West, particularly from the written records of the early civilizations of the Ancient Near East and the later worlds of Greece and Rome. These cultures form part of our heritage and their influence is reflected in mild versions of earlier taboos and beliefs. Western culture has become increasingly secular over the course of the last hundred years. There has been a decline in the numbers of religious believers and a watering down of what the remaining adherents believe, so naturally fewer and fewer people feel constrained by religious taboos. However, a Christian view of the universe is still an important part of our culture. Literature regularly alludes to life after death and the idea that heaven is up and hell is down, a belief that does not sit easily with the notion of a spherical world. The Christian universe is peopled by angels with wings and horned devils with pitchforks. This view is enshrined in the language. When we say, 'Damn you!' or 'Go to hell', we are using expressions that once referred to wishing someone an eternity in the fires of hell. When we say, 'You're an angel' or 'The child has an angelic smile', we are alluding to the goodness and beauty of angels.

There has also been a decline in those beliefs that mainstream religion brands as superstition. However, many people still avoid black cats, green paint, and walking under ladders. If they spill salt, which is supposed to bring bad luck, they throw a pinch of salt over their left shoulder to counteract the 'curse'. Some numbers are considered lucky and others unlucky. Many buildings avoid having floors or rooms numbered 13. Astrology lives on in the horoscopes published in many newspapers and magazines, and contagious magic persists in the practice of touching someone who has, say, won the lottery in the hope that some of their luck will 'rub off'. If challenged about the folly of these practices, people usually claim that they do not take superstitions seriously. Nevertheless, superstitious beliefs are as enshrined in the language as the Christian view. Sometimes when people say something like 'I've never broken a bone in my life', they will add 'Touch wood' and proceed to touch something made of wood in the hope of not tempting fate. And the very phrase 'tempting fate' reflects a pre-Christian belief.

As mainstream Christianity has declined in the West, there has been a rise in interest in a variety of other belief systems, some borrowed from various pre-Christian religions of the Ancient Near East and Europe, and others from Third World religions. These systems often go under the label **New Age**, and they embrace belief in the supernatural and in natural forces and energies other than those detectable by current science. They include I Ching, Feng Shui, nature worship, witchcraft, and satanism, though this last is in fact an offshoot of Christianity. Some of those who are involved in the revival of ancient religious practices and witchcraft make use of herbs, gemstones, cleansing rituals with fire and water, and spells old and new. The volume of literature on the occult being published in print and on the Web outweighs what was produced in the heyday of the grimoire. All the features of the old literature are preserved: word play, anagrams, palindromes, acrostics, and the like, as well as a belief in an iconic relationship between performance and effect. Some Web sites, for instance, recommend reversing a spell to undo its effect.

The decline of religion in the West has not ushered in a new era of linguistic freedom. Though few people today fear curses and we are no longer likely to be prosecuted for blasphemy, as is still the case in some Islamic countries, we do have new taboos on politically incorrect language, particularly in regard to race. One can be legally penalized for using language that is considered racially abusive, and there is no doubt that words like *nigger* have become loaded with negative connotations and can be deeply offensive. On the other hand attempts to impose new, politically correct terminology can be repressive and authoritarian. For instance, basic words such as *blind*, *deaf*, and *dumb* have sometimes been proscribed, as have a variety of terms for mental illness ranging from *mad* to *lunatic*. It is common to reprimand speakers and writers who are thought to have erred, and even to publish their offences in shame files. A cryptic crossword compiler has been cited for using expressions such as *troppo*, *non compos mentis*, and *a screw loose*. We saw in Chapter 8 that colloquial language is particularly rich with respect to human impairments, so the PC lobby is likely to have an uphill battle.

Chapter 7 included examples of cultures where names were considered an integral part of a person and were concealed from enemies for fear of sorcery. We in the present-day West do not share this apprehension, but given names are important, and it is significant that when people make a major change of lifestyle, they often change their given name. Although in general we feel no inhibition about using names, there is some taboo connected with the names of enemies. People often become distressed at the mention of the name of someone who has caused them pain in the past, be it the perpetrator of a crime or simply an ex-partner where there has been a bitter falling out. They refrain from mentioning the enemy by name, and relatives, friends, and acquaintances are expected to observe the taboo. Circumlocutions such as 'you know who' or 'a certain person' are used instead, or in some cases derogatory phrases.

A mild taboo sometimes surrounds the names of authority figures. A manager or employer may be referred to anonymously as 'the boss', 'his nibs', 'her nibs', or 'you know who'. Other forms of reference may be shortened versions of a title or office (the CEO, the CO, the VC) or nicknames. The names of controversial figures are also sometimes avoided. I can recall meetings of an organization where an important but opinionated figure was often absent. The absentee's conduct and views were inevitably the subject of discussion, but he was not mentioned by name. Members would say things like, 'Someone wouldn't stand for that', 'It won't get whatisname's vote', or 'That won't go down well in some quarters'.

Whereas in the past only governments and businesses had to concern themselves with secure means of communication, it has become relevant to all of us who use any form of electronic communication for confidential or sensitive purposes. Most of us have user names and passwords to access the Web sites of employers, banks and other financial institutions, clubs, societies, and so on. We are conscious of the need to think up passwords that can be kept in memory without being easy to guess, to change them from time to time, and to keep them secure if written down. Most of us have no direct experience of ciphers, but we trust that the financial transactions we carry out via the internet are enciphered securely by some kind of random key.

A new form of obscure language which developed in the twentieth century is what is known to the public as 'modern poetry'. Whereas poetry up to the early twentieth century had been metered in form and transparent in meaning, it became common to write free verse in a kind of asyndetic, stream-of-consciousness style. The result was often vague or ambiguous, rather like the language of the traditional prophet. There was also experimental poetry with extreme liberties of morphology and attempts to maximize sound symbolism, as in the work of the Russian futurist poet Velimir Khlebnikov (1885–1922). As we saw in Chapter 2, palindromic poetry has become popular in Eastern Europe, and various form of word play are a feature of modern poetry. The American poet Harryette Mullen, for instance, likes to juxtapose similar sounding words (*emblems of motion muted amused mulish*) and to use the occasional anagram: *tomboy girl with cowboy boots takes coy bow in prom gown* (Mullen 1996: 642, 646).

In thinking about secret and oblique language it may be illuminating to consider a modern news broadcast. It is normally in a national language, it is explicit, and it is spoken slowly and clearly—essentially a form of written language that is read aloud. This is a variety of language found in many public speeches and lectures. It represents one extreme of clear communication to a wide audience. At the other extreme we have close acquaintances, friends, or family speaking some form of in-group language, perhaps a dialect or argot, or a mixture of both, using a teasing, jocular style, full of abusive banter, making heavy use of pronouns rather than specific nouns, sprinkled with local allusions and double entendres, not at all explicit because speakers can assume a lot about what addressees know, and marked by a lot of phonetic reduction. This form of language is also a means of communication, one that is more sophisticated than the formal language in the way it exploits shared knowledge, but one that seems obscure if not secret to outsiders. Most spoken language falls between these extremes, and most of us litter our speech with the some local slang, the odd pun, a bit of irony, or an occasional allusion. To the extent that we do so, we too are using 'secret language'.

APPENDIX:
ANSWERS TO THE PROBLEMS

Chapter 2

The solution to the acrostic crossword in Figure 2 is 'Mary had a little lamb. She had it with mint-sauce'.

The solution to the cryptic crossword in Figure 8 is as follows:

B	R	O	N	C	O	█	A	B	E	T	T	O	R	S
I	█	P	█	L	█	█	E	█	E	█	V	█	█	T
L	I	P	P	I	E	█	S	T	A	M	P	E	D	E
I	█	R	█	F	█	B	█	A	P	█	R	█	█	N
O	N	O	X	F	O	R	D	█	P	O	N	T	I	C
U	█	B	█	S	█	E	█	C	█	R	█	█	█	I
S	P	I	T	█	E	A	C	H	C	A	R	T	E	L
█	█	U	█	A	█	K	█	A	L	█	I	█	█	█
A	D	M	I	S	S	I	O	N	S	█	A	G	R	A
U	█	█	I	█	N	█	E	█	S	█	E	█	█	P
G	I	R	D	L	E	█	C	L	A	P	T	R	A	P
M	█	E	█	L	█	C	█	S	A	█	K	█	█	O
E	V	E	R	Y	M	A	N	█	S	T	R	I	P	S
N	█	F	█	B	█	T	█	█	I	█	L	█	█	E
T	E	S	T	A	T	O	R	█	F	O	W	L	E	R

Chapter 3

1. Why is a publican like a prisoner?
   Because both are behind bars.

2. Why is the figure nine like a peacock?
   Because it is nothing without its tail.

3. What gets wetter the more it dries?
   A towel.

4. If you have me, you want to share me. If you share me, you haven't got me. What am I?
   A secret.

5. What can run but never walks, has a mouth but never talks, has a head but never weeps, has a bed but never sleeps?
   A river.

6.
   > My life can be measured in hours,
   > I serve by being devoured.
   > Thin, I am quick
   > Fat, I am slow
   > Wind is my foe.
   > What am I?

   A candle.

7. What is it the more you take away the larger it becomes?
   A hole.

8.
   > Old Mother Twitchett had but one eye,
   > And a long tail which she let fly;
   > And every time she went over a gap,
   > She left a bit of her tail in a trap.

   A needle and thread.

9. I have many feathers to help me fly. I have a body and head, but I'm not alive. It is your strength which determines how far I go. You can hold me in your hand, but I'm never thrown. What am I?
   An arrow.

10. What always speaks the truth but doesn't say a word?
    A mirror.
11. Why are naked people hard to see?
    Because they are barely visible.
12. What's the greatest worldwide use of cowhide?
    To keep cows together.

Chapter 4

The first cipher is a substitution cipher using *Turing* as the keyword, as in the following:

T	U	R	I	N	G	A	B	C	D	E	F	H	J	K	L	M	O	P	Q	S	V	W	X	Y	Z
a	b	c	d	e	f	g	h	i	j	k	l	m	n	o	p	q	r	s	t	u	v	w	x	y	z

The cipher text and plain text are shown below.

KJNHN	QBKIK	GLOKI	SRCJA	TRCLB	NOTFL	BTUNQ	PKHNW
oneme	thodo	fprod	ucing	aciph	eralp	habet	somew

BTQFN	PPPYP	QNHTQ	CRTFF	YONFT	QNIQK	QBNLF	TCJQN
hatle	sssys	temat	icall	yrela	tedto	thepl	ainte

XQTFL	BTUNQ	CPQKS	PNTRK	INWKO	ITLOT	RQCRN	QBTQB
xtalp	habet	istou	seaco	dewor	dapra	ctice	thath

TPUNN	JCJSP	NPCJR	NQBNP	NVNJQ	NNJQB	RNJQS	OYUDU
asbee	ninus	esinc	ethes	event	eenth	centu	rybjb

The second cipher is a transposition. The plain text was written out across ten columns and these were rearranged in the order shown by the key given in the last line of the table. Zero was treated as ten and the tenth column placed last. To decrypt the message you need to rearrange the columns of the cipher text in the following order.

2	6	1	3	4	7	9	8	5	0

The best clue was the digraph *qu* in the word *question*.

1	2	3	4	5	6	7	8	9	0
t	h	e	m	i	n	i	s	t	e
r	w	i	l	l	a	r	r	i	v
e	a	t	t	e	n	a	m	a	n
d	w	i	l	l	a	d	d	r	e
s	s	t	h	e	c	o	n	f	e
r	e	n	c	e	s	t	o	p	s
h	e	w	i	l	l	l	e	a	v
e	i	m	m	e	d	i	a	t	e
l	y	a	f	t	e	r	h	e	r
p	r	e	s	e	n	t	a	t	i
o	n	a	n	d	w	i	l	l	n
o	t	t	a	k	e	q	u	e	s
t	i	o	n	s	s	t	o	p	x
3	1	4	5	9	2	6	8	7	0

Chapter 10

The allusions in the various titles are taken from the following sources.

Eyeless in Gaza
Novel by Aldous Huxley (1936)
From Milton's *Samson Agonistes*:

> Promise was that I
> Should Israel from Philistian yoke deliver.
> Ask for that great deliverer now and find him
> Eyeless in Gaza at the mill with slaves...

Till Human Voices Wake Us

Film with Guy Pearce and Helena Bonham-Carter (2002)

Last line of T.S. Eliot's *The Love Song of J. Alfred Prufock*: 'Till human voices wake us and we drown'.

A Price above Rubies

Film starring Renée Zellweger (1988)

Proverbs 31:10 'Who can find a virtuous woman? For her price is far above rubies'.

Arms and the Man

Play by George Bernard Shaw (1894)

First line of Virgil's *Aeneid*: *Arma virumque cano* 'Arms and the man I sing'

Far from the Madding Crowd

Novel by Thomas Hardy (1874) and film (1967)

From 'Elegy Written in a Country Churchyard' by Thomas Gray:

> Far from the madding crowd's ignoble strife,
> Their sober wishes never learn'd to stray;
> Along the cool sequester'd vale of life
> They kept the noiseless tenour of their way.

Devices and Desires

Crime fiction by P.D. James (1989)

From the general confession in *The Book of Common Prayer*: 'We have followed too much the devices and desires of our own hearts'.

One Fine Day

Film with George Clooney and Michelle Pfeiffer (1996)

From the aria 'One fine day' (*Un bel dì*) from Puccini's *Madame Butterfly*.

The empress strikes back (*The Empire Strikes Back*)

Scent and scentuality (Jane Austen, *Sense and Sensibility*)

The line in winter (*The Lion in Winter* 1966 play, 1968 film, and 2003 teleplay)

The woes of Kilmanjaro (Ernest Hemingway, *The Snows of Kilimanjaro*)

Climb every mountain (song from *The Sound of Music*)

The ever so easy rider (1969 film *Easy Rider*)

Round the world in less than 80 days (Jules Verne, *Around the World in 80 Days*)

Beware of Greeks bearing guns (Virgil, *timeo Danaos et dona ferentes* 'I fear Greeks even bearing gifts')

SELECT BIBLIOGRAPHY

Abrahams, R.D. (1962). 'Playing the Dozens'. *Journal of American Folklore* 75: 209–20.

Adams, M. (2003). *Slayer Slang: A Buffy the Vampire Slayer Lexicon*. New York: Oxford University Press.

Agrippa von Nettesheim, H.C. (1992) (orig. 1531). *De Occulta Philosophia Libri Tres* ed. V.P. Compagni. Leiden: Brill.

Aikhenvald, A. (2003). *A Grammar of Tariana*. New York: Cambridge University Press.

Allan, K. and Burridge, K. (1991). *Euphemism and Dysphemism: Language Used as Shield and Weapon*. New York: Oxford University Press.

————— (2006). *Forbidden Words: Taboo and the Censoring of Language*. Cambridge: Cambridge University Press.

Anthon, C. (1850). *Q. Horatii Flacci Opera Omnia* [explanatory notes]. London: Longman.

Atkinson, J.M. (1984). ' "Wrapped Words": Poetry and Politics among the Wana of Central Sulawesi, Indonesia', in Brenneis and Myers (eds.), 33–68.

Augarde, T. (1984). *The Oxford Guide to Word Games*. Oxford: Oxford University Press.

Bacher, W. and Eisenstein, J.D. (2002). The *JewishEncyclopedia. com.*

Barb, A.A. (1948). 'St Zacharias the Prophet and Martyr: A Study in Charms and Incantations'. *Journal of the Warburg and Courtauld Institutes* 11: 35–67.

Basso, E.B. (2007). 'The Kalapalo Affinal Civility Register'. *Journal of Linguistic Anthropology* 17: 161–83.

Bavin, E. (1996). 'Body Parts in Acholi: Alienable and Inalienable Distinctions and Extended Uses', in H. Chappell and W. McGregor, *The Grammar of Inalienability: A Typological Perspective on Body Part Terms and the Part–Whole Relation.* Berlin: Mouton de Gruyter, 841–64.

Bergerson, H.W. (1973). *Palindromes and Anagrams.* New York: Dover.

Berndt, R.M. and C.H. (1964). *The World of the First Australians.* Sydney: Ure Smith.

Bierce, A. (1984) (orig. 1911). *The Enlarged Devil's Dictionary*, ed. E.J. Hopkins. Harmondsworth: Penguin.

Birnbaum, P. (1964). *A Book of Jewish Concepts.* New York: Hebrew Publishing Co.

Blake, B. (2007). *Playing with Words: Humour in the English Language.* London: Equinox.

—— (2008). *All about Language.* Oxford: Oxford University Press.

Bradūnas, E. (1975). 'If you Kill a Snake, the Sun will Cry, Folktale Type 425-M: A Study in Oicotype and Folk Belief'. *Lituanus* 21.1 (available at www.lituanus.org).

Brenneis, D.L. and Myers, F.R. (eds.) (1984). *Dangerous Words: Language and Politics in the Pacific*. New York: New York University Press.

Brown, K. (ed.) (2006). *Elsevier Encyclopedia of Language and Linguistics* (2nd edn.) Oxford: Elsevier.

Brown, P. and Levinson, S. (1987). *Politeness: Some Universals in Language Usage*. Cambridge: Cambridge University Press.

Bruce, S.G. (2007). *Silence and Sign Language in Medieval Monasticism: The Cluniac Tradition*. Cambridge: Cambridge University Press.

Budge, E.A.W. (1899). *Egyptian Magic*. London: Routledge and Kegan Paul.

—— (1978). *Amulets and Superstitions*. New York: Dover (orig. edn. Oxford University Press, London, 1930).

Burns, T.A. (1976). 'Riddling: Occasion to Act'. *Journal of American Folklore* 89. 352: 139–65.

Cameron, A. (1995). 'Ancient Anagrams'. *American Journal of Philology* 116.3: 477–84.

Cavendish, R. (1967). *The Black Arts*. New York: Perigree.

Clark, S. (2002). 'Witchcraft and Magic in Early Modern Culture', in B. Ankarloo, S. Clark, and W. Monter, *Witchcraft and Magic in Europe, vol. 4: The Period of the Witch Trials*. London: Athlone, 97–169.

Conklin, H.C. (1964). 'Linguistic Play in its Cultural Context', in D. Hymes (ed.), *Language, Culture and Society: A Reader in*

Linguistics and Anthropology. New York: Harper and Row, 295–300.

Curr, E.M. (1886). *The Australian Race* (4 vols). Melbourne: John Ferres and London: Truebner.

Dawson, J. (1881). *Australian Aborigines: The Languages and Customs of Several Tribes of Aborigines in the Western District of Victoria, Australia*. Melbourne: George Robertson.

Dixon, R.M.W. (1972). *The Dyirbal Language of North Queensland*. Cambridge: Cambridge University Press.

—— (1990). 'The Origin of "Mother-in-law Vocabulary" in Two Australian Languages'. *Anthropological Linguistics* 32: 1–56.

Drosnin, M. (1997). *The Bible Code*. London: Weidenfeld and Nicolson.

Dundes, A., Leach, J., and Özkök, B. (1972). 'The Strategy of Turkish Boys' Verbal Dueling Rhymes', in J. Gumperz and D. Hymes (eds.) *Directions in Sociolinguistics: The Ethnography of Communication*. New York: Holt, Rinehart and Winston, 130–60.

Eble, C. (2006). 'Slang, Argot and Ingroup Codes', in K. Brown (ed.) vol. 11: 412–14.

Elliott, R. (1957). 'Runes, Yews, and Magic.' *Speculum* 32.2: 250–61.

Endicott, K.M. (1991). *An Analysis of Malay Magic*. Singapore: Oxford University Press.

Errington, J.J. (1988). *Structure and Style in Javanese*. Philadelphia: University of Pennsylvania Press.

Evans-Pritchard, E.E. (1954). 'A Zande Slang Language'. *Man* 54: 185–6.

Farb, P. (1974). *Word Play: What Happens when People Talk*. New York: Knopf.

Finlayson, R. (1982). 'Hlonipa; The Women's Language of Avoidance among the Xhosa'. *South African Journal of African Linguistics*, supplement 35–60.

Fison, L. and Howitt, A.G. (1880). *Kamilaroi and Kurnai*. Melbourne: George Robertson.

Flint, V. (1991). *The Rise of Magic in Early Medieval Europe*. Princeton: Princeton University Press.

Flom, G. (1930). *Introductory Old English Grammar and Reader*. Boston: Heath.

Florey, M. (2005). 'A Cross-Linguistic Perspective on Emergent Possessive Constructions in Central Moluccan Languages'. *Australian Journal of Linguistics* 25: 59–84.

Fowler, H.W. (1983) (orig. 1926). *A Dictionary of Modern English Usage*. New York: Greenwich House.

—— and Fowler, F.G. (1931) (orig. 1906). *The King's English*. Oxford: Clarendon Press.

Frankfort, H., Frankfort, H.A., Wilson, J.A., and Jacobsen, T. (1949). *Before Philosophy: The Intellectual Life of Ancient Man*. Harmondsworth: Penguin.

Frazer, J.G. (1911*a*). *The Golden Bough: The Magic Art and the Evolution of Kings*. London: Macmillan.

—— (1911*b*). *The Golden Bough: Taboo and the Perils of the Soul*. London: Macmillan.

Fryer, P. (1964). *Mrs Grundy: Studies in English Prudery*. London: Dennis Dobson.

Gager, J.G. (ed.) (1992). *Curse Tablets and Binding Spells in the Ancient World*. New York: Oxford University Press.

Geipel, J. (1995). 'Caló: The Secret Language of the Gypsies', in P. Burke and R. Porter (eds.) *Languages and Jargons: Contributions to a Social History of Language*. Cambridge MA: Polity Press, 102–32.

Georges, R.A. and Dundes, A. (1963). 'Towards a Structural Definition of the Riddle'. *Journal of American Folklore* 76.300: 111–18.

Glazer, M. (1976). 'On Verbal Dueling among Turkish Boys'. *Journal of American Folklore* 89.351: 87–9.

Glazier, J. and Glazier, P.G. (1976). 'Ambiguity and Exchange: The Double Dimension of Mbeere Riddles'. *Journal of American Folklore* 89.352: 189–238.

Gotti, M. (1999). *The Language of Thieves and Vagabondes: 17th and 18th Century Canting Lexicography in England*. Tübingen: Max Niemeyer.

Greber, E.A [no date]. Chronotope of Revolution: The Palindrome from the Perspective of Cultural Semiotics. http://www.realchange.org/pal/semiotic.htm.

Green, T.A. and Pepicello, W.J. (1980). 'Sight and Spelling Riddles'. *Journal of American Folklore* 93.367: 23–34.

Green, T.A. and Pepicello, W.J. (1984). 'The Riddle Process'. *Journal of American Folklore* 97.384: 189–203.

Greenough, J.B. and Kittredge, L. (1931) (orig. 1902). *Words and their Ways in English Speech*. London: Macmillan.

Grimm, J. and W. (2002) (orig. 1812). *The Complete Fairy Tales*. London: Routledge.

Grose, [F]. (1811) (orig. 1785). *A Dictionary of the Vulgar Tongue*. London: Chappel.

Guérios, R.F.M. (1956). *Tabus Lingüísticos*. Rio de Janeiro: Organização Simões Editora.

Guiraud, P. (1985, c1956). *L'Argot* (9th edn.). Paris: Presses Universitaires de France.

Hajek, J. (2002). 'Parlaree: un Gergo Italianizzante in Inglese'. *Rivista di Dialettologia in Italia* 26: 169–89.

Hale, K. (1971). 'A Note on a Warlbiri Tradition of Antonymy', in D.D. Steinberg and L.A. Jakobovits (eds.) *Semantics, an Interdisciplinary Reader in Philosophy, Linguistics and Psychology*. Cambridge: Cambridge University Press, 472–82.

—— (1973). 'Deep-Surface Canonical Disparities in Relation to Analysis and Change', in T. Sebeok (ed.) *Current Trends in Linguistics* 11, The Hague: Mouton, 401–58.

Halliday, M.A.K. (1976). 'Anti-Languages'. *American Anthropologist* (New Series) 78: 570–84.

Hamnett, I. (1967). 'Ambiguity, Classification and Change: The Function of Riddles'. *Man* (New Series) 2: 379–92.

Hancock, I. (1984*a*). 'Romani and Angloromani', in P. Trudgill (ed.) *Language in the British Isles*. Cambridge: Cambridge University Press, 367–83.

—— (1984*b*). 'Shelta and Polari', in P. Trudgill (ed.) *Language in the British Isles*. Cambridge: Cambridge University Press. 384–403.

—— (1986). 'The Cryptolectal Speech of the American Roads: Traveler Cant and American Angloromani'. *American Speech* 61: 206–20.

Harman, T. (1567). 'A Caveat or Warening for Common Cvrsetors Vvlgarely Called Vagabondes'. Repr. in E. Viles and F.J. Furnivall (eds.) (1937) (orig. 1869). *The Fraternitye of Vacabondes*. London: Early English Text Society, 17–91.

Harries, L. (1971). 'The Riddle in Africa'. *Journal of American Folklore* 84. 334: 377–93.

Harrison, S.J. (1990). *Stealing People's Names: History and Politics in a Sepik River Cosmology*. Cambridge: Cambridge University Press.

Haviland, J. (1979*a*). 'Guugu-Yimidhirr Language'. *Language and Society* 8: 385–93.

—— (1979*b*). 'How to Talk to your Brother-in-law in Guugu-Yimidhirr', in T. Shopen (ed.) *Languages and their Speakers*, Cambridge MA: Winthrop, 161–239.

Heath, J., Merlan, F., and Rumsey, A. (eds.) (1982). *Languages of Kinship in Aboriginal Australia*. Sydney: University of Sydney Oceania Linguistic Monograph 24.

Herbert, R.K. (1990a). 'The Relative Markedness of Click Sounds: Evidence from Language Change, Acquisition and Avoidance'. *Anthropological Linguistics* 32: 120–38.

—— (1990b). 'The Sociohistory of Clicks in Southern Bantu'. *Anthropological Linguistics* 32: 295–315.

Hewett, J.W. (ed.) (1861). *Hymnorum Latinorum Delectus*. London: J. and F.H. Rivington.

Hotten, J.C. (1864). *The Slang Dictionary or The Vulgar Words Street Phrases and 'Fast Expressions' of High and Low Society*. London: Hotten (reproduced by Eliborn Classics).

—— (1874) (orig. 1859). *The Slang Dictionary: Etymological, Historical and Anecdotal*. London: Chatto and Windus.

Hudson, K. (1978). *The Jargon of the Professions*. London: Macmillan.

Jennings, G. (1965). *Personalities of Language*. New York: Crowell.

Jolly, K. (2002). 'Medieval Magic: Definitions, Beliefs, Practices', in K. Jolly, C. Raudvere, and E. Peters. *Witchcraft and Magic in Europe: vol. 3, The Middle Ages*. London: Athlone, 1–71.

Kahn, D. (1966). *The Codebreakers: The Story of Secret Writing*. London: Weidenfeld and Nicolson.

Keane, W. (1997). 'Religious Language'. *Annual Review of Anthropology* 26: 47–71.

Keenan, E. (1974). 'Norm-makers, Norm-breakers: Uses of Speech by Men and Women in a Malagasy Community', in R. Bauman and J. Sherzer (eds.) *Explorations in the Ethnography of Speaking*. New York: Cambridge University Press, 125–43.

Khanittanan, W. (2005). 'An Aspect of the Origins and Development of Linguistic Politeness in Thai', in R. Lakoff and S. Ide (eds.) *Broadening the Horizons of Linguistic Politeness*. Amsterdam: Benjamins, 315–35.

Kieckhefer, R. (1989). *Magic in the Middle Ages*. Cambridge: Cambridge University Press.

—— (1994). 'The Specific Rationality of Medieval Magic'. *American Historical Review* 99.3: 813–36.

Kinser, S. (1979). 'Saussure's Anagrams: Ideological Work'. *Modern Language Notes* 94: 1105–38.

Klerk, de, V. (2006). 'Slang, Sociology', in K. Brown (ed). vol. 11: 407–12.

Lambdin, T.O. (1973). *Introduction to Biblical Hebrew*. London: Darton, Longman, and Todd.

Langlois, A. (2006). 'Wordplay in Teenage Pitjatjantjara'. *Australian Journal of Linguistics* 26.2: 181–92.

Laycock, D. (1972). 'Towards a Typology of Ludlings, or Play Languages'. *Linguistic Communications* (Monash University) 6: 21–54.

Lehmann, A.C. and Myers, J.E. (eds.) (1993) (3rd edn.). *Magic, Witchcraft, and Religion: An Anthropological Study of the Supernatural*. Mountain View CA: Mayfield.

Lowe, K.A. (2006). 'Runes', in K. Brown (ed.) vol. 10: 688–91.

Luck, G. (1985). *Arcana Mundi: Magic and the Occult in the Greek and Roman Worlds*. Baltimore: Johns Hopkins University Press.

Maranda, E.K. (1976). 'Riddles and Riddling: An Introduction'. *Journal of American Folklore* 89.352: 127–37.

Matthews, W. (1938). *Cockney Past and Present: A Short History of the Dialect of London*. London: Routledge and Kegan Paul.

Maxwell-Stuart, P.G. (ed.) (1999). *The Occult in Early Modern Europe: A Documentary History*. New York: St Martin's Press.

Mayhew, H. (1851). *London Labour and the London Poor*. Vol 1. London.

McBryde J.M. Jr (1907). 'The Sator-Acrostic'. *Modern Language Notes* 22: 245–9.

McConvell, P. (1982). 'Neutralisation and Degrees of Respect in Gurindji', in Heath et al. (eds.), 86–106.

McKnight, G.H. (1928). *Modern English in the Making*. New York: Appleton-Century-Crofts.

Meggitt, M.J. (1962). *Desert People*. Sydney: Angus and Robertson and Chicago: University of Chicago Press.

Messenger, J.C. Jr (1960). 'Anang Proverb-Riddles'. *Journal of American Folklore* 73.289: 225–35.

Milner, G.B. (1961). 'The Samoan Vocabulary of Respect'. *Journal of the Royal Anthropological Institute* 91: 2.

Moody, E.J. (1993). 'Urban Witches', in A.C. Lehmann and J.E. Myers (eds.), 231–41.

Mullen, H. (1996). '*Muse and Drudge*: Selections'. *Callaloo* 19: 639–47.

Nha Trang Pensinger (2001). 'Versification of Vietnamese Riddles'. Website: Cong Huyen Ton Nu Nha Trang—Research Articles.

Niceforo, A. (1912). *Le Génie de l'argot*. Paris.

Ogden, D. (1999). 'Binding Spells: Curse Tablets and Voodoo Dolls in the Greek and Roman Worlds', in V. Flint, R. Gordon, G. Luck, and D. Ogden, *Witchcraft and Magic in Europe, vol. 2: Ancient Greece and Rome*. London: Athlone.

Ohl, R.T. (1928). *The Enigmas of Symphosius*. Philadelphia.

Olsan, L. (1992). 'Latin Charms of Medieval England: Verbal Healing in a Christian Oral Tradition'. *Oral Tradition* 7: 116–42.

Ostler, N. (2007). *Ad Infinitum: A Biography of Latin*. London: Harper.

Pálsson, H. and Edwards, P. (trans.) (1976). *Egil's Saga*. Harmondsworth: Penguin.

Partridge, E. (1960). *Slang To-Day and Yesterday: With a Short Historical Sketch, and Vocabularies of English, American and Australian Slang* (3rd edn.). New York: Bonanza.

Peek, P.M. (1981). 'The Power of Words in African Verbal Arts'. *Journal of American Folklore* 94.371: 19–43.

Peters, E. (2002). 'The Medieval Church and State on Superstition, Magic and Witchcraft: From Augustine to the Sixteenth Century', in K. Jolly, C. Raudvere, and E. Peters. *Witchcraft and Magic in Europe: vol. 3, The Middle Ages*. London: Athlone, 173–245.

Pettit, E. (ed. and trans.) (2001). *Anglo-Saxon Remedies, Charms, and Prayers from British Library MS 585: The 'Lacnunga'*, 2 vols., Lewiston NY: Mellen.

Price, G. (1984). *The Languages of Britain*. London: Edward Arnold.

Radcliffe-Brown, A.R. (1965) (orig. 1939). 'Taboo', in W.A. Lessa and E.V. Vogt (eds.) *Reader in Comparative Religion: An Anthropological Approach*. New York: Harper and Row, 72–82.

Rankin, I. (1997). *Black and Blue: An Inspector Rebus Mystory*. London: Orion.

Reuchlin, J. (1993) (orig. 1517). *On the Art of the Kabbalah* (*De Arte Cabalistica*), text with a trans. by G. Lloyd Jones. Lincoln NE and London: University of Nebraska Press (Bison Books).

Roper, J. (2003*a*). 'Towards a Poetics, Rhetorics and Proxemics of Verbal Charms'. *Folklore* (Tartu) 24: 7–49. www.folklore.ee/folklore/vol24/verbalcharm.pdf.

—— (2003*b*). 'English Orature, English Literature: The Case of Charms'. *Folklore* (Tartu) 24: 50–60. www.folklore.ee/folklore/vol24/engcharm.pdf.

—— (2005). *English Verbal Charms*. Folklore Fellows Communications 136, No. 288. Helsinki: Academia Scientiarum Fennica.

Roth, C. (ed.) (1966). *The Standard Jewish Encyclopedia*. London: W.H. Allen.

Rumsey, A. (1982). 'Gun-Gunma: An Australian Avoidance Language and its Social Functions', in Heath et al. (eds.), 160–81.

Rushton, P. (1980). 'A Note on the Survival of Popular Christian Magic'. *Folklore* 91: 115–18.

Russell, J.B. (1993). 'Witchcraft', in A.C. Lehmann and J.E. Myers (eds.), 190–9.

Sáenz-Badillos, A. (1993). *A History of the Hebrew Language* (trans. J. Elwolde). Cambridge: Cambridge University Press.

Sarton, G. (1936). 'Notes on the History of Anagrammatism'. *Isis* 26: 132–8.

Sherzer, J. (1982). 'Play Languages: with a Note on Ritual Languages, in L.K. Obler and L. Menn (eds.) *Exceptional Language and Linguistics*. New York: Academic Press, 175–99.

Shumaker, W. (1972). *The Occult Sciences in the Renaissance: A Study in Intellectual Patterns*. Berkeley: University of California Press.

—— (1982). *Renaissance Curiosa*. Binghamton, NY: Center for Medieval and Early Renaissance Studies.

Simmons, D.C. (1958). 'Cultural Functions of the Efik Tone Riddle'. *Journal of American Folklore* 71: 123–38.

Sinclair, A.T. (1909). 'The Secret Language of Masons and Tinkers'. *Journal of American Folklore* 22.86: 353–64.

Singh, S. (1999). *The Code Book: The Science of Secrecy from Ancient Egypt to Quantum Cryptography*. New York: Anchor Books (Random House).

—— (2000). *The Science of Secrecy: The Secret History of Codes and Codebreaking*. London: Fourth Estate.

Singh, S. (2001). *The Code Book: How to Make it, Break it, Hack it, Crack it*. New York: Delacorte Press (Random House).

Skemer, D.C. (2006). *Binding Words: Textual Amulets in the Middle Ages*. Pennsylvania: Penn State University Press.

Smith, L.D. (1955) (orig. 1943). *Cryptography: The Science of Secret Writing*. New York: Dover.

Stevenson, J. and Davidson, P. (eds.) (2001). *Early Modern Women Poets (1520–1700): An Anthology*. Melbourne: Oxford University Press.

Stewart, S. (1979). *Nonsense: Aspects of Intertextuality in Folklore and Literature*. Baltimore: Johns Hopkins University Press.

Taylor, A. (1943). 'The Riddle'. *California Folklore Quarterly* 2: 129–47.

Teit, J.A. (1917). 'Kaska Tales'. *Journal of American Folklore* 30: 427–73.

Thomsen, M. (2001). 'Witchcraft and Magic in Ancient Mesopotamia', in F. Cryer and M.-L. Thomsen, *Witchcraft and Magic in Europe, vol. 1: Biblical and Pagan Societies*. London: Athlone, 1–95.

Thomson, D. (1935). 'The Joking Relationship and Organized Obscenity in North Queensland'. *American Anthropologist* 37: 460–90.

Treis, Y. (2005). 'Avoiding their Names, Avoiding their Eyes: How Kambaata Women Respect their In-laws'. *Anthropological Linguistics* 47.3: 292–320.

Ullmann, S. (1957). *The Principles of Semantics*. Glasgow: Jackson and Oxford: Blackwell.

Vatuk, V.P. (1969). 'Amir Khusro and Indian Riddle Tradition'. *Journal of American Folklore* 82.324: 142–54.

Ward, J.D.U. (1957). 'Tramps' Sign Language'. *Western Folklore* 16: 137–9.

Weiner, A.B. (1984). 'From Words to Objects to Magic: "Hard Words" and the Boundaries of Social Interaction', in Brenneis and Myers (eds.), 161–91.

Wentworth, H. and Flexner, S.B. (1960). *Dictionary of American Slang*. New York: Thomas Y. Cromwell.

Werbolowsky, R.J.Z. and Wigoder, G. (eds.) (1997). *The Oxford Dictionary of the Jewish Religion*. New York: Oxford University Press.

Westcott, W.W. (1910). *An Introduction to the Kabalah*. Whitefish MT: Kessinger.

Weston, L.M.C. (1995). 'Women's Medicine, Women's Magic: The Old English Metrical Childbirth Charms'. *Modern Philology* 92: 279–93.

White, C.M.N. (1955). [untitled letter following Evans-Pritchard 1954]. *Man* 55: 96.

Williams, T.R. (1963*a*). 'The Forms and Functions of Tambunan Dusun Riddles'. *Journal of American Folklore* 76.300: 95–110.

—— (1963*b*). 'Tambunan Dusun Riddles'. *Journal of American Folklore* 76.300: 141–81.

Williamson, C. (ed.) (1977). *The Old English Riddles of the Exeter Book*. Chapel Hill: University of North Carolina Press.

Winslade, J.L. (2000). 'Techno-Kabbalah: The Performative Language of Magick and the Production of Occult Knowledge'. *Drama Review* 44.2: 84–100.

Wolfe, J.R. (1970). *Secret Writing: The Craft of the Cryptographer*. New York: McGraw-Hill.

Zika, C. (1976). 'Reuchlin's *De Verbo Mirifico* and the Magic Debate of the Late Fifteenth Century'. *Journal of the Warburg and Courtauld Institutes* 39: 104–38.

Zipes, J. (trans.) (1991). *Beauties, Beasts, and Enchantment: Classic French Fairy Tales*. New York: Meridian.

INDEX